JUSTICE FOR ALL

Justice for All identifies ten central flaws in the criminal justice system and offers an array of solutions – from status quo to evolution to revolution – to address the inequities and injustices that far too often result in courtrooms across the United States.

From the investigatory stage to the sentencing and appellate stages, many criminal defendants, particularly those from marginalized communities, often face procedural and structural barriers that taint the criminal justice system with the stain of unfairness, prejudice, and arbitrariness. Systematic flaws in the criminal justice system underscore the inequitable processes by which courts deprive citizens of liberty and, in some instances, their lives. Comprehensive in its scope and applicability, the book focuses upon the procedural and substantive barriers that often prohibit defendants from receiving fair treatment within the United States criminal justice system. Each chapter is devoted to a particular flaw in the criminal justice system and is divided into two parts. First, the authors discuss in depth the underlying causes and effects of the flaw at issue. Second, the authors present a wide range of possible solutions to address this flaw and to lead to greater equality in the administration of criminal justice. The reader is encouraged throughout to consider and assess all possible options, then defend their choices and preferences. Confronting these issues is critical to reducing racial disparities and guaranteeing Justice for all.

Describing the problems and assessing the solutions, *Justice for All* does not identify all problems or all solutions, but will be of immeasurable value to criminal justice students and scholars, as well as attorneys, judges, and legislators, who strive to address the pervasive flaws in the criminal justice system.

Charles E. MacLean, J.D., Ph.D., is an Associate Professor in the School of Law Enforcement and Criminal Justice at the Metropolitan State University in Brooklyn Park, Minnesota. Prior to entering the Academy, Chuck served for twenty years as a state felony prosecutor in Minnesota.

Adam Lamparello, J.D., LL.M., is an Assistant Professor of Public Law at Georgia State College and University in Milledgeville, Georgia. Adam has published over seventy-five law review articles and three textbooks that focus on constitutional law, criminal law, and legal education.

JUSTICE FOR ALL

Repairing American Criminal Justice

Charles E. MacLean and Adam Lamparello

Routledge
Taylor & Francis Group
LONDON AND NEW YORK

Cover image: © Kwanchai Lerttanapunyaporn / EyeEm / Getty Images

First published 2022
by Routledge
2 Park Square, Milton Park, Abingdon, Oxon OX14 4RN

and by Routledge
605 Third Avenue, New York, NY 10158

Routledge is an imprint of the Taylor & Francis Group, an informa business

British Library Cataloguing-in-Publication Data
A catalogue record for this book is available from the British Library

Library of Congress Cataloging-in-Publication Data
Names: MacLean, Charles (Professor of criminal justice), author. |
Lamparello, Adam, author.
Title: Justice for all : repairing American criminal justice / Charles
MacLean and Adam Lamparello.
Description: Milton Park, Abingdon, Oxon; New York,
NY: Routledge, 2022. | Includes bibliographical references and index.
Identifiers: LCCN 2021043938 (print) | LCCN 2021043939 (ebook) |
ISBN 9780367756567 (hardback) | ISBN 9780367756536 (paperback) |
ISBN 9781003163411 (ebook)
Subjects: LCSH: Criminal justice, Administration of–United States. |
Discrimination in criminal justice administration–United States. |
Equality–United States. | Equality before the law–United States.
Classification: LCC HV9950 .M239 2022 (print) | LCC HV9950 (ebook) |
DDC 364.973–dc23
LC record available at https://lccn.loc.gov/2021043938
LC ebook record available at https://lccn.loc.gov/2021043939

ISBN: 978-0-367-75656-7 (hbk)
ISBN: 978-0-367-75653-6 (pbk)
ISBN: 978-1-003-16341-1 (ebk)

DOI: 10.4324/9781003163411

Typeset in Bembo
by Taylor & Francis Books

CONTENTS

ILLUSTRATIONS

Figures

Tables

ACKNOWLEDGEMENTS

Chuck MacLean acknowledges the unwavering support of his wife and partner, Marie, without whom I – and perhaps all – would be lost.

Adam would also like to acknowledge and dedicate this book to Marc Lamparello, who passed away on April 17, 2020.

Marc, you were loved and will always be a part of the lives that you touched. I miss you and I hope to one day see you again.

Chuck MacLean acknowledges the stellar research work of Laura Hierlmaier, student researcher at Metropolitan State University.

Adam Lamparello would like to thank Daria Brown, a student at Georgia College and State University, for her helpful research and insights, particularly regarding the death penalty.

The authors also thank Chandler West for her invaluable edits and revisions, although the authors retain responsibility for any errors that remain.

PREFACE

This book highlights infirmities in the criminal justice system that have led to pervasive unfairness, inequality, and injustice. But make no mistake. No one is a victim. Your choices, not your circumstances, determine your destiny.

Notwithstanding, unfairness, injustice, and inequality plague the criminal justice system in many areas, such as in policing, adjudication, and sentencing. Identifying the problem, however, is not sufficient. Likewise, it is not sufficient to simply acquire knowledge and regurgitate facts.

Anyone can do that.

But it solves nothing.

It helps no one.

Developing practical and sustainable solutions is imperative if injustice is to become a thing of the past and equality a reality in the present and a staple of the future.

Leaders propose *solutions*. And leaders recognize that, no matter how compelling or sensible a policy proposal, real change requires great people. Talented people. Visionary people. As the legendary football coach Woody Hayes said, "You win with people."

Leaders are bold, creative, and courageous. They strive to effectuate meaningful change that improves people's lives.

That is the point of this book: to develop meaningful solutions that address the flaws in the criminal justice system. To that end, each chapter challenges *you* to be a leader by proposing solutions that will change the lives of others and reaffirm the values on which this country is based: equality, fairness, and justice – for all.

This book has neither a liberal nor conservative bias. Unfortunately, some professors are ideologically biased and strive to impose their views on students. This is professionally irresponsible and unethical. Professors should teach students *how* to think, not *what* to think. They should welcome diverse perspectives from across the political spectrum and encourage civil discourse. Sadly, many professors and universities have made the decision to replace instruction with ideology, and emphasize conformity over critical thinking. In so doing, the quality of education – and its ability to train students for the real world – has been compromised. If you experience this at your university, you are not alone – but you are not helpless. On any given issue, research and respect all perspectives. Form your views based on facts and evidence, not emotion and bias.

We have no ideological agendas and have no regard for people whose opinions are driven more by underlying agendas than critical analysis and study. We likewise rely on facts and evidence. We hope you will too.

Most importantly, we hope that you embrace the challenge of not merely learning, but creating ideas and solving problems.

And in that process, you will discover if you really can be the change you want to see in the world.

ABBREVIATIONS

For sake of brevity and clarity, the authors use the following conventions throughout this volume.

ABA	American Bar Association
CJS	United States criminal justice system
DOJ	United States Department of Justice
FBI	Federal Bureau of Investigation
LEA	law enforcement agency
LEMAS	Law Enforcement Management and Administrative Statistics
LEO	law enforcement officer
MRPC	Model Rules of Professional Conduct
NDAA	National District Attorneys Association
Police	except as specifically limited within the text, "police" includes all types of law enforcement officers

PART I
Law Enforcement

This part of the book discusses the roles of law enforcement officers (peace officers) in ensuring that their functions in the criminal justice system are always delivered in a fair, impartial, and reliable manner. The chapters in this section will require you to propose solutions that address the infirmities and inequities in law enforcement today along three dimensions: de-escalation and use of excessive force (chapter 1); reforming, transforming, reimagining, or defunding the police (chapter 2); and mental health of United States law enforcement officers (chapter 3). Each chapter provides the factual backdrop for the issue addressed, proposes a number of solutions, then calls on you to devise the wisest course of action.

Furthermore, as stated in the Preface, this book is intended not merely to help you acquire knowledge, but to require you to offer workable solutions that make a positive difference in people's lives. Put differently, it is not sufficient to merely complain about a problem. Transformative thinkers offer solutions that make a difference in people's lives.

DOI: 10.4324/9781003163411-1

1

DE-ESCALATION AND POLICE USE OF EXCESSIVE FORCE[1]

Officer-involved shootings of civilians in the 2010s appeared to skyrocket, the appearance, at least, exacerbated by the ubiquity of cell phone, squad, and body-worn cameras, trumpeted and magnified by the 24-hour news cycle and spread widely on social media and elsewhere on social media and the Internet more broadly. Excessive force incidents of virtually all types seemed to be on the rise, too.

The use-of-force continuum identifies a series of perceptions by the officer regarding threats posed by those with whom they interact and with each perception higher up the continuum justifying the officer to use increased force in response. The problem is that much use-of-force continuum training does not adequately question the officers' perceptions, which may be colored by implicit race bias, adrenaline, fear, inadequate training, and other factors. On the contrary, and far too frequently, use-of-force continuum training merely trains the officers that their perception – no matter how flawed – justifies their response based on the continuum's escalating categories.

Over 18 million new criminal cases were filed (United States Courts, 2020) and over 61 million contacts with the public were made by law enforcement in 2018 (nearly 29 million of those contacts were police-initiated) (Harrell & Davis, 2020). The vast majority of those cases were developed, and contacts were effected constitutionally by ethical officers without excessive force; four percent of Blacks and two percent of Whites experienced threats or use of force during their police contacts in 2018 (Harrell & Davis, 2020, n. 2, Table 3). However, subjective fears, misperceptions, stereotyped fear assessments, and racist or force-centric training have no place in the equation when the downside is an errant on-the-spot risk assessment that needlessly causes civilian injury or death. The use-of-force continuum and other use-of-force and de-escalation trainings, too often black-and-white and bathed in absolutes, must be softened with judgment, flexibility, understanding, and re-assessment at the scene coupled with a far more

DOI: 10.4324/9781003163411-2

objective and less subjective perception trigger. After all, execution is a potential consequence only for the most serious crimes and only in a dwindling number of states, and cruel and unusual punishment is unconstitutional even after trial, yet too many civilians are being shot and killed or assaulted by police for lesser or no crimes, without any due process and with no procedural justice. On average, nearly 19 civilians are shot and killed by police for every one police officer shot and killed by a civilian. This must stop.

Chapter Highlights

- Case Spotlight: The 2015 police killing of Walter Scott.
- Excessive force may be defined applying a "reasonable person" standard; thus, excessive force is the use of types or degrees of force beyond that which a reasonable person in the officer's situation would deem reasonable and necessary.
- In the United States in 2018, 55 law enforcement officers were killed in the line of duty and 1,165 civilians were killed by law enforcement officers.
- African American civilians were killed by U.S. law enforcement officers at twice the rate White civilians were killed.
- Geographic variations in excessive force demonstrate substantial lack of uniformity across the states, with the highest rate of officer-involved killings found in the Southwest (the five states with the highest incidence of officer-involved killings are all in the American Southwest: Arizona, Colorado, New Mexico, Nevada, and Oklahoma).
- Training, rules of thumb, and the use-of-force continuum all may exacerbate the excessive force problem.

Case Spotlight: The 2015 Police Killing of Walter Scott

On the morning of April 4, 2015, [North Charleston Police Department] Officer Michael Slager stopped Walter Scott's vehicle after observing that its center brake light was not functioning. After the stop, Scott fled on foot, and Slager pursued him for approximately 200 yards. During the chase, Slager shot his taser probes [at Scott] twice. The first shot was unsuccessful, but the second brought Scott to the ground. An altercation ensued, the details of which were heavily disputed during the sentencing hearing. The district court credited the testimony of Feidin Santana,[2] a bystander who witnessed the incident. Santana testified that he was walking to work when he noticed Slager chasing Scott on foot. Santana testified that he lost sight of Slager and Scott briefly. When he saw them again, Scott was on the ground facing down, and Slager was on top of Scott. Santana testified that he then heard something that sounded like electricity and that Scott sounded like he was being hurt. Santana also saw Slager punch Scott in the back. He testified that Scott was at no point face-up and that Scott was never on top of Slager. He did not see Scott punch or fight with Slager at any point. Nor did he witness Scott take control of Slager's taser, charge toward Slager, or attempt to hurt Slager. Santana described Scott's actions during the ground altercation as "[j]ust trying to get away, just trying to leave." Santana testified that after the ground altercation, Scott got up quickly, like "a man determined to just get away" (*United States v. Slager*, Appellee United States Brief).

Slager was still holding Scott when the two got up, but Scott managed to break free and run. At that point, Slager pulled out his service weapon and fired multiple times. When Slager began firing, Scott was at least 16 feet away from him, and when Slager fired his last shot, Scott was approximately 40 feet away from him. Five shots hit Scott, all entering from behind. Scott fell to the ground. Slager put handcuffs on Scott but did not administer any medical treatment. Santana filmed parts of the incident, including the shooting, on his cell phone. His video footage shows Slager firing eight shots at Scott, all while Scott was unarmed and running away from Slager. Scott died on the scene due to injuries from the gunshots.

South Carolina's murder prosecution against Slager ended in a mistrial. Federal prosecutors then presented the case to a grand jury on charges related to deprivation of Walter's civil rights. Slager ultimately pleaded guilty to the federal charge and was sentenced to twenty years imprisonment.

Law Enforcement Lore and Excessive Force

One need not interact much with American law enforcement officers before hearing some of the following maxims:

- I would rather be judged by twelve than carried by six.
- Shoot first and let God sort it out.
- Shoot center-mass.
- Shoot until the threat is eliminated; that is, until the source of the threat is dead.
- Shooting the subject in the leg is bad policy and unsafe.
- Anyone can kill you at any time (Brooks, 2021).
- Black people are just predisposed to violence (LaForgia & Valentino-DeVries, 2021).
- We have to bend the rules to beat those who break the rules.
- First, we ask; then, we tell; then, we make – "Ask – Tell – Make."

Indeed, in the Roll Call topic in a recent edition of Police1, an online magazine aimed at law enforcement officers, one commentator spun out many of those old bromides as gospel (Sumpter, 2021). But imagine all the assumptions that must be made before even considering those arguments:

- American police officers should be armed – even those on traffic patrol.
- Each officer's assessment of risk is perfect and free of bias.

- Even if the officer is biased, we judge the officer's conduct based on what a reasonable officer in his situation would have deemed permissible or necessary; the individual officer's subjective intent is irrelevant.
- Each officer has the power and right to end a life even though our criminal justice system is framed by assumptions including innocence until proven guilty and due process that are the antithesis of "shoot first and ask questions later."
- All previously unassigned governmental obligations that involve some risk must be assigned to armed law enforcement officers.
- We must mainstream those suffering from mental illness.
- Warrior police training prepares officers to shoot to kill but does not mandate it.

Excessive Force as an Outgrowth of Police Culture

No truisms regarding law enforcement officers – good or bad – are universal. In fact, many researchers have found that "problem officers" are a relatively small subset of law enforcement officers who tend to violate the norms, rules, laws, and policies repeatedly (Walker, Alpert, & Kenney, 2001). Others decry that "bad apples" analysis as short-sighted and inaccurate (Chalfin & Kaplan, 2021). The kernel from which that subset grew is subject to more dispute. Some argue problem officers, prone to using excessive force, are a natural result of the law enforcement evolution in the United States beginning with slave patrols, traversing the lynching era, and arriving today serving communities often torn by interracial and interethnic strife compounded by a vocal political climate where lines are drawn and honored, and compromise is the exception rather than the rule (Durr, 2015). Those theorists argue that so-called "problem officers" are doing exactly what many members of the majority want them to do: control the underclass – clean up the streets – and subjugate minorities. In a word, they argue, today's police are expected to protect the ruling class and the majority group by doing whatever it takes to suppress minority groups and protect the status quo a large share of the majority craves.

Other theorists argue that police strive to survive in a risky and uncertain profession where each shift can be their last and where survival requires quick action to defend against real and perceived risks from the public.[3] Low pay drives some police officers toward petty ethical violations, such as receiving and sometimes demanding favors, free meals, better prices on used cars, and worse. Low pay also adds stress at home for officers struggling to pay the bills, feed the children, and keep their families solvent. Those theorists argue that police absorb stress – and trauma – on the street during every shift and each shift's stress has not fully relented when a new shift must begin. That is a prescription for compound and unrelenting trauma leading toward mental health issues and psychological challenges that can – at some times and in some circumstances – lead some police to act out with excessive force toward those with whom they interact on the job.

The often too-broad array of duties law enforcement officers must bear and rules and policies they must follow add to the stress. As just one example, discussed in chapter 4, officers in many jurisdictions handle all critical incident calls with mentally ill subjects. That stress is often amplified by the minimal training many officers receive on mental health – in themselves and in those with whom they interact on the job. Training officers in handling critical incidents (McShane, 2019) [4] with subjects on the autism spectrum and civilians with other acute and chronic mental health issues has helped in some areas, and some cities are moving away from exclusively sending law enforcement officers to mental health calls, but there is a long way to go (Nelson, 2016).

That compound stress faced by many officers is often exacerbated by an "us versus them" mindset with officers siloing their professional and personal lives around fellow law enforcement officers and their families, whom they deem to be the only people they can trust and the only people who understand what police face every day. Some officers in this vein feel the public is too afraid to defend themselves and too politically correct to understand the excessive force that "real police work" at times "requires."

Finally, there is a variable, but in some areas quite strong, undercurrent of toxic masculinity and overt celebration of toughness and violence among some police officers and law enforcement agencies (Rawski & Workman-Stark, 2018). Certainly, officers are sometimes taunted by civilians, but even a cursory review of YouTube will reveal dozens of bodycam and citizen cell phone footage clips showing officers taunting, assaulting, and laughing at civilians as the officers appear all too willing to join the celebration of violence and "power over" (Hall, 2021; Levin, 2021).[5] Officers must be physically fit to serve well and protect themselves, fellow officers, and the public, so many officers habitually work out and many law enforcement agencies pay for them to do so or provide exercise equipment for that purpose. Of course, there are salutatory benefits to officers staying healthy – reduced stress, improved health, fewer heart and pulmonary challenges, and the like. However, slavish worship of toughness and bicep circumference can lead some officers to argue their career quest is *to be the toughest person any civilian will ever encounter*. Thus, siloed, stressful, and risky circumstances faced by law enforcement officers can express as outward directed violence toward those the officers are or should be in uniform to serve.

Of "Bad Apples," "Bad Cases," "Bad Barrels," and "Bad Orchards"

At least since the Lexow (1890s), Curran (1910s), Seabury (1930s), Helfand (1940s), Knapp (1970s), and Mollen (1990s) Commissions examining New York City policing (Grennan, 2001), public officials and scholars have struggled to define and manage police misconduct and identify whether police misconduct and excessive use of police force is caused by: (1) "bad apples" (Obasogie, 2019), individual unethical officers lurking in police departments; (2) "bad cases" that pushed officers into untenable situations where they were compelled to use excessive force; (3) "bad barrels," referring to the Chief, top officials, and senior officers in a police department enabling misconduct by failing to compel, mandate, and model ethical behavior, failing to protect whistleblowers, and protecting and failing to punish officers who use excessive force; or (4) "bad orchards,"[6] defined as communities – or at least the majorities or power-brokers in communities that want and expect police to clean up the streets and keep crime suppressed no matter the means employed.

Certainly, bad apples exist in many police departments. Likewise, some cases are tough, split-second calls. And some communities want the streets cleaned up, no matter the cost or means. So, the problems and solutions related to use of excessive force by police rest with the barrels, the top officials and senior officers in a police department who can exhibit ethical conduct on every shift and institute transparency requirements and disciplinary procedures that ensure whistleblower protection and swift discipline – even termination – for problem officers. Some bad cases will occur now and then, but a rotten apple cannot last long in an ethical barrel that hires, trains, and promotes ethical officers, and retrains, disciplines, or terminates unethical officers. Similarly, an ethical barrel can exist and thrive even while serving a community (a bad orchard) that wants results without worrying much about the Constitution, procedures, or means. Nonetheless, civil service and union protections hamstring many police administrators' power to intercede to improve behavior and better manage use of force. Police departments are top-down organizations and the solution to excessive use of force must be solved from the top-down where the department's leadership demand and model ethical behavior on every shift (Armacost, 2016; Wilson, 1978; Wood, Tyler, & Papachristos, 2020).

Use-of-force Training and the Continuum

Generally speaking, new police officers are trained by more senior or retired officers. Thus, lessons improvidently learned and stories repeated in the stationhouse as lore of "how we do things," are replicated and handed down – perpetuated, if you will – with each new cohort of recruits. Cultural competence, de-escalation, negotiation, and soft skills, if taught at all, can be relegated to subordinate positions with little class time. Instead, an extraordinary amount of class time is assigned to hand-to-hand fighting, incapacitation, personal defense, and firearms use (Blumberg, Papazoglou, & Schlosser, 2020). Thus, the exciting parts of law enforcement training – fighting and firearms – are front and center, while ethics, judgment, de-escalation, and cultural awareness are relegated to special topics and are too often quickly forgotten. Moreover, with training focused on old officers teaching new ones, the old lessons are too-often perpetuated and honored while the newer approaches are diminished and ridiculed.

Even today, notwithstanding the warrior versus guardian debates, warrior training has retained a foothold in some law enforcement training. As stated by Dave Grossman, a warrior trainer who has taught officers in up to 200 training sessions nationwide per year,

> "The only way to make a frightened [officer] respond in a certain way is to make it a conditioned response [as soon as you see an enemy, you kill] … . We train

officers to create a symphony of death and destruction … . Only a killer can hunt a killer … . Are you emotionally, spiritually, psychologically prepared to snuff out a human life in defense of innocent lives – if you can't make that decision, you need to find a different job … . Do you understand you can be sued for not shooting? The one that dies next might be you. Know the law and know it well. Don't be afraid of getting sued – it's just a chance for overtime."

(Atkinson & Hartrick, 2017)

Within that cauldron of warrior training (Cowen, 2021) insufficiently leavened by de-escalation and cultural competency training, officers are often taught to apply a use-of-force continuum that takes on various guises such as that depicted in Figure 1.1. Officer and agency application of use-of-force continuums is supported by the National Institute of Justice branch of the United States Department of Justice, the

---

- Officer Presence – No force is used. Considered the best way to resolve a situation.
  - The mere presence of a law enforcement officer works to deter crime or diffuse a situation.
  - Officers' attitudes are professional and nonthreatening.
- Verbalization – Force is not-physical.
  - Officers issue calm, nonthreatening commands, such as "Let me see your identification and registration."
  - Officers may increase their volume and shorten commands in an attempt to gain compliance. Short commands might include "Stop," or "Don't move."
- Empty-Hand Control – Officers use bodily force to gain control of a situation.
  - *Soft technique.* Officers use grabs, holds and joint locks to restrain an individual.
  - *Hard technique.* Officers use punches and kicks to restrain an individual.
- Less-Lethal Methods – Officers use less-lethal technologies to gain control of a situation.
  - *Blunt impact.* Officers may use a baton or projectile to immobilize a combative person.
  - *Chemical.* Officers may use chemical sprays or projectiles embedded with chemicals to restrain an individual (e.g., pepper spray).
  - *Conducted Energy Devices (CEDs).* Officers may use CEDs to immobilize an individual. CEDs discharge a high-voltage, low-amperage jolt of electricity at a distance.
- Lethal Force – Officers use lethal weapons to gain control of a situation. Should only be used if a suspect poses a serious threat to the officer or another individual.
  - Officers use deadly weapons such as firearms to stop an individual's actions.

Figure 1.1: The Use-of-Force Continuum[1]

[1] United States Department of Justice (2009). The Use-of-Force Continuum. Available at https://nij.ojp.gov/topics/articles/use-force-continuum

International Association of Chiefs of Police (Canterbury & Cunningham, 2016), and other police unions, law enforcement agencies, and interest groups.

Use-of-force continuums (United States Commission on Civil Rights, 2018; United States Department of Justice, 2009) depict graphically the following principle (Congressional Research Service, 2020): as the degree of perceived threat posed to the officer and others increases, the degree of force the officer may use in response concomitantly increases. Thus, as the degree of threat rises on the threat scale, the degree of "authorized" force rises on the response scale.

That construct is obviously grounded on a presumption that officers accurately perceive the threat, but what if the officer misperceives the threat? If the officer accurately perceives the threat and uses deadly force, if you accept that officers should use deadly force when they deem that necessary, that is at least defensible. However, if the officer overestimates the threat posed – if the officer thinks a lighter is a gun or a distraught person poses a lethal threat or any young Black child wearing a hoodie is a gangster-thug – the officer will overestimate the degree of force the continuum permits in response.[7] Four scenarios are presented below to set out the dilemma and to present the fatal flaw in use-of-force continuum training and approaches.

Scenario 1: A Somali officer, new to the Minneapolis Police Department and rushed into street duty to fill a perceived racial/ethnic gap on the force, was called to a late-night suspicious person call. After the new Somali officer, already very nervous, arrived at the scene in a two-officer squad, he heard a loud bang and fired his weapon in response directly across the inside of the squad car and in front of his partner. This scenario is based on the actual case (*State of Minnesota v. (Mohamed) Noor*, 2021) where Justine Ruszczyk was killed by newly recruited Somali Officer Mohamed Noor after Ruszczyk called 9-1-1 to report a suspicious person near her home at about 11:30 p.m. on July 15, 2017. Officer Noor reported that he was afraid so he fired his weapon, killing Ruszczyk. Noor had misperceived the threat and responded with deadly force drastically out of step with the actual degree of threat posed. Noor was convicted and sentenced to serve 12.5 years in prison.

Scenario 2: An officer was called to the scene of a young Black male reportedly carrying a gun at a park. The reporting party told dispatchers that the gun was probably fake and the subject was probably a juvenile, but that information may not have been relayed to the responding officers. Within two seconds of the officer's arrival at the park, the officer fired at the young male, killing him. The boy's weapon was a toy gun. This scenario is based on the actual case (United States Department of Justice, 2020) where twelve-year-old Tamir Rice was shot and killed by Cleveland Police Officer Timothy Loehmann on November 22, 2014. Officer Loehmann had misperceived the threat and therefore responded with impermissible and deadly force. Cleveland police and federal prosecutors deemed the shooting justified and declined to seek charges against the officer, but Officer Loehmann was ultimately fired for lying on his job application (not for the shooting) (Associated Press, 2021). The officer's partner (Ferrise, 2019) and a 9-1-1 dispatcher (Associated Press, 2017) were suspended, and Tamir Rice's family later settled with the City of Cleveland for a reported $6 million (Smith, 2015). In April 2021, Tamir Rice's family asked the Department of Justice to reopen the investigation (Long, 2021).

Scenario 3: An officer stopped a Black motorist with an inoperable taillight. The motorist, pursuant to legal requirements, told the officer – without prompting – that he (the motorist) possessed a firearm in the vehicle. The officer told the motorist to provide his driver's license and registration. When the motorist reached into the car to retrieve the requested paperwork, the officer shot and killed the motorist, who had not been retrieving the firearm at all. This scenario is based on the actual case (*State of Minnesota v. (Jeronimo) Yanez*, 2016; Minnesota Public Radio News, 2017) where St. Anthony (Minnesota) officer Jeronimo Yanez shot and killed Philando Castile in July 2016. Officer Yanez had misjudged the threat and therefore misjudged the degree of authorized force. Yanez was later acquitted of manslaughter (Smith, 2017).

Scenario 4: Three young Black males, all wearing hoodies, were standing together on a sidewalk when an officer approached them to find out what they were up to. The officer, who believes all Black males, especially those wearing hoodies, are drug dealers and possibly carrying weapons, unsnaps his holster and prepares to pull his firearm. What may happen next? This scenario is an exemplar, not based on any particular incident, but should create the mental picture for the reader: how do bias, fear, stress, inadequate training, ethical lapses, and the like lead officers such as this generic officer to misperceive the threat and take a life without justification?

The "Noble Cause" Position

Many officers consider themselves to be manning the thin line, protecting the weak and innocent majority from the violent and criminal minority (Caldero, Dailey, & Withrow, 2018). Those officers consider that a noble cause; they run toward the risk instead of away and swear an oath to protect those who do not, cannot, or will not protect themselves. Some of those noble cause officers are predisposed to favor action over reflection, and defenders of the noble cause sometimes argue that predisposition is essential and even imperative, since officers have an existential right to preserve their lives when threatened.

Defenders of the "noble cause" concept often argue that we must accept that law enforcement officers have dangerous jobs and must interact with those the rest of us would sooner avoid, thus making use of force inevitable and use of excessive force at least occasionally likely and sometimes permissible.

The Response to the "Noble Cause" Position

On the other hand, and as noted by many others, law enforcement's noble cause can be coopted and lead some officers toward corrupt means in service of that noble cause:

- We need to bend the rules to catch those who break the rules.
- Courts allow us to deceive suspects to get confessions.
- The Constitution is a technicality put in our way by bleeding hearts.
- We are paid poorly and are entitled to free meals, coffee, and the gifts some citizens provide.

- We must be ready to kill or be killed.
- The public does not understand what we do – we are their only protectors.

Given their predisposition toward action over reflection, action-oriented folks flock to law enforcement careers they see as a chance to serve a greater cause. Some have long family histories of law enforcement service. Others previously served in the military and may see a law enforcement career as a continuation of the action orientation, regimentation, and camaraderie they experienced.

In service to the noble cause of law enforcement, some officers come to believe they are – or should be deemed – above the law.

As in the Walter Scott shooting presented in the Case Spotlight above, some officers believe that if a subject fails to comply with their commands, officers are free to shoot them if they flee. Even the United States Supreme Court came fairly close to blessing such actions in *Tennessee v. Garner* (1985) and *Graham v. O'Connor* (1989), where the Court held that although police must deem deadly force necessary to use it on a fleeing felon and must have probable cause to believe the subject posed a threat or death or serious injury to the officer or others, the officer's actions must be judged by what a reasonable officer would have deemed reasonable and necessary under the circumstances. That contributes to the lopsided statistics one finds in officer-involved killings: although officers shoot and kill about 1,000 people in the United States each year,[8] most are deemed justified and fewer than eight officers per year are charged criminally. Less than half of those officers charged are convicted, often for an offense less than the most severe original charge (Dewan, 2021).

Data on Officer-involved Killings Are Incomplete, Inadequate, and Regionally Varied

The Federal Bureau of Investigations (n.d.) ("FBI") has long struggled to create a national use-of-force database from voluntary reports to be submitted by the 18,000+ law enforcement agencies ("LEAs") in the United States. That quest began in earnest when Congress enacted the Violent Crime Control and Law Enforcement Act of 1994 and compelled then-United States Attorney General Janet Reno to "acquire data about the use of excessive force by law enforcement officers" (H.R. 3355 (Violent Crime Control and Law Enforcement Act of 1994)). The FBI's efforts have been plagued by recalcitrant LEAs, some of which would rather not report use-of-force data that may expose problems they would prefer remain undisclosed. In 2020, just 5,030 of the 18,514 federal, state, local, and tribal LEAs provided use-of-force data to the FBI (Jackman, 2020). The limited FBI data depicts a use-of-force situation in the United States where only about twenty percent of responding entities reported at least one civilian complaint of excessive police use-of-force, but fewer than ten percent of reported use-of-force incidents resulted in officer discipline and all but a small percent were unfounded or dismissed. One may rightly wonder whether that poor reporting rate skews the data away from discovering the use-of-force hotspots that are most in need of reform.

The federal government likewise does not yet maintain an official nationwide database of civilians shot and killed by law enforcement, but the *Washington Post* has informally gathered those data and the circumstances of each shooting since 2015 (note this does not include civilian deaths by officers using means other than firearm, such as by knife or strangulation) (*Washington Post* – Fatal Force).[9] Over the period from 2015 through April 2021, the *Washington Post* reports that over 5,000 civilians were shot by police in the United States. Of that number, 128 of those killed by police were unarmed Black males and 153 were unarmed White males. Given that White males outnumber Black males by 5.4:1 in the United States' general population, unarmed Black males are 4.5 times more likely to be shot and killed by law enforcement than unarmed White males. Considering that statistic, little wonder that the abolitionists and the Black Lives Matter movement have called for revolution in police reform, not mere evolution alone. More details from the *Washington Post* database are presented in Tables 1.1 and 1.2.

The data in Tables 1.1 and 1.2 reveal the tragedy and geographical variation of officer-involved shooting deaths. That geographic variation is to be expected given

TABLE 1.1 Officer-involved ("O-I") Killings in the United States, January 1, 2015 to June 18, 2021

States over 12 O-I killings per year:	*States under 5 O-I killings per year:*
1-California – 941 (145/year)	40-Hawaii – 34 (5 per year)
2-Texas – 567 (87/year)	41-Nebraska – 31 (5/year)
3-Florida – 421 (65/year)	42-Maine – 25 (4/year)
4-Arizona – 297 (46/year)	43-Connecticut – 24 (4/year)
5-Colorado – 229 (35/year)	44-South Dakota – 20 (3/year)
6-Georgia – 226 (35/year)	45-District of Columbia – 18 (3/year)
7-Oklahoma – 189 (29/year)	46-New Hampshire – 18 (3/year)
8-Ohio – 181 (28/year)	47-Delaware – 16 (2/year)
9-North Carolina – 179 (28/year)	48-Wyoming – 15 (2/year)
10-Washington – 175 (27/year)	49-North Dakota – 14 (2/year)
11-Tennessee – 168 (26/year)	50-Vermont – 9 (1/year)
12-Missouri – 159 (24/year)	51-Rhode Island – 4 (1/year)

TABLE 1.2 Officer-involved Killings in the United States per capita, January 1, 2015 to June 18, 2021

Top 5 O-I States per 100,000:	*Bottom 5 O-I states per 100,000:*
1-Alaska (6.01 per 100,000)	47-New Jersey (0.83 per 100,000)
2-New Mexico (5.82)	48-Connecticut (0.67)
3-Oklahoma (4.78)	49-Massachusetts (0.61)
4-Arizona (4.08)	50-New York (0.61)
5-Colorado (3.98)	51-Rhode Island (0.38)

that each of the 18,000+ law enforcement agencies in the United States is led by a different chief or sheriff with differing viewpoints on race, equity, procedural justice, and the role of force in policing, as well as differing hiring and discipline processes, and differing willingness to protect whistle-blowers or support or squelch excessive force by officers. As a result, the state with the highest rate of officer-involved civilian shooting deaths (Alaska with 6.01 per 100,000 population) has a rate nearly 16 times higher than the state with the lowest rate (Rhode Island with 0.38).

The data in Table 1.3 reveal the tragedy and racial disparity of officer-involved shooting deaths where the civilian was unarmed when killed. Whether mistakes or intentional acts, in one-third of the states, unarmed, non-Hispanic Black civilians are more than twice as likely to be shot and killed by a law enforcement officer as would be predicted from the non-Hispanic Black share of the total population.

There are clear racial disparities in police use of excessive force and deadly force against civilians (Goff, Lloyd, Geller, Raphael, & Glaser, 2016; Lee, Weitzer, & Martínez, 2018; Newton, 2018; Peoples, 2019; Ross, 2015; Smith & Holmes, 2014; Terrill & Reisig, 2014; Trinkner, Kerrison, & Goff, 2021–2022; Wihbey & Kille, 2016). The time is now to acknowledge that and devise training, recruiting, selection, and discipline methods for weeding out racially biased and violence-prone officers as successfully as possible.

Perhaps the most telling data of all compare the number of civilians shot and killed by officers each year against the number of officers shot and killed by civilians each year as depicted in Table 1.4. The number of officers shot and killed in the line of duty

TABLE 1.3 Most Racially Disparate States for Officer-involved Shooting Deaths, 2015–2021[10]

1 Wisconsin – 9.2 times more likely
2 Washington State – 4.1
3 New Jersey – 3.8
4 New York – 3.5
5 Tennessee – 3.5
6 Illinois – 3.4
7 California – 3–4
8 Indiana – 3.4
9 Pennsylvania – 3.3
10 Arizona – 3.3
11 Virginia – 3–1
12 Oklahoma – 3.0
13 Florida – 2.9
14 Kentucky – 2.5
15 Texas – 2.2
16 Colorado – 2.1
17 Maryland – 2.0

TABLE 1.4 Police Shot and Killed by Civilians and Civilians Shot and Killed by Police, 2015–2021

Year	*Civilians shot and killed by officers*	*Officers shot and killed by civilians*	*Ratio Civilian: Officer Shot and killed*
2015	993	43	23:1
2016	960	67	14:1
2017	986	46	21:1
2018	990	53	19:1
2019	999	50	20:1
2020	1021	48	21:1
2021 (est)	915	57	16:1
TOTAL	**6864**	**364**	**18.8:1**

by civilians is derived from the National Law Enforcement Memorial Museum (2021a, 2021b); the Federal Bureau of Investigations Uniform Crime Report ("UCR"), and LEOKA (Law Enforcement Officers Killed and Assaulted) reports (United States Department of Justice, 2015–2019; 2021, Spring; 2021, July 8), and lists a slightly lower number of firearm-related officer deaths each year and cumulatively (for example, cumulatively from 2015–2020, 278 officers were reported killed by civilian firearms in the UCR versus 307 reported by the Museum). Over the period 2015–2020, on average, nearly 18.8 civilians were shot and killed by an officer for every officer shot and killed by a civilian (using the UCR data, the ratio was 20.6:1). Consider whether officers are facing lethal threats as often as they report.

The Role for De-escalation Training, Procedures, and Legislation

Some commentators have persuasively argued that law enforcement officers in the United States too often and too early resort to using deadly force when most situations can be de-escalated as is done throughout much of the rest of the world, especially where officers serve unarmed. The argument goes that although deadly force may be authorized, de-escalation measures may yet reduce or eliminate the imminent threat and avoid a tragedy.

Several states have already promulgated or enacted or are considering adoption of policies and legislation requiring police to train officers in de-escalation methods and techniques and to apply them in every situation where feasible. An excerpt from one such legislative enactment (Oregon HB 4301; 2020, 2d Spec. Sess.) follows:

> A peace officer may use deadly physical force upon another person only when it is objectively reasonable, under the totality of circumstances known to the peace officer, to believe that the person poses an imminent threat of death or

> serious physical injury to the peace officer or to a third person and the use of deadly physical force is necessary … .
>
> Prior to using deadly physical force upon another person, if the peace officer has a reasonable opportunity to do so, the peace officer shall [c]onsider alternatives such as verbal de-escalation, waiting, using other available resources and techniques if reasonable, safe and feasible, or using a lesser degree of force; and [g]ive a verbal warning to the person that deadly physical force may be used and provide the person with a reasonable opportunity to comply.

Other states have delegated to peace officer standards and training ("POST") boards the obligation to promulgate procedures and standards related to de-escalation. An example is contained in the Minnesota Peace Officers Standards and Training Board (2020) Use of Force and Deadly Force Model Policy, excerpted below, which all Minnesota law enforcement agencies were required to adopt by December 15, 2020.

> De-Escalation [defined]: Taking action or communicating verbally or non-verbally during a potential force encounter in an attempt to stabilize the situation and reduce the immediacy of the threat so that more time, options, and resources can be called upon to resolve the situation without the use of force or with a reduction in the force necessary. De-escalation may include the use of such techniques as command presence, advisements, warnings, verbal persuasion, and tactical repositioning… .
>
> An officer shall use de-escalation techniques and other alternatives to higher levels of force consistent with their training whenever possible and appropriate before resorting to force and to reduce the need for force… .
>
> All officers shall receive training, at least annually, on this agency's use of force policy and related legal updates … . In addition, training shall be provided on a regular and periodic basis and designed to … [p]rovide techniques for the use of and reinforce the importance of de-escalation … .

Superlative examples of de-escalation, particularly in contexts where officers deal with persons suffering from chronic or acute mental health issues, are presented in the NBC Left Field (2019) documentary, *A Different Kind of Force: Policing Mental Illness*, and in a heart-rending June 2017 video (CNN, 2017) showing Bangkok Officer Anirut Malee listening to, disarming, then hugging a distraught, knife-wielding musician whose guitar had just been stolen and who had not been paid for his recent work. Officer Malee asked that the man not be criminally charged.

Mandating de-escalation training, policies, and measures is already underway in many jurisdictions and will likely continue in the near future if not beyond (Hutton, 2021; Moon, 2018; Mora, 2019; National Conference on State Legislatures, n.d.; Obasogie & Newman, 2017; Peoples, 2019; Police Use of Force Project, n.d.; Pugh, Rauenzahn, Wang, Chung, Jacobs, & Kaufman, 2020; Sherman, 2020a, 2020b; Sinyangwe, 2016; Terrill & Paoline, 2016). Nonetheless, according to the most recent Law Enforcement Management and Administrative

Statistics data (LEMAS, 2016), which were released in 2020, and based on a survey of 2,784 law enforcement agencies across the United States, there is still room for improvement regarding law enforcement agency use of force policies, reporting, and investigation as evidenced in Table 1.5.

The national decertified law enforcement officer index is gaining momentum (International Association of Directors and Law Enforcement Standards and Training, n.d.). Policies alone do not ensure procedural justice or reasonable use of force, but they can be an important star in the constellation of tools to achieve both goals.

Police Enjoy Multiple Protections that Shield them from Consequences

Although the U.S. Supreme Court's *Tennessee v. Garner* (1985) and *Graham v. O'Connor* (1989) decisions sketched out the bases for allowable deadly force by peace officers, and although Title 42 of United States Code section 1983 and the Court's *Bivens v. Six Unknown Federal Narcotics Agents* (1971) decision appeared to open the window for injured civilians to seek compensation, the Court's *Saucier v. Katz*

TABLE 1.5 Law Enforcement Policies on Use of Force Policies and Investigation as of 2016

With any use of force	
97%	Have writing policies or directives on using non-lethal force
96%	Have written policies or directives on reporting any use of force
77%	Maintain computerized files on all use of force
52%	Require external investigation for use of force causing serious injury
With use of weapon or other deadly force	
98%	Have written policies or directives on use of deadly force or weapon discharge
78%	Require external investigation for use of force causing death
51%	Require external investigation for discharge of firearm at or toward another
Regarding all civilian complaints against officers	
12%	Civilian complaint review board or other external agency used for all complaints
5%	Require review outside chain of officer's command for use of force complaint
3%	Civilian complaint review board has independent subpoena power

(2001), then *Pearson v. Callahan* (2009) decisions narrowed the injured civilian's ability to show that an officer's excessive force violated the civilian's constitutional rights, effectively creating at least qualified immunity for law enforcement officers (Reuters, 2020–2021). Those cases required that the officers violated a civilian's clearly established right, usually under the Fourth Amendment, and required, in essence, that a virtually identical case occurred before and yielded a damage award. The recently proposed George Floyd Justice in Policing Act (2021–2022) would curtail and end officers' qualified immunity, respectively, but both languish without passage in Congress (see Hill, Tiefenthäler, Triebert, Jordan, Willis, & Stein, 2020, for discussion of Floyd's death, and Ending Qualified Immunity Act (2021–2022)).

Furthermore, prosecutors are prone to condone and thus refrain from charging cases involving excessive force by officers, and both grand juries and petit (trial) juries usually accord officers great latitude in choosing to use force while protecting and serving the communities from which those grand and petit jurors were selected (Trac Reports, n.d.). Furthermore, prosecutors, too, are virtually immune from suit in all but the most egregious and patterned circumstances (*Connick v. Thompson*, 2011). All in all, victims of procedural abuse or misconduct at the hands of both police officers and prosecutors are largely unable to secure civil damages for those professional misdeeds, although the *State of Minnesota v. (Derek) Chauvin* (2020–2021) case (and a handful of other cases) may be an outlier or may finally indicate that criminal consequences for police officer use of excessive force may at least be available in extraordinary circumstances.

Against that backdrop of police use of excessive force, the following problems guide the reader toward beginning to address the excessive force issue from prevention, tactical, training, public safety, procedural justice, and public policy perspectives.

Exercises

Exercise One

Consider at least seven of the fourteen principles identified near the beginning of this chapter, as follows:

- I would rather be judged by twelve than carried by six.
- Shoot first and let God sort it out.
- Shoot center-mass.
- Shoot until the threat is eliminated.
- Shooting the subject in the leg is bad policy and unsafe.
- We have to bend the rules to beat those who break the rules.
- First, we ask; then, we tell; then, we make – "Ask – Tell – Make."
- American police officers should be armed – even those on traffic patrol.
- Each officer's assessment of risk is perfect and free of bias.

- Even if the officer is biased, we judge the officer's conduct based on what a reasonable officer in his situation would have deemed permissible or necessary.
- Each officer has the power and right to end a life even though our criminal justice system is framed by assumptions including innocence until proven guilty and due process that are the antithesis of shoot first and ask questions later.
- All previously unassigned governmental obligations that involve some risk must be assigned to armed law enforcement officers.
- We must mainstream those suffering from mental illness.
- Warrior police training prepares officers to shoot to kill but does not mandate it.

For each of the seven principles of lore you select, discuss in detail the flaws in reasoning implicit in each, then propose seven sound and ethical principles of your own design that would better guide law enforcement behavior and would help reduce law enforcement use of excessive force.

Exercise Two

Watch the short video presented at https://youtu.be/qMdcxkEIDEM, then describe your observations and reactions to it in detail. Next, propose a path that might be used involving hiring, discipline, training, policies, or otherwise in this police department to reduce the likelihood that similar events would occur in this city police department again. Be specific and detailed.

Exercise Three

Watch the extensive video entitled *A Different Kind of Force – Policing Mental Illness* (2019) presented at https://youtu.be/DnOLvKEYIQI or *Ernie & Joe: Crisis Cops* (2019). Describe in detail in your own words whether the solutions, in your view, rest with better trained, sworn, and armed law enforcement officers responding to these sorts of calls for service or whether mental health professionals, perhaps with armed law enforcement as backup or at a distance, would handle these calls with better results and fewer tragedies.

Exercise Four

Considering the continuum of force and law enforcement officer use-of-force training, policies, and procedures, (A) what flaws and unnecessary risks do you perceive in the current situation; (B) what changes would you recommend for improvements to training, policies, and procedures; and (C) how would each change you propose improve use-of-force outcomes and practices if applied? If you deem no changes necessary or advisable, please explain in detail why that is your position on this issue.

Exercise Five

Watch the bodycam video at https://youtu.be/0jDy2Uod-1E from an Albany Police encounter in 2019. Draft a three-page reflection based on that video. Among other topics, consider addressing the nature of the force used by police in this encounter, the "ask-tell-make" approach used by those officers, the group-think apparent in the officers' behaviors inside and outside the dwelling, the degree to which the police violence betrayed one or several rotten apples, a rotten barrel (the agency encouraging or accepting that behavior), or proper police work. If time permits, also present your recommendations for those officers and that agency in terms of training, discipline, tactics, use of force, de-escalation, and procedural justice.

Notes

1 Chuck MacLean was the principal author of this chapter.
2 Feiden Santana's smartphone video of the Walter Scott shooting is chilling in its stark intentionality and lack of credible threat. *NBC News* (2015, April 9). Dissecting the Walter Scott shooting (video, 3:49). Available at https://youtu.be/c6UzGIxQ_Qg.
3 See chapter 4.
4 See also, *Ernie & Joe: Crisis Cops* (video: 1:38:00) (2019); A different kind of force – Policing mental illness (video: 1:04:18) (2019). Available at https://youtu.be/DnOLvKEYIQI.
5 Example videos may be found at https://www.youtube.com/watch?v=f3TFV2bTj38, https://www.youtube.com/watch?v=zFfrbLYVYgU, https://www.youtube.com/watch?v=2Q2M0qDyagQ, https://www.youtube.com/watch?v=y3Gh7DZ6eSc, https://www.youtube.com/watch?v=9tjPmupjws8, https://www.youtube.com/watch?v=RM-7LpmfM-w, https://www.youtube.com/watch?v=Zd8V3nmQGJg.
6 Sometimes these concepts have been referred to as rotten apples, rotten barrels, and rotten orchards.
7 See chapter 4 for research demonstrating that police, especially in stressful situations, are unable to accurately perceive the risk and thus to accurately measure the appropriate response.
8 See Table 1.4.
9 See also, *Guardian* (2015). The counted: People killed by police in the U.S. Available at http://www.theguardian.com/us-news/series/counted-us-police-killings.
10 Table 1.3 lists, based on likelihood ratios, all States where unarmed non-Hispanic Black persons are at least twice as likely to be shot to death by police as would be expected based on the Black share of the non-Hispanic population. For example, in Wisconsin, unarmed non-Hispanic Black persons are 9.1 times more likely to be shot to death by police than the non-Hispanic Black share of the population.

References

Armacost, B. (2016, August 19). The organizational reasons police departments don't change. *Harvard Business Review Online*. Available at https://hbr.org/2016/08/the-organizational-reasons-police-departments-dont-change.

Associated Press (2021, March 11). Appeal by ex-officer who killed Tamir Rice dismissed. Available at https://apnews.com/article/shootings-police-tamir-rice-timothy-loehmann-cleveland-d2344d69a0bcf1e4f6000772ed378504.

Associated Press (2017, March 14). 911 dispatcher in Tamir Rice case suspended for 8 days; mother call that "unacceptable." Available at https://www.chicagotribune.com/nation-world/ct-tamir-rice-911-dispatcher-suspended-20170314-story.html.

Atkinson, C. & Hartrick, L. (2017). Conditioned response: The police trainer who teaches cops to kill (video: 6:52). *The New Yorker*. Available at https://youtu.be/ETf7NJOMS6Y.

Bivens v. Six Unknown Federal Narcotics Agents, 403 U.S. 388 (1971).

Blumberg, D. M., Papazoglou, K., & Schlosser, M. D. (2020). Organizational solutions to the moral risks of policing. *International Journal of Environmental Research and Public Health*, 17(20). Available at https://www.mdpi.com/855234. doi:10.1521/jsyt.2017.36.3.1.

Brooks, R. (2021). *Tangled up in blue: Policing the American city*. New York: Penguin Books.

Caldero, M. A., Dailey, J. D., & Withrow, B. L. (2018). *Police ethics: The corruption of noble cause* (fourth edition). New York NY: Routledge/Taylor & Francis Group.

Canterbury, C., & Cunningham, T. (2016). Statement of the Fraternal Order of Police and the International Association of Chiefs of Police on use of force standards. *Fraternal Order of Police and International Association of Chiefs of Police*. Available at https://mtu1.com/news/2527/informational-bulletin–statement-of-the-iacp-and-fop-on-use-of-force-standards.

Chalfin, A. & Kaplan, J. (2021). How many complaints against police officers can be abated by incapacitating a few "bad apples?" *Criminology & Public Policy*, 20(2), 351–370.

CNN (2017, June 30). Cop stops man with knife, hugs him. Available at https://youtu.be/qv-OSyQkPXM.

Congressional Research Service (2020, July 10). Police use of force: Overview and considerations for Congress. Available at https://www.hsdl.org/?view&did=841436.

Connick v. Thompson, 563 U.S. 51 (2011).

Court Statistics Project (2020). *State court caseload digest: 2018 data*. National Center for State Courts. Available at https://www.courtstatistics.org/__data/assets/pdf_file/0014/40820/2018-Digest.pdf.

Cowen, T. W. (2021, April 22). Footage of police trainer teaching cops how to kill resurfaces amid ongoing brutality. *Complex*. Available at https://www.complex.com/life/footage-of-police-trainer-teaching-cops-how-to-kill-resurfaces-ongoing-brutality/.

Dewan, S. (2021, April 12). Few police officers who cause deaths are charged or convicted. *The New York Times*. Available at https://www.nytimes.com/2020/09/24/us/police-killings-prosecution-charges.html.

Durr, M. (2015). What is the difference between slave patrols and modern day policing? Institutional violence in a community of color. *Critical Sociology*, 41(6), 873–879.

Ending Qualified Immunity Act, 117th Congress (2021–2022), HR 1470 [pending, not enacted].

Federal Bureau of Investigation (n.d.). National use-of-force data collection. Available at https://www.fbi.gov/services/cjis/ucr/use-of-force.

Ferrise, A. (2019, January 30). Cleveland officer Frank Garmback's suspension halved for role in Tamie Rice shooting. *Cleveland.com*. Available at https://www.cleveland.com/metro/2018/07/cleveland_officer_frank_garmba.html.

George Floyd Justice in Policing Act, 117th Congress (2021–2022), HR 1280, § 102 [pending; not enacted at press time].

Goff, P. A., Lloyd, T., Geller, A., Raphael, S., & Glaser, J. (2016). *The science of justice: Race, arrests, and police use of force*. Center for Policing Equity. Available at https://policingequity.org/images/pdfs-doc/CPE_SoJ_Race-Arrests-UoF_2016-07-08-1130.pdf.

Graham v. O'Connor, 490 U.S. 386 (1989).

Grennan, S. (2001). Historical perspective on police corruption in New York City in Palmiotto, M. J. (ed.) (2001) *Police misconduct: A reader for the 21st century*. New York NY: Prentice-Hall.

Guardian (2015). The counted: People killed by police in the US. Available at http://www.theguardian.com/us-news/series/counted-us-police-killings.

Hall, B. (2021, May 20). "You shouldn't be able to breathe," officer tells man before he dies. *NewsChannel5-Nashville*. Available at https://www.newschannel5.com/news/newschannel-5-investigates/you-shouldnt-be-able-to-breathe-officer-tells-man-before-he-dies.

Harrell, E. & Davis, E. (2020, December). Contacts between police and the public, 2018 – Statistical tables – Table 1. United States Department of Justice, Office of Justice Programs, Bureau of Justice Statistics. Available at https://bjs.ojp.gov/content/pub/pdf/cbpp18st.pdf.

Hill, E., Tiefenthäler, A., Triebert, C., Jordan, D., Willis, H., & Stein, R. (2020). How George Floyd was killed in police custody. *The New York Times*. Available at https://nyti.ms/2XMtUMa.

Hutton, A. (2021, May 16). Brooklyn Center in Minneapolis votes through sweeping police reform after fatal shootings of Black men: The bill will be named after Daunte Wright and Kobe Dimock-Heisler who were killed during encounters with city law enforcement officers. *Independent TV (UK)*. Available at https://www.independent.co.uk/news/world/americas/police-shooting-brooklyn-center-daunte-wright-b1848397.html.

Imbler v. Pachtman, 424 U.S. 409 (1976).

Jackman, T. (2020, June 17). FBI launched database on police use of force last year, but only 40 percent of police participated. *The Washington Post*. Available at https://www.washingtonpost.com/crime-law/2020/06/17/fbi-launched-database-police-use-force-last-year-only-40-percent-police-participated/.

International Association of Directors of Law Enforcement Standards and Training (n.d.). The National Decertification Index. Available at https://www.iadlest.org/our-services/ndi/about-ndi.

LaForgia, M. & Valentino-DeVries, J. (2021, May 15). How a genetic strain in Black people can give the police cover. *The New York Times*. Available at https://www.nytimes.com/2021/05/15/us/african-americans-sickle-cell-police.html?smid=nytcore-ios-share.

Law Enforcement Management and Administrative Statistics ("LEMAS") (2016). *Database and documentation*. Available at https://www.icpsr.umich.edu/web/NACJD/studies/37323/datadocumentation#.

Lee, A. S., Weitzer, R., & Martínez, D. E. (2018). Recent police killings in the United States: A three-city comparison. *Police Quarterly*, 21(2), 196–222. doi:10.1177/1098611117744508.

LEMAS (2016). See Law Enforcement Management and Administrative Statistics (2016).

Levin, S. T. (2021, May 4). "We're terrorized": LA sheriffs frequently harass families of people they kill, says report. *The Guardian* (UK). Available at https://www.theguardian.com/us-news/2021/may/04/los-angeles-sheriffs-harass-families-of-victims-report.

Long, C. (2021, April 16). Family asked feds to reopen case on 12-year-old Tamir Rice, who was shot and killed by Cleveland police in 2014. *Chicago Tribune*. Available at https://www.chicagotribune.com/nation-world/ct-aud-nw-tamir-rice-shooting-20210416-cnlzwresbbfw7m5b7kt6hdqx2q-story.html.

McShane, J. (2019). *Ernie & Joe: Crisis Cops* (video: 1:38:00). Available on HBO.

Minnesota Peace Officer Standards and Training Board(2020). Use of Force and Deadly Force Model Policy. Available at https://dps.mn.gov/entity/post/model-policies-learning-objectives/Documents/pdf.pdf.

Minnesota Public Radio News (2017, June 20). Squad car video: Officer Yanez pulls over Philando Castile. Available at https://www.youtube.com/watch?v=_pXWe4xFO04.

Moon, J. (2018, September 20). Police use of force policy analysis. *Campaign Zero*. Available at https://static1.squarespace.com/static/56996151cbced68b170389f4/t/57e1b5cc2994ca4ac1d97700/1474409936835/Police+Use+of+Force+Report.pdf.

Mora, V. (2019, Fall). As California goes, so does the nation: The state's new police use of deadly force law. *The Western Criminologist*, 17–18.

National Conference on State Legislatures (n.d.). Law enforcement statutory database. Available at https://www.ncsl.org/research/civil-and-criminal-justice/law-enforcement-statutory-database.aspx.

National consensus policy on use of force (2020, July). *National consensus policy and discussion paper on use of force*. Available at https://www.theiacp.org/sites/default/files/2020-07/National_Consensus_Policy_On_Use_Of_Force%2007102020%20v3.pdf.

National Law Enforcement Memorial and Museum (2021a). *2020 law enforcement officers fatalities report*. Available at http://nleomf.org/wp-content/uploads/2021/01/2020-LE-Officers-Fatalities-Report-opt.pdf.

National Law Enforcement Memorial and Museum (2021b). *Causes of law enforcement deaths over the past decade, 2010–2019*. Available at https://nleomf.org/facts-figures/causes-of-law-enforcement-deaths.

NBC Left Field (2019). *A different kind of force – Policing mental illness*. Available at https://youtu.be/DnOLvKEYIQI.

NBC News (2015, April 9). *Walter Scott shooting: Video analysis* (video, 3:49). Available at https://youtu.be/c6UzGIxQ_Qg.

Nelson, C. A. (2016). Frontlines: Policing at the nexus of race and mental health. *Fordham Urban Law Journal*, 43(3), 615–684.

Newton, S. (2018). The excessive use of force against blacks in the United States of America. *The International Journal of Human Rights*, 22(8), 1067–1086.

Obasogie, O. K. (2019, August 2). The bad-apple myth of policing. *The Atlantic*. Available at https://www.theatlantic.com/politics/archive/2019/08/how-courts-judge-police-use-force/594832/.

Obasogie, O. K., & Newman, Z. (2017). Police violence, use of force policies, and public health. *American Journal of Law & Medicine*, 43, 279–295.

Oregon HB 403I (2020, 2d Spec. Sess.). Available at https://olis.oregonlegislature.gov/liz/2020S2/Measures/Overview/HB4301.

Pearson v. Callahan, 555 U.S. 223 (2009).

Peoples, L. (2019, September 5). What the data say about police shootings. *Nature*. Available at https://www.nature.com/articles/d41586-019-02601-9.

Police Use of Force Project (n.d.). How police use of force policies can help to end police violence. Available at http://useofforceproject.org/#project.

Pugh, H., Rauenzahn, B., Wang, J., Chung, J., Jacobs, P., & Kaufman, A. (2020, June 13). Preventing police use of excessive force. *The Regulatory Review*. Available at https://www.theregreview.org/2020/06/13/preventing-police-excessive-force/.

Rawski, S. L. & Workman-Stark, A. L. (2018). Masculinity context cultures in policing organizations and recommendations for training interventions. *Journal of Social Issues*, 74(3), 607–627.

Reuters (2020–2021). Shielded: How an obscure legal doctrine called qualified immunity protects police accused of excessive force. Available at https://www.reuters.com/investigates/section/usa-police-immunity/.

Ross, C. T. (2015). A multi-level Bayesian analysis of racial bias in police shootings at the county level in the United States, 2011–2014. *PLoS ONE*. doi:10.1371/journal.pone.0141854.

Saucier v. Katz, 533 U.S. 194 (2001).

Schwartz, M. A. (2020, June 5). How the Supreme Court enables police excessive force. *New York Law Journal*. Available at https://www.law.com/newyorklawjournal/2020/06/05/how-the-supreme-court-enables-police-excessive-force/.

Sherman, L. W. (2020a). Evidence-based policing and fatal police shootings: Promise, problems, and prospects. *The ANNALS of the American Academy of Political and Social Science*, 687(1), 8–26. doi:10.1177/0002716220902073.

Sherman, L. W. (2020b). Preventing avoidable deaths in police encounters with citizens: Immediate priorities. *The ANNALS of the American Academy of Political and Social Science*, 687(1), 216–226. doi:10.1177/0002716220904048.

Sinyangwe, S. (2016, September 20). Examining the role of use of force policies in ending police violence. Available at https://papers.ssrn.com/sol3/papers.cfm?abstract_id=2841872.

Smith, B., & Holmes, M.D. (2014). Police use of excessive force in minority communities: A test of the minority threat, place, and community accountability hypotheses. *Social Problems*, 61, 83–104.

Smith, M. (2015, April 25). Tamir Rice's family to receive $6 million from Cleveland. *The New York Times*. Available at https://www.nytimes.com/2016/04/26/us/tamir-rice-family-cleveland-settlement.html.

Smith, M. (2017, June 16). Minnesota officer acquitted in killing of Philando Castile. *The New York Times*. Available at https://www.nytimes.com/2017/06/16/us/police-shooting-trial-philando-castile.html.

State of Minnesota v. (Derek) Chauvin, No. 27-CR-20–12646. Criminal Complaint (Minn. D. Ct. Hennepin County, June 3, 2020).

State of Minnesota v. (Mohamed) Noor, No. A19–1089, 2021 WL 317740 (Minn. Ct. App. 2021, Feb. 1).

State of Minnesota v. (Jeronimo) Yanez, No. 62-CR-16–8110, Criminal Complaint (filed 2016, Nov. 15).

Sumpter, K. (2021, May 13). Should cops shoot to incapacitate? The answer is "Yes!" Police1 Role Call. Available at https://www.police1.com/police-training/articles/should-cops-shoot-to-incapacitate-nPxv9KnlMwOUTnSo/.

Tennessee v. Garner, 471 U.S. 1 (1985).

Terrill, W., & Paoline, E. A. (2016). Police use of less lethal force: Does administrative policy matter? *Justice Quarterly*, 34(2), 193–216.

Terrill, W., & Reisig, D. M. (2014). Neighborhood context and police use of force. *Crime and Delinquency*, 40(30), 291–321.

Trac Reports, Inc. (n.d.). Police officers rarely charged for excessive use of force in federal court. Available at https://trac.syr.edu/tracreports/crim/615/#:~:text=Despite%20growing%20popular%20unrest%20and,242)%20against%20law%20enforcement.

Trinkner, R., Kerrison, E. M., & Goff, P. A. (in press 2021–2022). The force of fear: Police stereotype threat, self-legitimacy, and support for excessive force. *Law and Human Behavior*, 43(5), 421–435. Available at https://psycnet.apa.org/fulltext/2019-36698-001.html. doi:10.1037/lhb0000339.

United States Commission on Civil Rights (2018). *Police use of force: An examination of modern policing practices*. Available at https://www.usccr.gov/pubs/2018/11-15-Police-Force.pdf.

United States v. (Michael) Slager, No. 18–4036, Appellee United States' Brief (4th Cir. 2018, July 5). Available at https://www.justice.gov/crt/case-document/united-states-v-slager-brief-appellee.

United States Courts (2020). *Federal judicial caseload statistics 2020 Table D*. Available at https://www.uscourts.gov/statistics-reports/federal-judicial-caseload-statistics-2020-tables.

United States Department of Justice (2020, December 29). Press release: Justice Department announces closing of investigation into 2014 officer involved shooting in Cleveland, Ohio. Available at https://www.justice.gov/opa/pr/justice-department-announces-closing-investigation-2014-officer-involved-shooting-cleveland.

United States Department of Justice Federal Bureau of Investigations (2015–2019). *Law enforcement officers killed and assaulted, 2015–2019.* Available at https://www.fbi.gov/services/cjis/ucr/publications#LEOKA.

United States Department of Justice Federal Bureau of Investigations (2021, July 8). *Law enforcement officers killed and assaulted, year-to-date 2021.* Available at https://crime-data-explorer.fr.cloud.gov/pages/le/leoka.

United States Department of Justice Federal Bureau of Investigations Crime Data Explorer (2021, Spring). *Law enforcement officers killed and assaulted, 2020.* Available at https://crime-data-explorer.fr.cloud.gov/pages/downloads.

United States Department of Justice (2009). *The use-of-force continuum.* Available at https://nij.ojp.gov/topics/articles/use-force-continuum.

United States Department of Justice National Institute of Justice (2020, March 5). *The use-of-force continuum.* Available at https://nij.ojp.gov/topics/articles/overview-police-use-force.

Violent Crime Control and Law Enforcement Act of 1994, H.R. 3355, P. Law 103–322, 103d Congress (1994). Available at https://www.congress.gov/103/statute/STATUTE-108/STATUTE-108-Pg1796.pdf.

Walker, S., Alpert, G. P., & Kenney, D. J. (2001). *Early warning systems: Responding to the problem police officer.* U.S. Department of Justice, Office of Justice Programs, National Institute of Justice (2% of officers commit 50% of the misconduct).

Washington Post (updated through June 18, 2021). *Fatal Force.* Available at https://www.washingtonpost.com/graphics/investigations/police-shootings-database/.

Wihbey, J., & Kille L. W. (2016, July 28). Excessive or reasonable force by police? Research on law enforcement and racial conflict. *Journalist's Resource.* Available at https://journalistsresource.org/criminal-justice/police-reasonable-force-brutality-race-research-review-statistics/.

Wilson, J. Q. (1978). *Varieties of police behavior: The management of law and order in eight communities.* Cambridge, MA: Harvard University Press.

Wood, G., Tyler, T. P., & Papachristos, A. V. (2020, May 5). Procedural justice training reduces police use of force and complaints against officers. *Proceedings of the National Academy of Sciences*, 117(18), 9815–9821.

2

REFORMING, TRANSFORMING, REIMAGINING, OR DEFUNDING THE POLICE[1]

Accelerated by the 2020 police killing of George Floyd in Minneapolis, Minnesota, many have called for defunding the police, a phrase that evades clear definition. Does it mean to abolish law enforcement all together or to reduce the breadth of roles we call upon police to play or to redirect resources away from law enforcement and toward social and economic investments? Calls to defund the police polarize law and order and procedural justice advocates and leave communities in need of law enforcement services wondering, "What about us?" Others have called for reforming the police, arguing that evolution – not revolution – is needed to improve law enforcement without defunding it entirely. Still others have said no meaningful change can occur without transforming or reimagining the police from the ground up, arguing that incremental tinkering with police tactics, power, and structure is doomed to fail, because, they explain, American policing was grounded on racist themes and protection of majority interests to the detriment of minorities. In this chapter, all three perspectives are illuminated and weighed while addressing police shootings of unarmed African Americans, the appropriateness of applying qualified immunity to cases involving police misconduct, the advisability and practicalities of defunding the police, the viability of alternatives, including providing increased resources for mental health treatment, and the impact of such reforms on public safety, and the costs and benefits of each option.

Summary

- Case Spotlight: The 2020 killing of George Floyd in Minneapolis.
- American law enforcement has long been called upon to shore up the majority power structure, thereby favoring the majority and disfavoring minorities and their communities.
- Strident calls for defunding the police would leave some troubled communities without the law enforcement resources they desperately need and, in many cases, want.

DOI: 10.4324/9781003163411-3

- Reforming the police calls for evolution by bending law enforcement toward greater procedural justice and redirecting tax dollars from law enforcement to social resources.
- Reimagining or transforming the police envisions a revolution yielding a quantum leap from today's policing toward a gentler, more equitable, less force-driven approach to enforcing criminal laws – a system where "law enforcement" is supplanted and replaced by public safety and peace officers.

Case Spotlight: Murder of George Floyd by Minneapolis Police Officer Derek Chauvin

FIGURE 2.1 George Floyd Street Art in Mauer Park
Source: https://commons.wikimedia.org/wiki/File:Wandbild_Portrait_George_-Floyd_von_Eme_Street_Art_im_Mauerpark_(Berlin).jpg

FIGURE 2.2 Abolish the Police Street Art
Source: https://commons.wikimedia.org/w/index.php?search=abolish+the+police&-title=Special:MediaSearch&go=Go&type=image

At about 8:00 p.m. on May 25, 2020, clerks with Cup Foods in Minneapolis, Minnesota, called 9-1-1 to report that a man had just purchased cigarettes at the store using an apparently counterfeit $20 bill. Two Minneapolis Police officers – Thomas Lane and J. Alexander Keung – arrived on the scene shortly thereafter and the clerks told the officers that the man who had passed the bill was seated in a car across the street from the store. Officers approached the car; George Floyd (a 46-year-old Black man) was in the driver's seat and there were two passengers. Officer Lane briefly drew his service weapon and ordered Floyd to show his hands and get out of the car. Once Floyd put his hands on the steering wheel, Officer Lane holstered his weapon, bodily pulled Floyd out of the car, and cuffed Floyd's hands behind his back. Officer Lane told Floyd he was being arrested for allegedly passing a single counterfeit bill. When the officers tried to place Floyd into their marked squad car, Floyd stiffened then crumpled to the ground indicating that he did not want to enter the squad car because he was claustrophobic. Minneapolis Police Officers Derek Chauvin and Tou Thao then arrived on the scene and tried to help the first two officers load Floyd into the backseat of the squad car. Floyd continued struggling and repeatedly indicated he could not breathe, then Officer Chauvin pulled Floyd through and out of the squad car and onto the pavement. Officer Chauvin then placed his knee on Floyd's neck and chest with two of the other officers' bodies placed on Floyd's chest and legs. Floyd continued saying he could not breathe, called for his "Mama," and said, "I'm about to die." The incident, which was videotaped from several angles, dragged on for over seven minutes with Officer Chauvin's knee on Floyd's neck. At least two of the other officers asked the senior officer Chauvin whether they should roll the man onto his side – Chauvin refused. During the last four minutes of that time, with Chauvin still holding his knee against Floyd's neck, Floyd closed his eyes and did not appear to be moving let alone actively resisting. Bystanders begged the officers to get off of Floyd's neck but Officer Chauvin kept his knee on Floyd's neck until EMTs arrived and told Officer Chauvin to get off Floyd's neck so the EMTs could load Floyd onto the stretcher then into the ambulance.[2]

Videos of the incident reverberated around the globe generating thousands of protests and calls for reform and abolition of law enforcement. That tragedy and the echoes of those protests continue to drive reform and abolition efforts and discussions in many communities and state and federal capitals.

The case against Officer Chauvin was tried to a jury in May 2021. After 21 days of testimony and about eight hours of deliberation, Chauvin was convicted on all counts – all of which required proof beyond a reasonable doubt that Chauvin unintentionally (not intentionally) killed George Floyd. On June 25, 2021, Chauvin was sentenced in state court to 22.5 years in prison,[3] a ten-year aggravated (that is, increased) durational departure from the presumptive guidelines sentence.[4] Chauvin and the other three officers on the scene have also been indicted by a federal grand jury for violating George Floyd's civil rights by killing Floyd without justification or excuse.[5] Chauvin later pleaded guilty to the federal charge.

Responses to Black Lives Matter, George Floyd, and Excessive Use of Police Force

Although defunding, reforming, reimagining, and transforming the police are often used almost interchangeably, they call for very different means, methods, solutions, and end-points (Akbar, 2020; Collins, 2020; Elbeshbishi & Quarshie, 2021; Fernandez, 2020; *Guardian*, 2020, June 22; Human Rights Watch, 2020; Jagannathan, 2020; Karakatsanis, 2019; Lowrey, 2020; National Research Center, 2021; O'Rourke & Binder, 2021; Searcey, 2020; Taylor, 2020; Terpstra, 2020; Weichselbaum & Lewis, 2020).

Some state legislatures, such as Michigan, have already lined up to oppose defunding efforts. As one example, Michigan Senate Resolution SR149, adopted in October 2020, and labelled "A resolution to discourage local units of government from defunding and abolishing police departments," provided:

> [L]aw enforcement is a necessary and vital function of our government at all levels … . Law enforcement officers are courageous individuals working in dangerous situations to enforce the laws enacted by the Legislature to ensure public safety, protect the health and possessions of our citizens, and prevent crime and disorder … . Defunding or abolishing police departments at any level of government will put citizens at risk, create chaos and disorder, and burden remaining departments that may be called upon to assist municipalities that no longer have the resources to respond to emergency calls …; and … [p] ast incidents of rioting and looting in our cities are further evidence of the need to properly fund law enforcement. The absence of law enforcement officers in our cities and rural areas could affect the state's economy, discouraging businesses from locating here and out-of-state residents from visiting; now, therefore, be it Resolved by the Senate, That we discourage local units of government from defunding or abolishing police departments.[6]

In the face of such opposition, defunding the police often starts with the assumption that there are too many police officers doing too much harm or that officers are too often being called upon to perform services they are patently ill-prepared to deliver. Those who supportively approach defunding the police can be arrayed along a spectrum from one extreme – abolishing the police all together – to the other extreme – substantially reducing funding that supports harmful police conduct and transferring those public funds to helpful and creative uses like increased educational, living-wage employment, and affordable housing opportunities; child and young adult activities; family supports; community-based mental health treatment; nutrition supports; and other social programming. The general defunding theory is that the law enforcement role in the United States grew out of slave patrols and continues to be in business in large part to protect majority interests by subjugating minorities (Al-Hashimi, 2021; Bryant, 2019; Gehring, 2020; Owusu-Bempah, 2017; Steinmetz, Schaefer, & Henderson, 2017;

Tensley, 2021). Other defunding proponents argue that, over time, police have been assigned many roles that could be better and less muscularly served by others who are trained and focused on each role (Sherman, 2020; Weiner, 2021): police have become first responders for mental health crises although caseworkers and psychologists could more safely respond to those crises with a better informed and less armed foundation (Everytown Research & Policy, 2021; NBC Left Field, 2019; Reuland, Draper, & Norton, 2012; Rogers, McNiel, & Binder, 2019; Vermeer, Woods, & Jackson, 2020, Weiner, 2021, Westervelt, 2020); police have been assigned school liaison and security roles better served by educators and school personnel (Homer & Risher, 2020; McKenna & White, 2018; Petteruti, 2011); drug enforcement by police could be more wisely and peaceably addressed through decriminalization, legalization of possession and use, and enhanced funding for treatment and aftercare (Ferreira, 2017); police intervention in many domestic abuse situations could be better provided by family supports, counselling, and therapy (Boyd-Barrett, 2020; Chinn, 2020; Reuland, Morabito, Preston, & Cheney, 2006); and so on. Reducing the police role in these and other situations would free up public dollars for peaceful interventions through non-police providers. As a corollary, each police intervention, especially those including arrest, charging, conviction, and sentencing, costs society and communities immeasurably and should be seen as more an opportunity cost and less a necessary government expenditure.

Status Quo: Isolated and Limited Modifications to Police Funding and Practice

Law enforcement in the United States is a reflection of its past and with over 18,000 separate law enforcement agencies in the country, each with independent leadership, there are over 18,000 unique reflections of that past. Some law enforcement agencies (LEAs) reflect a slave tradition, while others mirror community inequities, and still others are built on a platform of slow and limited modifications to past practice and even then, only when compelled by circumstances. Thus, the status quo is a crazy quilt of over 18,000 unique approaches to LEA practice, procedure, and personality, comfortable in its stability but unable and often unwilling to respond to new evidence-based approaches, evolving popular sentiment, and new legislative or judicial guidance.

> Reforming police, as it turns out, is a lot harder than reforming the military, because of the decentralized way in which thousands of police departments across the country operate, the historical affinity of certain police departments with the same racial ideologies espoused by extremists, and an even broader reluctance to do much about it.
>
> *(Speri, 2017)*

Evolution – The Middle Ground: Reforming the Police

In the middle, one finds a group largely satisfied with the LEA approach but focused on optimizing procedural justice and racial-ethnic equity throughout the criminal justice system and mitigating the sharp racial and ethnic disparities in how persons of color ("POCs") are treated by law enforcement and prosecutors, and by judges in bail setting, sentencing, sentence mitigation, and post-conviction remedies. These advocates, in other words, seek to reform the police. Many of these advocates recognize the difficulties to be encountered in reforming the police, which requires reform in 18,000+ independent LEAs.

What Has Been Tried to Date and to What Effect?

The National Conference of State Legislatures (NCSL Database) (updated regularly) found that more than thirty states, between January 2020 and April 2021, had enacted nearly 150 police reforms ranging from restricting neck restraint techniques to mandating and funding body-worn cameras.

Table 2.1 betrays the true challenge of trying to evolve or transform American law enforcement when it is a disjointed amalgam of more than 50 separate federal and state jurisdictions and no less than 18,000 separate law enforcement agencies and about 800,000 individual law enforcement officers. As Table 2.1 illustrates, nearly 20 states have not enacted any substantive police reform from January 2020 through April 2021 (see Figure 2.3) – in spite of George Floyd, Breonna Taylor, Tamir Rice, and all the other victims of police overreach and error – and in spite of the tens of millions of dollars in civil settlements already paid out to those victims' surviving relatives.

Even those states that have enacted police reform have largely shown limited legislative willingness to wade too deeply into telling reform. Indeed, only a handful of states (notably, California, Kentucky, Minnesota, New York, Oregon, Utah, and Virginia) have enacted broad and impactful police reforms. A couple of exemplars follow. California (NCSL Database, updated regularly) has prohibited LEAs from authorizing LEOs to wear uniforms resembling military issue; required LEOs to be evaluated by physicians or psychologists regarding their race, ethnicity, gender, sexual orientation, or religious biases; compelled LEAs to deemphasize paramilitary aspects of LEOs' jobs; authorized creation of a County Sheriff's Oversight Board with subpoena power; prohibited carotid restraints and chokeholds; required the state attorney general to investigate all officer-involved killings of unarmed civilians and post resulting reports on a public website; and required the state attorney general to maintain a Police Practices Division to review LEA use of deadly force policies. Minnesota (NCSL Database, updated regularly) addressed peer counseling and stress management resources after stressful incidents; adopted LEO residency incentives; mandated critical incident and autism spectrum training; reformed POST membership and practices; required LEOs to intervene and report when other LEOs engage in use of excessive force; regulated LEO use of force; and prohibited warrior-style LEO training.

TABLE 2.1 Police Reform-Related Legislation by State post-George Floyd

	AL	AK	AZ	AR	CA	CO	CT	DE	DC	FL	GA	HI	ID	IL	IN	IA	KS	KY	LA	ME
Authorize Civilian Recording of LE Activity																				
Autism Spectrum Training Reform																				
Body-Worn Camera Reform																				
Chokehold Reform					■			■							■	■				
Civilian Oversight Board Reform					■															
Civilian Review Board Reform																				
Comprehensive Policing and Justice Reforms									■											
Critical Incident Training and Procedures Reform															■					
De-Escalation Policies/Training Reform															■					
Disciplineded/Discharged LEO Transparency & Procedures Reform												■		■	■			■		
Evidence Reform																				
First Responder Mental Health Reform																		■		
Law Enforcement Integrity/Accountability Reform						■	■													
LEA Drug & Alcohol Testing of LEOs Reform																				
LEA Paramilitary Focus in Recruitment/Job Descriptions Reform					■															
LEA Purchase of Military Surplus Equipment Reform														■						
LEA Staffing, Organization, and Personnel Reform				■																

LEA Use of Arrest Quotas Reform																				
LEO Background Investigations Reform																				
LEO Cultural Awareness Training Reform																				
LEO Duty Hours Reform																				
LEO Evaluation for Racial, Ethnic, Gender, Religious Bias Reform																				
LEO Intervention to Prevent Excessive Force Reform																				
LEO Mental Health Reform																				
LEO Minimum Qualifications Reform																				
LEO Requirement to Report Misconduct by Other LEOs Reform																				
LEO Residency Reform																				
LEO Sex Misconduct with Arrestee Reforms																				
LEO Training Requirements Reform																				
LEO Use of Teargas & Long-Range Acoustic Devices Reform																				
LEO Vehicle Stop Procedures Reform																				
Mental Health & Critical Incident Training/ Procedures Reform																				
Mental Health Diversion Pilot Program Reform																				
Militarized LEA Uniforms Reform																				
Mobile Crisis Co-Response Team Reform																				

No-Knock Warrants Reform																				
NO SUBSTANTIVE REFORM																				
Officer Care to Arrestee Reform																				
Officer-Involved Civilian Death Investigation Reform																				
Other POST Board Reforms																				
Peace Officer Bill of Rights Repeal																				
Police Reform Commission Reform																				
Police Training Reform																				
Reporting of Incident Against Protected Class Reform																				
Search Warrant Reform																				
Trauma-Informed Care Reform																				
Use of Force Reform																				
Warrior-Style LEO Training Reform																				
Whistleblower Protections Reform																				

	MD	MA	MI	MN	MS	MT	NE	NV	NH	NJ	NM	NY	NC	ND	OH	OK	OR	PA	RI	SC
Authorize Civilian Recording of LE Activity																				
Autism Spectrum Training Reform																				
Body-Worn Camera Reform																				
Chokehold Reform																				
Civilian Oversight Board Reform																				
Civilian Review Board Reform																				
Comprehensive Policing and Justice Reforms																				
Critical Incident Training and Procedures Reform																				
De-Escalation Policies/Training Reform																				
Disciplineded/Discharged LEO Transparency & Procedures Reform																				
Evidence Reform																				
First Responder Mental Health Reform																				
Law Enforcement Integrity/Accountability Reform																				
LEA Drug & Alcohol Testing of LEOs Reform																				
LEA Paramilitary Focus in Recruitment/Job Descriptions Reform																				
LEA Purchase of Military Surplus Equipment Reform																				
LEA Staffing, Organization, and Personnel Reform																				
LEA Use of Arrest Quotas Reform																				
LEO Background Investigations Reform																				

	MD	MA	MI	MN	MS	MT	NE	NV	NH	NJ	NM	NY	NC	ND	OH	OK	OR	PA	RI	SC
LEO Cultural Awareness Training Reform																				
LEO Duty Hours Reform																				
LEO Evaluation for Racial, Ethnic, Gender, Religious Bias Reform																				
LEO Intervention to Prevent Excessive Force Reform								■									■			
LEO Mental Health Reform				■																
LEO Minimum Qualifications Reform																				
LEO Requirement to Report Misconduct by Other LEOs Reform									■											
LEO Residency Reform				■																■
LEO Sex Misconduct with Arrestee Reforms																				
LEO Training Requirements Reform																				
LEO Use of Teargas & Long-Range Acoustic Devices Reform																	■			
LEO Vehicle Stop Procedures Reform								■												
Mental Health & Critical Incident Training/Procedures Reform			■	■																
Mental Health Diversion Pilot Program Reform																				
Militarized LEA Uniforms Reform																				
Mobile Crisis Co-Response Team Reform																				
No-Knock Warrants Reform	■																			
NO SUBSTANTIVE REFORM																				
Officer Care to Arrestee Reform												■								

	MD	*MA*	*MI*	*MN*	*MS*	*MT*	*NE*	*NV*	*NH*	*NJ*	*NM*	*NY*	*NC*	*ND*	*OH*	*OK*	*OR*	*PA*	*RI*	*SC*
Officer-Involved Civilian Death Investigation Reform												■								
Other POST Board Reforms			■	■		■	■										■	■		■
Peace Officer Bill of Rights Repeal	■																			
Police Reform Commission Reform																	■			
Police Training Reform																				
Reporting of Incident Against Protected Class Reform												■								
Search Warrant Reform																				
Trauma-Informed Care Reform												■								
Use of Force Reform				■													■			
Warrior-Style LEO Training Reform				■																
Whistleblower Protections Reform																				

Authorize Civilian Recording of LE Activity	*SD*	*TN*	*TX*	*UT*	*VT*	*VA*	*WA*	*WV*	*WI*	*WY*
Autism Spectrum Training Reform										
Body-Worm Camera Reform										
Chokehold Reform										
Civilian Oversight Board Reform										
Civilian Review Board Reform										
Comprehensive Policing and Justice Reforms										
Critical Incident Training and Procedures Reform										
De-Escalation Policies/Training Reform										
Disciplineded/Discharged LEO Transparency & Procedures Reform										
Evidence Reform										
First Responder Mental Health Reform										
Law Enforcement Integrity/Accountability Reform										
LEA Drug & Alcohol Testing of LEOs Reform										
LEA Paramilitary Focus in Recruitment/Job Descriptions Reform										
LEA Purchase of Military Surplus Equipment Reform										
LEA Staffing, Organization, and Personnel Reform										
LEA Use of Arrest Quotas Reform										

Authorize Civilian Recording of LE Activity	*SD*	*TN*	*TX*	*UT*	*VT*	*VA*	*WA*	*WV*	*WI*	*WY*
LEO Background Investigations Reform										
LEO Cultural Awareness Training Reform										
LEO Duty Hours Reform										
LEO Evaluation for Racial, Ethnic, Gender, Religious Bias Reform										
LEO Intervention to Prevent Excessive Force Reform										
LEO Mental Health Reform										
LEO Minimum Qualifications Reform										
LEO Requirement to Report Misconduct by Other LEOs Reform										
LEO Residency Reform										
LEO Sex Misconduct with Arrestee Reforms										
LEO Training Requirements Reform										
LEO Use of Teargas & Long-Range Acoustic Devices Reform										
LEO Vehicle Stop Procedures Reform										
Mental Health & Critical Incident Training/ Procedures Reform										
Mental Health Diversion Pilot Program Reform										
Militarized LEA Uniforms Reform										

	SD	*TN*	*TX*	*UT*	*VT*	*VA*	*WA*	*WV*	*WI*	*WY*
Authorize Civilian Recording of LE Activity										
Mobile Crisis Co-Response Team Reform						■				
No-Knock Warrants Reform										
NO SUBSTANTIVE REFORM										
Officer Care to Arrestee Reform										
Officer-Involved Civilian Death Investigation Reform				■						
Other POST Board Reforms						■				
Peace Officer Bill of Rights Repeal										
Police Reform Commission Reform										
Police Training Reform		■								
Reporting of Incident Against Protected Class Reform										
Search Warrant Reform						■				
Trauma-Informed Care Reform										
Use of Force Reform				■	■					
Warrior-Style LEO Training Reform										
Whistleblower Protections Reform										

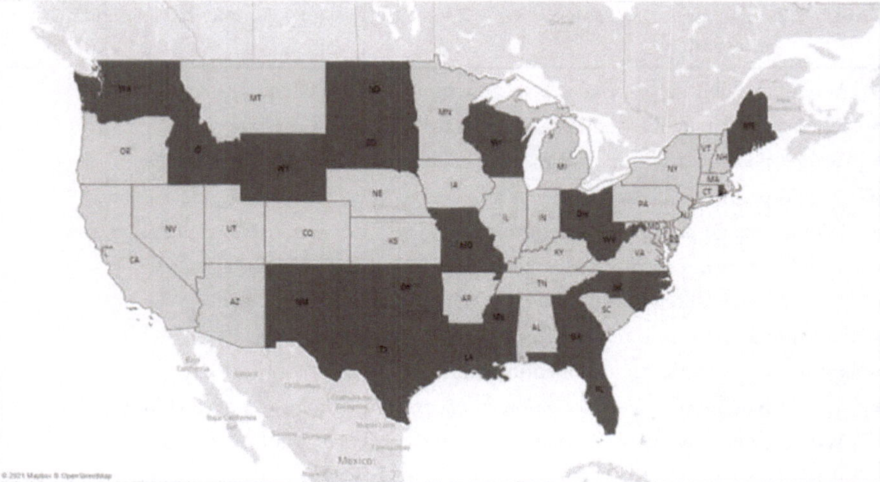

FIGURE 2.3 States (Dark Gray) Without Substantive Police Reform Legislation Between January 2020 and April 2021

Several police reform initiatives gained multistate support. At least seven states (CA, DE, IN, IA, OR, UT, VA) restricted or eliminated LEO use of neck restraints and chokeholds. Eleven states (HI, IL, IN, KY, MD, NV, NJ, NY, OR, UT, VA) modified and improved the transparency of LEO discipline, suspension, and termination for misconduct. Six states (AL, AR, KY, MI, MN, UT) required mental health and critical incident training for LEOs. At least eight states (MI, MN, MT, NE, OR, PA, SC, VA) adopted substantial peace officer standards and licensing board reforms. Seven states (CA, CT, HI, MN, OR, UT, VT) adopted use-of-force policy and procedure reforms. Other key legislative quests are to enact whistle-blower protections, and duties for officers to intervene and report fellow officer misconduct. Some also recommend all officers receive bias training (which many commentators deem to be an ineffectual "feel-good" Band-Aid).

Perhaps the paradigm evolutionary proposal for police reform, the George Floyd Justice in Policing Act (2020–2021 – not enacted at press time), is bogged down in Congress as this book goes to press. The Act's highlights, as identified by the Congressional Research Service (2020), are presented in Table 2.2.

Among the early leaders in evolutionary police reform, Washington State, in May 2021, enacted a sweeping set of statutory amendments[8] to begin to address procedural justice and disparate outcomes in law enforcement activities. Some highlights of Washington's enacted and sweeping though evolutionary police reforms are presented in Table 2.3.

Those evolutionary changes in Washington State and potential changes in the George Floyd Justice in Policing Act are obviously important improvements, but have left many stones unturned. Some of those other stones are presented in Table 2.1, above. Of course, those incremental changes leave some core law enforcement problems unaddressed, including White supremacy in law enforcement, the military-to-policing pipeline, and

TABLE 2.2 Highlights of George Floyd Justice in Policing Act of 2021 [pending, not enacted]

- Would prohibit racial, religious, and discriminatory profiling
- Would ban chokeholds and no-knock warrants at the federal level
- Would penalize states that fail to ban chokeholds and no-knock warrants
- Would permit deadly force only as a last resort and would require de-escalation
- Would change permissible use of force standard from reasonable to necessary
- Would limit transfer of military equipment to law enforcement agencies
- Would require body-word cameras at the federal level
- Would penalize states that fail to mandate body-worn cameras
- Purports to "eliminate" qualified immunity for officers[7]
- Would require improved law enforcement training to address police culture issues
- Would gather better data on law enforcement practices and use of force
- Would establish DOJ task force to coordinate responses to officer misconduct
- Would create a nationwide police misconduct registry
- Would require use of force reports by race, sex, disability, religion, and age

TABLE 2.3 Washington's Sweeping Police Reform Act as Enacted – Highlights

- Bans chokeholds and neck restraints
- Bans no-knock warrants
- Requires officers to intervene if fellow officers engage in excessive force
- Creates an independent office to review use of deadly force incidents
- Requires use of de-escalation procedures
- Restricts police vehicle chases
- Restricts use of teargas
- Improves certification and background checks for police officers
- Creates new and independent office to investigate use of force incidents
- Mandates recording of custodial interrogations

the impact of President Donald Trump and his Department of Justice opposition to substantive police reform during his presidency. Those are addressed below.

Ridding Law Enforcement of White Supremacists. White supremacists have long been known to affiliate with law enforcement officers and agencies; indeed, some police officers are white supremacists and other police officers actively sympathize with white supremacists and their organizations (Speri, 2017). Michael German (2020a, 2020b), himself a former FBI agent, reported that the white supremacy connection to law enforcement has been shown since the FBI Counterterrorism Division report (2006) and was reflected again in a classified FBI counterterrorism policy guide cited by Speri (2017), which stated "domestic terrorism investigations focused on militia extremists, white supremacist extremists, and sovereign citizen extremists often have identified active links to law enforcement officers." Quoted in Speri (2017), Chapman University Professor Pete Simi noted, "If you look at the history of law enforcement in the United States, it is a history of white supremacy, to put it bluntly." That spirit was echoed by John Marshall Law School Professor Samuel Jones, also cited in Speri (2017): "When somebody holds a belief that indicates that they do not see all Americans are worthy of equal protection under the law, it compromises their ability to be a police officer."

The Military-to-Policing Pipeline. A related concern many have identified revolves around militarization of policing and the military as a feeder for the police profession (Weichselbaum & Schwartzapfel, 2017). As police budgets grew increasingly strained in the 1990s, police agencies, some pressed into serving the "War on Terror," often turned to government surplus equipment, authorized by Section 1033 of the National Defense Authorization Act of 1997[9] to fill some of the gap. That resulted in a dramatic increase in military-grade equipment (armed personnel carriers, assault weapons, tanks, helicopters, etc.) owned by law enforcement serving America's cities – reaching about $2 billion by mid-2020 (McCartney, Murray, & Roganasakul, 2020).

In a similar vein, military service, particularly military police service, often is seen as a perfect feeder for law enforcement careers. It seems logical. Both military and law enforcement are top-down, regimented careers. Even the ranks are similar: Commander, Captain, Lieutenant, Sergeant, and so on. However, problems can arise when veterans carry their military training and mindsets into police service. America's streets are not battlefields. Every person with a gun or knife or screwdriver in America is not a lethal threat to a police officer as would be more likely the case in a theatre of war. The rules of engagement in a military theatre are not the same as the rules of engagement for police officers. The imagined rough equivalence between military service and police service carries over into police culture almost without leavening. For example, the theory implicit in the "blue code of silence" (Center on Media, Crime, and Justice at John Jay College: The Crime Report, 2021) and "the thin blue line," that officers are reliant on other officers for their very lives and the corollary that an officer cannot rat on a fellow officer, because each relies on the other to have their back and to save their life, is a theory born of battle (the Crimean War in 1854, to be precise), not police service (Hernandez, 2020). Thankfully, even that Blue Code of Silence is broken from time to time.[10] Theories giving superordinate value to the prime directive and self-preservation, commonplace and relevant in a theatre of war, are misleading and poor guideposts when protecting and serving civilians in an American city. Those who explore these militarization and military–police pipeline concerns explain that while most veterans can become terrific public servants as law enforcement officers, other veterans can struggle to differentiate between the rules of war and the realities on America's streets (International Association of Chiefs of Police, 2009).

The Anti-Reform Policing Legacy of Donald Trump and his DOJ. Consent decrees, which were authorized by the President Clinton era 1994 crime bill (Federal Violent Crime

Control and Law Enforcement Act of 1994), which ushered in some very unfortunate over-incarceration problems with some of its other provisions, then flourished under the Obama administration before disintegrating under Donald Trump and then-United States Attorney General Jeff Sessions in 2018 (Attorney General Jeff Sessions, 2018). A rebirth of consent decrees may be another evolutionary path forward. Under a consent decree, generally, the United States Department of Justice and a local city and its police department reach an agreement to reform local police operations to better ensure constitutional law enforcement and procedural justice. A sample consent decree from the Obama era may be reviewed at *United States v. Cleveland*, Settlement Agreement (2015). Consider also the following section identifying some evolutionary steps that have been taken in other countries.

International Police Reform Innovations. Other nations have responded in varying degrees to police accountability and reform, and with varying levels of sincerity and success (Kleinfeld, 2020; United Nations Office on Drugs and Crime, 2011). Perhaps we should consider or adopt some of their reforms in the United States. Some countries have:

- hired more women in law enforcement as done in Peru (Jones, 2000);
- fired all officers and rehired only those passing exacting tests (El Salvador, the country of Georgia, and the city of Bogotá, Colombia) (Kleinfeld, 2020);
- disciplined or terminated officers accepting bribes (country of Georgia (Saakashvilli, 2020));
- vastly expanded training rigor and duration; Portugal requires 260 weeks of police training; Finland, 135 weeks; Germany, 101 weeks; Australia, 87 weeks; England, 56 weeks; and in the United States, just 21 weeks (Institute for Criminal Justice Training Reform, n.d.);
- abolished the police force as Estonia did in 1990 (Saar, 1999), followed by Georgia in 2004 and Ukraine in 2014 (Trofimov, 2020);
- centralized their police forces; Canada has fewer than 200 police forces (Statistics Canada, 2020) and the Netherlands (Government of the Netherlands, n.d.) and France (Council on Foreign Relations, 2021) each has a single national police force compared to the United States with over 18,000 separate law enforcement agencies largely untethered from each other;
- disarmed most police officers, such as in Britain, Ireland, New Zealand, Norway, and Iceland (Commander, 2018; Goldhill, 2016), plus 14 other countries;[11]
- dramatically reduced situations where police are authorized to use extensive force, such as in Denmark (Centre for Human Rights: University of Pretoria, n.d.) and Finland (Centre for Human Rights: University of Pretoria, n.d.); see also the European Convention on Human Rights (1950 and as amended thereafter), ratified by 47 countries (Scotland Equality and Human Rights Commission, n.d.), that restricts officer use of deadly force to when it is "absolutely necessary," instead of based on "reasonable belief" as in most U.S. states; and the United Nations (1979) Code of Conduct for Law Enforcement Officials, which permits police use of force only as a "last resort";

- banned neck restraints and chokeholds in most European countries (Berger & Noack, 2021);
- elevated crisis intervention and de-escalation training to a central pillar in police training compared to the United States where those topics are often more afterthought than pillar (Serhan, 2020);
- among many other examples.

Many argue that communities of color see law enforcement as a system that controls them but does not protect or value them. Indeed, at least one commentator has argued that the source of Black distrust of law enforcement lies in this "legal estrangement," living in a society where one is the object of much law enforcement focus but very little law enforcement protection and respect (Bell, 2017).[12] Evolutionary law enforcement reform may be able to capitalize on many of the options above. Revolutionary police reform efforts – perhaps enough to address this estrangement – could require transformation of law enforcement that would be much more wide ranging.

Revolution: Reimagining, Transforming, or Abolishing the Police

Advocates of reimagining the police posit that armed law enforcement officers should be applied only when circumstances require their presence and their weapon. For example, social workers could respond to homeless or truancy situations. Psychologists and counselors could respond to critical incidents involving mentally ill subjects. Non-sworn and unarmed officers could hand out parking and traffic tickets. By reducing the footprint of law enforcement responsibilities, dollars are freed to meet those other societal needs, and the tragedies that can accompany firearm-wielding officers can be averted.

Further along the police reform spectrum are LEAs operating in communities unwilling (or, at least, no longer willing) to abide by the status quo and who are driven, instead, to envision and adopt an entirely new approach to public safety (note the seismic shift from the "law enforcement" label and paradigm to "public safety"). Advocates within those communities seek to jettison past practices and create an entirely new approach to public safety grounded on community investment, dramatic reductions in police presence and warrior persona, and redirection of responsibilities and funding away from LEAs and toward community organizations better able to (1) provide resources communities and residents need to feed their children, earn educational advancement, achieve greater equality of housing, occupational, and financial equity, and (2) more peaceably approach critical mental health incidents, minor traffic violations, community patrols, and de-escalation that often heavily armed LEOs seem unable or unwilling to manage without unreasonable coercion, intervention, and force.

Defunding has started to occur in some cities, but those efforts, to date, are characterized much more by slightly reduced (and sometimes, re-directed) budget dollars (Akinnibi, Holder, & Cannon, 2021; McEvoy, 2020; Mulvihill, 2020). By early 2021, the fifty largest United States cities had reduced their police budgets by an estimated 5.2% overall. Some examples are presented in Table 2.4 (Akinnibi, Holder, & Cannon, 2021):

TABLE 2.4 Police Budget Cuts in Selected Cities, 2020–2021

- Austin, Texas – cut $150 million from the city's police budget (-33% reduction)
- Minneapolis, Minnesota – cut $28 million (-14.8%)
- New York City – cut $1 billion (-14.8%) [New York later increased the budget]
- Seattle, Washington – cut $3.5 million (-11.2%)
- Denver, Colorado – cut $25 million (-9.8%)
- Las Vegas, Nevada (-8%)
- Arlington, Texas (-7.5%)
- New Orleans, Louisiana (-7%)
- Chicago, Illinois (-6%)
- Baltimore, Maryland – cut $22 million (-4%)
- San Francisco, California – cut $120 million (-4%)
- Portland, Oregon – cut $16 million (-3%)
- Los Angeles, California – cut $150 million (-2%)
- Philadelphia, Pennsylvania – cut $33 million (-2%)

Despite those individual cities reducing police budgets and often reinvesting or reallocating some of the savings to social programming, virtually no U.S. city has disbanded its police force,[13] and several cities that appeared to be on the road to defunding have since reversed course as increased crime rates have captured legislators' attentions (Arango, 2021; Holder, Akinnibi, & Cannon, 2020; Smerconish, 2021). Thus, defunding – so far – is a euphemism, at best.

That is a great disappointment to many who seek true defunding and abolition, who bemoan that to honor inertia, tradition, status quo, and majority control over minority communities and individuals, police budgets stay bloated, while employment, housing, nutrition, community empowerment, and other key programs remain underfunded. Proponents of defunding the police run the gamut. At one end of the "defund the police" spectrum may be found those who support measured reallocation of public resources away from traditional law enforcement and toward nutrition, education, community investment, jobs creation, income balancing, Medicare for All, work skills education, and equity. At the other extreme are those activists who favor abolition of the police all together, to be replaced not by a new or reconstituted or re-assigned law enforcement agency, but by unarmed community patrols and a wide range of community and individual investments to create a less violent, less coercive, and more self-empowering community from the ground up. The abolitionists argue that existing LEAs must be disbanded as they are incapable of or pathologically resistant to reform. Conversely, abolitionists argue that White supremacist LEOs, who inherited the historical American tradition of minority suppression and the wholly American law enforcement context of having been born out of slave patrols and the slave trade, must be rooted out and removed from public safety all together. The following section addresses proposals made by abolition advocates from across much of that range.

Abolitionists' Arguments

Abolitionists are no longer willing to wait patiently for time-tested and evidence-based but modest evolution of United States law enforcement. The stream of new incidents of excessive police use of force have taken too many young and unarmed Black lives. Many of the names of the victims of deadly police violence are now household names.

How many of these victims' names in Figure 2.4 do you recognize and how many names could you add to this list?

Abolitionists' and other commentators' arguments run far deeper than even that list of Black people killed by LEOs. They maintain that superficial or stepwise and incremental changes are too little, too late. They point to entrenched and unrelenting over-policing in predominantly Black neighborhoods (Boehme, Cann, & Isom, 2020; Jackson, McKay, Cheliotis, Bradford, Fine, and Trinkner, 2021; Weichselbaum & Lewis, 2020); Black-targeting stop-and-frisk policies (Purdno, White, & Fradella, 2020); police use of excessive force (Schwartz & Jahn, 2020); racially disparate vehicle stop (Harris, Ash, & Fagan, 2020), arrest (Webb & Savard, 2021), charging (Sommers & Marotta, 2014), conviction and sentencing (Omori &

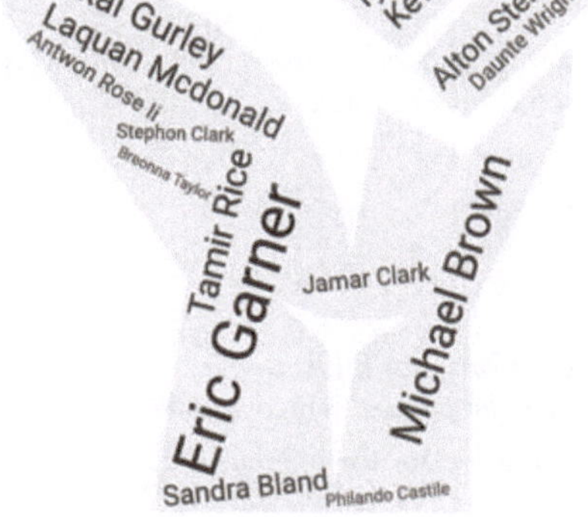

FIGURE 2.4 Selected Names of Young Black Victims of Officer-Involved Killings

Peterson, 2020), and capital punishment statistics (American Civil Liberties Union, n.d.; Baldus, Woodworth, Zuckerman, & Weiner, 1998; Center for Capital Litigation, 2008; Hoag, 2020; Kovara, 2019; *McCleskey v. Kemp*, 1987; Ndulue, 2020); racially unequal bail setting (Arnold, Dobbie, & Yang, 2018) and pretrial diversions (Schlesinger, 2013); and so on, as issues we can no longer ignore or withstand. It is time, abolitionists argue, to redirect police budgetary dollars to community needs and to put an end to the U.S. law enforcement establishment that was born in slavery and exists to protect the rights of the majority over the rights and interests of those in the minority. Abolitionists believe that police culture and the U.S. law enforcement system, grounded as it is in slavery and oppression, is incapable of meaningful reform (Gimbel & Muhammad, 2019); thus, it is time to defund the police and reallocate those public funds.

Some government officials, commentators, and even residents of minority neighborhoods oppose abolition as it fails to recognize that Black people and neighborhoods need and want some police presence. Indeed, many fear that defunding/abolition would leave some – especially minority-majority – neighborhoods at risk and exposed to rampant crime without a centralized force of officers authorized to protect and serve all. They argue that mitigating racially biased policing and excessive force and redirection of at least some police budget dollars toward family and community needs would reduce crime rates, thus rendering full abolition unnecessary, unwise, and indefensible. Instead, they argue, do not throw the baby out with the bath water by abolishing law enforcement all together – improve law enforcement and tailor it to meeting true community needs with less

TABLE 2.5 Abolitionists' Common Targets for Reallocation of Funds

- Social workers
- Community empowerment
- Self-defense training
- Mental health treatment
- Low-cost housing
- Low-cost medical care
- Redirect law enforcement funds toward person crimes and away from recreational drug use and possession, which should be decriminalized
- Domestic abuse shelters
- Early childhood nutrition
- Prenatal nutrition
- Decarceration
- Redirect law enforcement efforts and funds toward person crimes and away from "quality of life" and *mala prohibitum* crimes, which should be decriminalized
- Creating non-armed response groups for mental health emergency calls
- Income balancing
- Economic and employment opportunities

propensity toward violence and fewer racial disparities. After all, there is no need to have an officer armed with a semi-automatic weapon and body armor issue tickets for faulty taillights and no need for officers wielding battering rams to enter a home to arrest an alleged welfare cheat or drug user. Surveys have revealed that as few as 18% of United States residents support the "defund the police" movement (Elbeshbishi & Quarshie, 2021), let alone abolition.

Critically, even most abolitionists describe abolition as a process starting with delegitimization, moving through alternative generation and creation, community and individual empowerment, police budget and personnel reductions, then on toward defunding and abolition (Akbar, 2020). They reason that if the factors that predispose toward criminality (such as poor educational attainment and opportunities, weak and unequal economic opportunities, limited housing choices, and income inequality and strain) are eased by wise social investments, then the need for huge police budgets and presence will erode over time as those alternatives take hold.

Exercises

As you consider the following "exercises," consider each of the three response categories identified in this chapter: status quo, evolutionary reform, and defunding/reimagining/abolishing in all its guises.

Before settling on the paths you deem appropriate – status quo, reform, reimagine, abolish, or any of their variants – consider the exercises below. While reviewing each exercise, determine whether the actions of all officers on scene were appropriate, constitutional, just, and equitable, and whether policies, procedures, and laws adequately drove the officers to act ethically, equitably, and in culturally sensitive ways. As you proceed through these exercises, identify the factors that support your position on each, including all relevant counterarguments. Finally, devise a policy or set of policies for an agency to prevent or reduce the frequency or severity of race-based or race-disparate police actions in the future. Be creative – do not confine yourself to the ideas posed in this chapter.

Exercise One[14]

In Lorain, Ohio, on September 4, 2014, officers (who later acknowledged they suspected a young Black man, Pele Smith, of drug possession) arrested Smith for jaywalking after realizing they had insufficient probable cause to arrest him on drug charges. After arresting Smith and placing Smith in handcuffs behind his back, one officer escorted Smith to a squad car as Smith called out to his Mother to watch Smith's young son. As the escorting officer came closer to the squad car, the officer slammed Smith, face first, into the squad car's windshield, shattering the windshield.

Note that rapper Ice Cube later used an excerpt from the Pele Smith squad video in the teaser video for his "Arrest the President" release (Ice Cube/Cubevision, 2018).

Imagine you are serving on the local police department's community outreach taskforce. What steps would you take to blunt the uproar from this particular incident and what reforms would you suggest to repair police–community relationships and trust and prevent recurrence of such officer behavior. Thoroughly consider and discuss your rationale.

Exercise Two[15]

On June 14, 2014, a Dallas mother called police for help managing her schizophrenic adult son. The mother warned the 9-1-1 operator that her son was mentally ill and needed to go to a hospital. She stated that she wanted only mental health-trained officers to respond. Officers arrived and the young man stood on the threshold of the house, holding a screwdriver at his side. The officers yelled for the young man to drop the screwdriver and when he did not drop the screwdriver, within ten seconds of the young man appearing at his doorway, the officers fired five rounds into the young man, two into his back. He died in his own driveway with his mother, who had called the police for help, watching helplessly as her son died. Both officers on the scene falsely claimed that the young man had lunged at the officers; the video indicated otherwise. One of the officers claimed, "We had to shoot. He came at us." Presumably having been trained in the "ask, tell, make" policing method, these officers asked him to drop the knife, then told him to drop it, and then when he did not drop the knife, they made him drop it by shooting him to death. A Dallas County Grand Jury declined to charge the officers in the case and a federal judge later dismissed the family's civil suit against the officers.

Imagine you are the Dallas Police Chief and wish to improve your Department's methods, procedures, approaches, and policies for training and responding to mental health critical incidents – perhaps in partnership with other community organizations and professionals. What steps would you take, and why?

Exercise Three

Imagine a predominantly Black neighborhood in a large U.S. city characterized by poor public schools, unkempt public parks, poor access to quality healthcare and even fresh produce, few employment prospects, high unemployment, high incarceration rates, and poor outcomes for children and families. Black males in the neighborhood, many of whom have felony records, cannot find work. Both parents, even if present in the home, have insufficient time to supervise the children, who find ways to get in trouble. Those poor prospects and that high stress yield a high degree of despair, and law enforcement increases patrols of the neighborhood to enforce order, suppress drug transactions, and "clean up" the streets. Thus, the cycle of poverty is perpetuated with absent parents lost to incarceration, poor education, weak employment prospects, and high crime rates. Reduction (not elimination) of the police presence and allocation of those dollars toward employment, education, neighborhood revitalization, parks, and local empowerment would reduce the rate at which the neighborhood's adults are lost to incarceration, reduce the criminal history records of the residents, improve educational, nutritional, and employment prospects, improve housing values, and reduce intergenerational despair, homelessness, and felony records. Note that reduction of police presence and budgets is central to those improved prospects.

The neighborhood and the city within which it is located differ on the path toward improving the neighborhood and the prospects of its residents. Discuss possible paths using each of the three categories discussed in this chapter: status quo, evolutionary reform, and revolution/defunding/abolition. Then choose your preferred path and explain, in detail, why you prefer that path.

Exercise Four

Imagine that you are Chair of the local Police Oversight Commission charged with overseeing police procedures and behavior and recommending improvements, and your local police department has just moved through an 18-month period where the number of excessive force complaints has risen 220%, and media outlets have focused on several egregious examples of officer excessive force against area minorities. Furthermore, the United States Department of Justice has indicated it may be visiting the city soon to investigate the police department's actions, policies, procedures, leadership, and oversight mechanisms with an eye toward a possible consent order compelling the city and the city police department to eliminate racially disparate treatment of civilians, reduce excessive force incidents and complaints, and recommit to constitutional protections for all those present in the city. The Police Chief has asked you to get out in front of this and propose ten specific steps the police department should take immediately to improve the quantum of procedural justice it delivers.

Identify those ten specific steps in detail and explain the rationale for each. If possible, also identify other steps you considered but rejected, and why.

Exercise Five

You are a community organizer in a predominantly Black and poor neighborhood in a major Northeast city. The neighborhood has a substantial crime problem and is served by mostly White police officers. You are interested in pressing for defunding law enforcement but wish to straddle the two polar positions among the neighborhood residents. About one-half want to defund law enforcement all together and transfer the funds to social programming to build a stronger community from the ground up by improving education and housing opportunities, and improving medical outcomes and nutrition for neighborhood residents. The other half fear defunding, because they believe it will result in less protection and less cohesion in the neighborhood and this second half predicts something close to anarchy and chaos if law enforcement is withdrawn.

Craft a brief position paper that sketches out a middle ground that "speaks" to both groups' wishes and concerns, and that is likely to attract supporters from both groups. Be sure to present your position paper not as a finished product but as a document that can provoke thought and discussion among the neighborhood residents from both groups as they work together to fill in the blanks of your sketch of that middle ground.

Notes

1 Chuck MacLean was the principal author of this chapter.
2 *State of Minnesota v. (Derek) Chauvin*, No. 27-CR-20–12646. Amended Criminal Complaint (Minn. D. Ct. Hennepin County, June 3, 2020). Available at https://www.mncourts.gov/mncourtsgov/media/High-Profile-Cases/27-CR-20-12646/AmendedComplaint06032020.pdf.
3 *State of Minnesota v. (Derek) Chauvin*, No. 27-CR-20–12646. Sentencing Order and Memorandum Opinion (Minn. D. Ct. Hennepin County, June 25, 2021). Available at https://mncourts.gov/mncourtsgov/media/High-Profile-Cases/27-CR-20-12646/MCRO_27-CR-20-12646_Sentencing-Order_2021-06-25_20210625145755.pdf.
4 The aggravated durational departure was based on two statutory aggravating factors: (1) abuse of position of trust and authority, and (2) treatment of the victim with particular cruelty. Minnesota Department of Corrections (2021, June 25). Departure Report regarding Derek Michael Chauvin. Available at https://www.mncourts.gov/mncourtsgov/media/High-Profile-Cases/27-CR-20-12646/DepartureReport06282021.pdf.
5 *United States Department of Justice* (2021, May 7). Press release: Four former Minneapolis police officers indicted on federal civil rights charges for death of George Floyd; Derek Chauvin also charged in separate indictment for violating civil rights of a juvenile. Available at https://www.justice.gov/opa/pr/four-former-minneapolis-police-officers-indicted-federal-civil-rights-charges-death-george.
6 Michigan Senate Resolution SR149 (adopted 2020, October). Available at http://legislature.mi.gov/documents/2019-2020/resolutionadopted/Senate/htm/2020-SAR-0149.htm.
7 See, e.g., Reinert, A. A. (2021, March 4). Qualified immunity of appeal: An empirical assessment. *Cardozo Legal Studies Research Paper* (No. 634), available at https://papers.ssrn.com/sol3/papers.cfm?abstract_id=3798024; Reinert, A. A. (2021, March 18). Unpacking a decade of appellate decisions on qualified immunity. *Lawfare Institute*, available at https://www.lawfareblog.com/unpacking-decade-appellate-decisions-qualified-immunity.
8 Including Washington HB 1054, 1267, SB 5051, among others; Johnson, G. (2021, May 18). Washington governor signs sweeping police reform measures. *Seattle Times*, available at https://www.seattletimes.com/seattle-news/gov-inslee-signs-sweeping-washington-state-police-bills-banning-choke-holds-creating-deadly-force-review-office/; *Washington State Governor Jay Inslee's Office* (2021, May 18). Inslee signs police accountability legislative package, available at https://medium.com/wagovernor/inslee-signs-police-accountability-legislative-package-515f82ffa77d; Washington HB 1054, available at http://lawfilesext.leg.wa.gov/biennium/2021-22/Pdf/Bills/House%20Passed%20Legislature/1054-S.PL.pdf?q=20210714133007; Washington State HB 1267, available at http://lawfilesext.leg.wa.gov/biennium/2021-22/Pdf/Bills/House%20Passed%20Legislature/1267-S.PL.pdf?q=20210714133107; Washington State SB 5051, available at http://lawfilesext.leg.wa.gov/biennium/2021-22/Pdf/Bills/Senate%20Passed%20Legislature/5051-S2.PL.pdf?q=20210714133241.
9 See also, Else, Daniel H. (2014, August 28). The "1033 program," Department of Defense support to law enforcement. Congressional Research Service, available at https://fas.org/sgp/crs/natsec/R43701.pdf.
10 See, e.g., Chavira, D. (2021, June 28). Greeley police officer Ken Amick accused of excessive force & charged with assault. *CBS-Denver*. Available at https://denver.cbslocal.com/2021/06/28/ken-amick-excessive-force-investigation-greeley-police/.

11 Godin, M. (2020, June 19). What the U.S. can learn from countries where cops don't carry guns. *Time.com*. Available at https://time.com/5854986/police-reform-defund-unarmed-guns/.
12 See also, Bernick, E. D. (2021). Policing as unequal protection, available at SSRN: https://ssrn.com/abstract=3850829, doi:10.2139/ssrn.3850829; see also, Bullock, J. R. M., Fain, C., Weeden, L. D., & SpearIt (2021). The U.S. Constitution: Reimagining "We the People" as an inclusive construct. *The Bridge: Interdisciplinary Perspectives on Legal & Social Policy, 6*, art. 5. Available at https://digitalscholarship.tsu.edu/thebridge/vol6/iss1/5.
13 Camden, New Jersey disbanded its police department in May 2013, only to re-establish law enforcement there under county control. Landergan, K. (2020, June 12). The city that really did abolish the police. *Politico Magazine*, available at https://www.politico.com/news/magazine/2020/06/12/camden-policing-reforms-313750; several other cities have announced plans to "defund" their police departments after the George Floyd murder, but all appear to only be reducing and not eliminating funding for police. McEvoy, J. (2020, August 13). At least 13 cities are defunding their police departments. *Forbes*, available at https://www.forbes.com/sites/jemimamcevoy/2020/08/13/at-least-13-cities-are-defunding-their-police-departments/?sh=4387755529e3.
14 This exercise is derived from an actual incident. See Cleveland.com (2017, April 21). Pele Smith incident (2014, September 4). Available at https://youtu.be/3DNdAyPSfh8.
15 This exercise is derived from actual case video. See *CNN* (2015, March 18). Dallas police shoot, kill mentally ill man (video: 4:23). Available at https://youtu.be/3FV53jLDlRQ.

References

Akbar, A. (2020). An abolitionist horizon for (police) reform. *California Law Review*, 108, 1781–1846.

Akinnibi, F., Holder, S., & Cannon, C. (2021, January 12). *Cities say they want to defund the police*. Their budgets say otherwise. Bloomberg CityLab. Available at https://www.bloomberg.com/graphics/2021-city-budget-police-funding/.

Al-Hashimi, M. (2021). The brazen daylight police murder of George Floyd and the racist origin of American policing. *Fourth World Journal*, 20(2), 34–46.

American Civil Liberties Union (n.d.). Race and the death penalty. Available at https://www.aclu.org/other/race-and-death-penalty.

Arango, T. (2021, May 23). A year after George Floyd: Pressure to add police amid rising crime. *New York Times*. Available at https://www.nytimes.com/2021/05/23/us/george-floyd-police.html?smid=nytcore-ios-share.

Arnold, D., Dobbie, W., & Yang, C. S. (2018, May). Racial bias in bail decisions. *The Quarterly Journal of Economics*, 133(4), 1885–1932. Available at https://scholar.harvard.edu/files/cyang/files/ady_racialbias.pdf.

Attorney General Jeff Sessions (2018, November 17). Memorandum to United States Attorneys: Principles and procedures for civil consent decrees and settlement agreements with state and local government entities. Available at https://www.justice.gov/opa/press-release/file/1109621/download.

Baldus, D. C., Woodworth, G., Zuckerman, D., & Weiner, N. A. (1998). Racial discrimination and the death penalty in the post-*Furman* era: An empirical and legal overview with recent findings from Philadelphia. *Cornell Law Review*, 83(6), 1638–1770.

Bell, M. (2017). Police reform and the dismantling of legal estrangement. *The Yale Law Journal*, 126(7), 2054–2150. doi:10.2307/45222555.

Berger, M. & Noack, R. (2021, April 21). From guns to neck restraint: How police tactics differ around the world. *The Washington Post*. Available at https://www.washingtonpost.com/world/2020/06/06/guns-neck-restraint-how-police-tactics-differ-around-world/.

Bernick, E. D. (2021, May 12). Policing as unequal protection. Available at https://papers.ssrn.com/sol3/papers.cfm?abstract_id=3850829.

Blacklivesmatter.com (2020). *What defunding the police really means*. Available at https://vimeo.com/435916734.

Boehme, H. M., Cann, D., & Isom, D. A. (2020, forthcoming). Citizens' perceptions of over- and under-policing: A look at race, ethnicity, and community characteristics. *Crime & Delinquency*. Available at https://www.researchgate.net/profile/Hunter-Boehme/publication/346629843_Citizens'_Perceptions_of_Over-and_Under-_Policing_A_Look_at_Race_Ethnicity_and_Community_Characteristics/links/6010221792851c2d4df50bfe/Citizens-Perceptions-of-Over-and-Under-Policing-A-Look-at-Race-Ethnicity-and-Community-Characteristics.pdf

Boyd-Barrett, C. (2020, December 11). Alternatives to calling the police for domestic violence survivors. *California Health Report*. Available at https://www.calhealthreport.org/2020/12/11/alternatives-to-calling-the-police-for-domestic-violence-survivors/.

Bryant, K. (2019), "Policing communities of color: An historical examination of social control and protest management strategies", in Rabe-Hemp, C. E. & Lind, N. S. (eds.) *Political Authority, Social Control and Public Policy* (*Public Policy and Governance, Vol.*31). Bingley UK: Emerald Publishing Limited, at 43–61.

Bullock, J. R. M., Fain, C., Weeden, L. D., & SpearIt (2021). The U.S. Constitution: Reimagining "We the People" as an inclusive construct. *The Bridge: Interdisciplinary Perspectives on Legal & Social Policy*, 6, art. 5. Available at https://digitalscholarship.tsu.edu/thebridge/vol6/iss1/5.

Center for Capital Litigation (2008, September). *Race and capital punishment: The need for a racial justice act in South Carolina*. Available at https://justice360sc.org/wp-content/uploads/2015/12/Report.Race-Capital-Punishment.RJA_.pdf.

Center on Media Crime and Justice at John Jay College*: The Crime Report* (2021, May 20). Policing task force: "Blue code of silence" harms communities. Available at https://thecrimereport.org/2021/05/20/policing-task-force-calls-for-ending-blue-code-of-silence/.

Centre for Human Rights: University of Pretoria (n.d.). The law on police use of force worldwide – Denmark. Available at https://www.policinglaw.info/country/denmark.

Centre for Human Rights: University of Pretoria (n.d.). The law on police use of force worldwide – Finland. Available at https://www.policinglaw.info/country/finland.

Chavira, D. (2021, June 28). Greeley police officer Ken Amick accused of excessive force & charged with assault. CBS-Denver. Available at https://denver.cbslocal.com/2021/06/28/ken-amick-excessive-force-investigation-greeley-police/.

Chinn, H. (2020, July 22). Intersecting issues: Supporting domestic violence survivors, defunding police. *Public Broadcasting System*. Available at https://whyy.org/articles/intersecting-issues-supporting-domestic-violence-survivors-defunding-police/.

Cleveland.com (2017, April 21). Pele Smith incident (2014, September 4). Available at https://youtu.be/3DNdAyPSfh8.

CNN (2015, March 18). Dallas police shoot, kill mentally ill man (video: 4:23). Available at https://youtu.be/3FV53jLDlRQ.

Collins, S. (2020, September 23). The financial case for defunding the police. *Vox.com*. Available at https://www.vox.com/the-highlight/21430892/defund-the-police-funding-abolish-george-floyd-breonna-taylor-daniel-prude.

Commander, E. (2018, July 6). Most UK police don't carry guns. What about other countries? *Euronews*. Available at https://www.euronews.com/2018/05/30/most-uk-police-don-t-carry-guns-what-about-other-countries-.

Congressional Research Service (2020, July 10). Police use of force: Overview and considerations for Congress. Available at https://www.hsdl.org/?view&did=841436.

Council on Foreign Relations (2021, April 21). How police compare in different democracies. Available at https://www.cfr.org/backgrounder/how-police-compare-different-democracies.

Elbeshbishi, S. & Quarshie, M. (2021, March 7). Fewer than 1 in 5 support "defund the police" movement, USA Today/IPSOS poll finds. *USA Today*. Available at https://www.usatoday.com/story/news/politics/2021/03/07/usa-today-ipsos-poll-just-18-support-defund-police-movement/4599232001/.

Else, D. H. (2014, August 28). The "1033 program," Department of Defense support to law enforcement. *Congressional Research Service*. Available at https://fas.org/sgp/crs/natsec/R43701.pdf.

European Court of Human Rights (1950 and as amended thereafter). *European Convention for the Protection of Human Rights and Fundamental Freedoms*, Article 2(2). Available at https://www.echr.coe.int/Documents/Convention_ENG.pdf.

Everytown Research & Policy (2021, June 4). Alternative dispatch programs: A strategy for improving emergency responses and reducing police violence. Available at https://everytownresearch.org/report/alternative-dispatch-programs/.

Federal Bureau of Investigation Counterterrorism Division (2015, April 1). *Counterterrorism policy directive and policy guide*. Available in redacted form at https://s3.documentcloud.org/documents/3423189/CT-Excerpt.pdf.

Federal Bureau of Investigation Counterterrorism Division (2006, October 17). White supremacist infiltration of law enforcement. Available in heavily redacted form at http://s3.documentcloud.org/documents/402521/doc-26-white-supremacist-infiltration.pdf.

Federal Violent Crime Control and Law Enforcement Act of 1994, P. Law 103–322. Available at https://www.congress.gov/103/statute/STATUTE-108/STATUTE-108-Pg1796.pdf.

Fernandez, P. (2020, June 11). Defunding the police will actually make us safer. *American Civil Liberties Union of Oregon*. Available at https://aclu-or.org/en/news/defunding-police-will-actually-make-us-safer.

Ferreira, S. (2017, December 5). Portugal's radical drugs policy is working. Why hasn't the world copied it? *The Guardian*. Available at https://www.theguardian.com/news/2017/dec/05/portugals-radical-drugs-policy-is-working-why-hasnt-the-world-copied-it.

Gehring, T. (2020). Relationships between racial slavery, incarceration, and policing, part I. *Journal of Prison Education and Reentry*, 6(3), 243–244.

George Floyd Justice in Policing Act, 117th Congress (2021–2022), HR 1280, § 102 [pending; not enacted at press time].

German, M. (2020a, August 27). Hidden in plain sight: Racism, White supremacy, and far-right militancy in law enforcement. *Brennan Center for Justice*. Available at https://www.brennancenter.org/our-work/research-reports/hidden-plain-sight-racism-white-supremacy-and-far-right-militancy-law#footnote4_t4ghcdb.

German, M. (2020b, September 1). White supremacist links to law enforcement are an urgent concern. *Brennan Center for Justice*. Available at https://www.brennancenter.org/our-work/analysis-opinion/white-supremacist-links-law-enforcement-are-urgent-concern.

Gimbel, V. N. & Muhammad, C. (2019). Are police obsolete? Breaking cycles of violence through abolition democracy. *Cardozo Law Review*, 40, 1453–1543.

Godin, M. (2020, June 19). What the U.S. can learn from countries where cops don't carry guns. *Time.com*. Available at https://time.com/5854986/police-reform-defund-unarmed-guns/.

Goldhill, O. (2016, July 9). How do police handle violence in countries where officers don't carry guns? *Quartz (qz.com)*. Available at https://qz.com/727941/how-do-police-handle-violence-in-countries-where-officers-dont-carry-guns/.

Government of the Netherlands (n.d.). Organisation of the Dutch police. Retrieved from https://www.government.nl/topics/police/organisation-of-the-dutch-police.

Guardian (UK) (2020, June 22). What does defund the police actually mean? Available at https://www.youtube.com/watch?v=xg6YV_5Om3s.

Harris, A. P., Ash, E., & Fagan, J. (2020, November). Fiscal pressures and discriminatory policing: Evidence from traffic stops in Missouri. *Journal of Race, Ethnicity, and Politics*, 450–480. Available at https://www.research-collection.ethz.ch/bitstream/handle/20.500.11850/453298/SSRN-id3192562%281%29.pdf?sequence=1.

Hernandez, D. (2020, July 6). The thin blue line: The history behind the controversial police emblem. *The San Diego Union-Tribune*. Available at https://www.sandiegounion tribune.com/news/public-safety/story/2020-07-06/the-thin-blue-line-the-complex-his tory-and-thoughts-behind-the-police-emblem.

Hoag, A. (2020). Valuing Black lives: A case for ending the death penalty. *Columbia Human Rights Law Review*, 51(3), 983–1007.

Holder, S., Akinnibi, F., & Cannon, C. (2020, September 22). America's big cities aren't defunding the police. *Bloomberg CityLab*. Available at https://www.bloomberg.com/grap hics/2020-city-budget-police-defunding/.

Homer, E. M. & Risher, B. W. (2020). Police in schools and student arrest rates across the United States: Examining differences by race, ethnicity, and gender. *Journal of School Violence*, 19(2), 192–204.

Human Rights Watch (2020, August 12). A roadmap for re-imagining public safety in the United States. Available at https://www.hrw.org/news/2020/08/12/roadmap-re-ima gining-public-safety-united-states.

Ice Cube/Cubevision (2018, November 6). Ice Cube–Arrest the President. Available at https://youtu.be/mFqksq9nhFg.

Institute for Criminal Justice Training Reform (n.d.). Required training for police internationally. Available at https://www.trainingreform.org/the-data.

International Association of Chiefs of Police (IACP) (2009, September 15). *Employing returning combat veterans as law enforcement officers*. Available at https://www.theiacp.org/sites/default/files/2018-08/IACPReturningCombatVeteransFINAL2009-09-15.pdf.

Jackson, J., McKay, T., Cheliotis, L., Bradford, B., Fine, A., & Trinkner, R. (2021 forthcoming). Centering race in procedural justice theory: Systematic racism and the under-policing and over-policing of Black communities. Available at https://osf.io/preprints/socarxiv/kgwhc/.

Jagannathan, M. (2020, June 19). As activists call to defund the police, mental-health advocates say 'the time is now' to rethink public safety. *MarketWatch*. Available at https://www.ma rketwatch.com/story/long-before-defund-the-police-mental-health-advocates-have-been-re defining-public-safety-2020-06-11.

Johnson, G. (2021, May 18). Washington governor signs sweeping police reform measures. *Seattle Times*. Available at https://www.seattletimes.com/seattle-news/gov-inslee-signs-sweep ing-washington-state-police-bills-banning-choke-holds-creating-deadly-force-review-office/.

Jones, P. M. (2000, April 23). To fight corruption, Peru turns to female cops. *Chicago Tribune*. Available at https://www.chicagotribune.com/news/ct-xpm-2000-04-23-0004230200-story.html.

Karakatsanis, A. (2019, March 28). The punishment bureaucracy: How to think about "criminal justice reform." *Yale Law Journal Forum*, 128. Available at https://www.yalela wjournal.org/forum/the-punishment-bureaucracy.

Kleinfeld, R. (2020, July 2). These countries reformed their brutal, biased police. The U.S. can, too. *Foreign Policy*. Available at https://foreignpolicy.com/2020/07/02/police-bruta lity-racism-reform-international/.

Kovara, M. B. (2019). Racial disparities in the criminal justice system. *Journal of Social Issues*, 75(4), 1139–1164.

Landergan, K. (2020, June 12). The city that really did abolish the police. *Politico Magazine*. Available at https://www.politico.com/news/magazine/2020/06/12/camden-policing-reforms-313750.

Lowrey, A. (2020, June 5). Defund the police: America needs to rethink its priorities for the whole criminal-justice system. *The Atlantic*. Available at https://www.theatlantic.com/ideas/archive/2020/06/defund-police/612682/.

McCartney, A., Murray, P., & Roganasakul, M. (2020, July 1). After pouring billions into militarization of U.S. cops, Congress weighs limits. *Bloomberg.com*. Available at https://www.bloomberg.com/graphics/2020-police-military-equipment/.

McEvoy, J. (2020, August 12). At least 13 cities are defunding their police departments. *Forbes*. Available at https://www.forbes.com/sites/jemimamcevoy/2020/08/13/at-least-13-cities-are-defunding-their-police-departments/?sh=4387755529e3.

McKenna, J. M. & White, S. R. (2018). Examining the use of police in schools: How roles may impact responses to student misconduct. *American Journal of Criminal Justice*, 43, 448–470.

McCleskey v. Kemp, 481 U.S. 279 (1987).

Michigan Senate Resolution SR149 (adopted 2020, October). Available at http://legislature.mi.gov/documents/2019-2020/resolutionadopted/Senate/htm/2020-SAR-0149.htm.

Minnesota Department of Corrections (2021, June 25). Departure Report regarding Derek Michael Chauvin. Available at https://www.mncourts.gov/mncourtsgov/media/High-Profile-Cases/27-CR-20-12646/DepartureReport06282021.pdf.

Mulvihill, G. (2020, October 1). Police departments seeing modest cuts, but not "defunding." *Associated Press*. Available at https://apnews.com/article/virus-outbreak-police-law-enforcement-agencies-local-governments-iowa -420d07148086f72bc255c676bfe214532#:~:text=%E2%80%9CPolice%20don't%20really%20solve,the%20Movement%20for%20Black%20Lives

National Conference on State Legislatures (NCSL Database) (updated regularly). Law enforcement statutory database. Available at https://www.ncsl.org/research/civil-and-criminal-justice/law-enforcement-statutory-database.aspx.

National Defense Authorization Act of 1997, section 1033, P. Law 104–201. Available at https://www.congress.gov/104/plaws/publ201/PLAW-104publ201.pdf.

National Research Center [Polco.us] (2021). How residents see public safety services within their communities. Available at https://unite.icma.org/wp-content/uploads/2020/09/How-Residents-See-Public-Safety-Services-Within-Their-Communities-1.pdf.

NBC Left Field (2019). *A different kind of force – Policing mental illness* (video: 1:04:18). Available at https://youtu.be/DnOLvKEYIQI.

Ndulue, N. (2020, September). *Enduring injustice: The persistence of racial discrimination in the U.S. death penalty*. Death Penalty Information Center. Available at https://documents.deathpenaltyinfo.org/pdf/Enduring-Injustice-Race-and-the-Death-Penalty-2020.pdf.

O'Rourke, A., Su, R., & Binder, G. (2021). Disbanding police agencies. *Columbia Law Review*, 121(4), 1327–1404.

Omori, M. & Petersen, N. (2020). Institutionalizing inequality in the courts: Decomposing racial and ethnic disparities in detention, conviction, and sentencing. *Criminology*, 58(4), 678–713.

Owusu-Bempah, A. (2017). Race and policing in historical context: Dehumanization and the policing of Black people in the 21st century. *Theoretical Criminology*, 21(1), 23–34.

Petteruti, A. (2011, November). Education under arrest: The case against police in schools. *Justice Policy Institute*. Available at http://www.justicepolicy.org/uploads/justicepolicy/documents/educationunderarrest_fullreport.pdf.

Purdno, J., White, M. D., & Fradella, H. F. (2020) Reforming stop and frisk for 21st Century policing, chapter 24 in *Critical issues in policing: Contemporary readings*. Long Grove IL: Waveland Press.

Torres, J. (2015). Race-ethnicity and stop-and-frisk: Past, present, future. *Sociology Compass*, 9(11), 931–939.

Reinert, A. A. (2021, March 4). Qualified immunity of appeal: An empirical assessment. *Cardozo Legal Studies Research Paper* (No. 634). Available at https://papers.ssrn.com/sol3/papers.cfm?abstract_id=3798024.

Reinert, A. A. (2021, March 18). Unpacking a decade of appellate decisions on qualified immunity. *Lawfare Institute*. Available at https://www.lawfareblog.com/unpacking-decade-appellate-decisions-qualified-immunity.

Reuland, M., Draper, L., & Norton, B. (2012, December). *Statewide law enforcement/mental health efforts: Strategies to support and sustain local initiatives*. Department of Justice Bureau of Justice Assistance. Available at https://csgjusticecenter.org/wp-content/uploads/2020/02/1.8.12_Statewide-LE-MH_web.pdf.

Reuland, M., Morabito, M. S., Preston, C., & Cheney, J. (2006). *Police-community partnerships to address domestic violence*. United States Department of Justice, Office of Justice Programs. Available at https://www.ojp.gov/ncjrs/virtual-library/abstracts/police-community-partnerships-address-domestic-violence.

Rogers, M. S., McNiel, D. E., & Binder, R. L. (2019). Effectiveness of police crisis intervention training programs. *Journal of the American Academy of Psychiatry and Law*, 47(4), 1–8.

Saakashvilli, M. (2020, June 11). I abolished and rebuilt the police. The United States can do the same. *Foreign Policy*. Available at https://foreignpolicy.com/2020/06/11/abolish-police-georgia-brutality-crime/.

Saar, J. (1999). Criminal justice system and process of democratization in Estonia. *NATO Democratic Institutions Research Fellowship Final Report*. Available at https://www.nato.int/acad/fellow/97-99/saar.pdf.

Schlesinger, T. (2013). Racial disparities in pretrial diversion: An analysis of outcomes among men charged with felonies and processed in state courts. *Race and Justice*, 3(3), 210–238.

Schwartz, G. L. & Jahn, J. L. (2020, June 24). Mapping police violence across U.S. metropolitan areas: Overall rates and racial/ethnic inequities, 2013–2017. *PLOS One*, 15(6): 30229686. doi:10,1371/journal.pone.0229686. Available at https://journals.plos.org/plosone/article?id=10.1371/journal.pone.0229686.

Scotland Equality and Human Rights Commission (n.d.). What is the European Convention on Human Rights? Available at https://www.equalityhumanrights.com/en/what-european-convention-human-rights.

Searcey, D. (2020, June 8). What would efforts to defund or disband police departments really mean? *The New York Times*. Available at https://www.nytimes.com/2020/06/08/us/what-does-defund-police-mean.html.

Serhan, Y. (2020, June 10). What the world could teach America about policing: Examples about of reforms that are seen as "radical" in the United States. *The Atlantic*. Available at https://www.theatlantic.com/international/archive/2020/06/america-police-violence-germany-georgia-britain/612820/.

Sherman, S. A. (2020, July 22). Many cities are rethinking the police, but what are the alternatives? *The Kinder Institute for Urban Research*. Available at https://kinder.rice.edu/urbanedge/2020/07/22/many-cities-are-rethinking-police-what-are-alternatives.

Smerconish, M. (2021, June 12). Police reform intersects with crime surge. *CNN.com*. Available at https://www.cnn.com/videos/tv/2021/06/12/smerconish-police-reform-intersects-with-crime-surge.cnn.

Sommers, S. R. & Marotta, S. A. (2014). Racial disparities in legal outcomes: On policing, charging decisions, and criminal trial proceedings. *Policy Insights from the Behavioral and Brain Sciences*, 1 (1), 103–111. Available at https://journals.sagepub.com/doi/pdf/10.1177/2372732214548431.

Speri, A. (2017, September 31). The FBI has quietly investigated white supremacist infiltration of law enforcement. *The Intercept*. Available at https://theintercept.com/2017/01/31/the-fbi-has-quietly-investigated-white-supremacist-infiltration-of-law-enforcement/.

State of Minnesota v. (Derek) Chauvin, No. 27-CR-20-12646. Amended Criminal Complaint (Minn. D. Ct. Hennepin County, June 3, 2020). Available at https://www.mncourts.gov/mncourtsgov/media/High-Profile-Cases/27-CR-20-12646/AmendedComplaint06032020.pdf.

State of Minnesota v. (Derek) Chauvin, No. 27-CR-20-12646. Sentencing Order and Memorandum Opinion (Minn. D. Ct. Hennepin County, June 25, 2021). Available at https://mncourts.gov/mncourtsgov/media/High-Profile-Cases/27-CR-20-12646/MCRO_27-CR-20-12646_Sentencing-Order_2021-06-25_20210625145755.pdf.

Statistics Canada (2020, December 8). Police resources in Canada, 2019. Available at https://www150.statcan.gc.ca/n1/pub/85-002-x/2020001/article/00015-eng.htm.

Steinmetz, K. F., Schaefer, B. P., & Henderson, H. (2017). Wicked overseers: American policing and colonialism. *Sociology of Race and Ethnicity*, 3(1), 68–81.

Taylor, K-Y. (2020, August 14). We should still defund the police. *The New Yorker*. Available at https://www.newyorker.com/news/our-columnists/defund-the-police.

Tensley, B. (2021, May 24). Legal scholar explains the origins of America's policing crisis and how it may change. *CNN.com*. Available at https://www.cnn.com/2021/05/20/politics/george-floyd-policing-race-deconstructed-newsletter/index.html.

Terpstra, J. (2020). Police reform as institutional change: Symbols and dilemmas. *International Journal of Law, Crime and Justice*, 60, 100359–. doi:10.1016/j.ijlcj.2019.100359.

Trofimov, Y. (2020, June 13). Two countries dismantled their police to start fresh. It worked-up to a point. *The Wall Street Journal*. Available at https://www.wsj.com/articles/two-countries-dismantled-their-police-to-start-fresh-it-workedup-to-a-point-11592040601.

United Nations (1979). *Code of Conduct for Law Enforcement Officials*. Available at https://www.cfr.org/backgrounder/how-police-compare-different-democracies.

United Nations Office on Drugs and Crime (2011). *Handbook on police accountability, oversight and integrity*. Available at https://www.unodc.org/pdf/criminal_justice/Handbook_on_police_Accountability_Oversight_and_Integrity.pdf.

United States v. City of Cleveland, Settlement Agreement (2015, May 26). Available at https://www.justice.gov/sites/default/files/crt/legacy/2015/05/27/cleveland_agreement_5-26-15.pdf.

United States Department of Justice (2021, May 7). Press release: Four former Minneapolis police officers indicted on federal civil rights charges for death of George Floyd; Derek Chauvin also charged in separate indictment for violating civil rights of a juvenile. Available at https://www.justice.gov/opa/pr/four-former-minneapolis-police-officers-indicted-federal-civil-rights-charges-death-george.

Vermeer, M. J. D., Woods, D., & Jackson, B. A. (2020, August). Would law enforcement leaders support defunding the police? Probably-if communities ask police to solve fewer problems. *Rand Corporation*. Available at https://www.rand.org/content/dam/rand/pubs/perspectives/PEA100/PEA108-1/RAND_PEA108-1.pdf.

Washington HB 1054. Available at http://lawfilesext.leg.wa.gov/biennium/2021-22/Pdf/Bills/House%20Passed%20Legislature/1054-S.PL.pdf?q=20210714133007.

Washington State HB 1267. Available at http://lawfilesext.leg.wa.gov/biennium/2021-22/Pdf/Bills/House%20Passed%20Legislature/1267-S.PL.pdf?q=20210714133107.

Washington State SB 5051. Available at http://lawfilesext.leg.wa.gov/biennium/2021-22/Pdf/Bills/Senate%20Passed%20Legislature/5051-S2.PL.pdf?q=20210714133241.

Washington State Governor Jay Inslee's Office (2021, May 18). Inslee signs police accountability legislative package. Available at https://medium.com/wagovernor/inslee-signs-police-accountability-legislative-package-515f82ffa77d.

Webb, P. & Savard, D. (2021). Officer observations and disproportionate minority youth arrest: Origins, outcomes, and opportunities. *Journal of Ethnicity in Criminal Justice*. doi:10.1080/15377938.2021.1934931.

Weichselbaum, S. & Lewis, N. (2020, June 9). Support for defunding the police department is growing. Here's why it's not a silver bullet. *The Marshall Project*. Available at https://www.themarshallproject.org/2020/06/09/support-for-defunding-the-police-department-is-growing-here-s-why-it-s-not-a-silver-bullet.

Weichselbaum, S. & Schwartzapfel, B. (2017, March 30). When warriors put on the badge; Many veterans make careers in policing – Some bring war home. *The Marshall Project*. Available at https://www.themarshallproject.org/2017/03/30/when-warriors-put-on-the-badge.

Weiner, R. (2021, May 17). D.C. to divert some mental health calls away from police. *The Washington Post*. Available at https://www.washingtonpost.com/local/public-safety/dc-mental-health-crisis-response/2021/05/17/2c761706-b746-11eb-96b9-e949d5397de9_story.html.

Westervelt, E. (2020, September 18). Mental health and police violence: How crisis intervention teams are failing. *National Public Radio [NPR] News*. Available at https://www.npr.org/2020/09/18/913229469/mental-health-and-police-violence-how-crisis-intervention-teams-are-failing.

3

MENTAL HEALTH OF UNITED STATES LAW ENFORCEMENT OFFICERS[1]

An officer's work life is often filled with high stakes, high stress, high risk, and uncertainty. Those features are exacerbated by a natural tendency of many police officers to silo into affinity groups made up mostly of fellow officers and their families. Low pay and bad hours coupled with the occupational hazard of bringing stress home leads many officers' home lives to be financially strapped and chaotic. Those stresses build and fester in the absence of timely professional care often foregone by officers concerned about the stigma and potentially adverse work consequences of seeking psychological help and what some officers see as admitting weakness.

Furthermore, our law enforcement officers have also been pressed into service as first-line responders for mainstreamed civilians suffering from their own mental health burdens and challenges. It is often challenging to instantaneously discern whether threatening appearances reflect an actual threat or an artifact of mental illness – and officers often do not have the training to make those calls, nor the luxury of time to consider the circumstances.

The solution includes providing mental health and family counseling for law enforcement while eliminating the stigmas sometimes attached to strong female and male officers acknowledging a psychological flaw or weakness. The repair for mental health issues plaguing civilians is for officers to train more extensively on appreciating, diagnosing, and understanding acute and chronic mental health challenges so they can recognize them and make more reasoned assessments and perceptions of threats and appropriate law enforcement responses.

Chapter Highlights

✓Case Spotlight: Mental Health of Dallas-Fort Worth area LEOs

✓Approximately 26% of officers exhibit hazardous alcohol consumption, about 10% suffer from anxiety disorder or suicidal thoughts, and over 14% suffer from

DOI: 10.4324/9781003163411-4

post-traumatic stress disorder or depression – all far in excess of the values for the general public
✓Officers suffer fear/anxiety, money stress, domestic strife, sleep disturbances, and suicide to degrees greater than the general public
✓Although virtually all LEAs report that they offer officers mental health support and intervention, the majority of LEAs have no formal intervention, assessment, or treatment resources for officers
✓Police's local role in anti-terrorism efforts increases risk and anxiety
✓Solutions include providing more identification, assessment, intervention, and treatment resources; more stress-reduction techniques and resources; better pay; and better hours

Case Spotlight: Mental Health of Dallas-Fort Worth Area LEOs

A telling study of mental health issues and care among licensed peace officers in a large Dallas-Fort Worth-area LEA (Jetelina, Molsberry, Gonzalez, Beauchamp, & Hall, 2020), revealed some troubling and sobering data about the mental health challenges of the law enforcement profession. Some 17% of the study participants reported seeking mental health services in the preceding year, 12% reported a lifetime mental health diagnosis, and 26% exhibited current mental health issues based on a screening test. The study also found that barriers to LEOs seeking mental health care included difficulty identifying an active mental illness problem, confidentiality concerns, a belief that counselors could not relate to LEOs, and stigmas to treatment that could yield a finding that the struggling LEO is unfit to serve. Of course, none of those concerns or statistics should be surprising; officers face uncertain risks daily, are exposed to violent crime scenes and injured or dead victims, and face financial and family difficulties related to shift work, depression, PTSD, PTSI, and financial challenges related to poor salaries. The study authors recommended further studies of law enforcement mental health to focus on PTSD as a serious officer mental health issue, but also on depression, anxiety, self-harm, and suicidal ideation to examine the scope of these problems. Many of the participants in this study expressed willingness and interest in seeking psychological help, but nonetheless, LEO reticence to seek mental health care is perhaps the greatest concern as evidenced by the fact that up to three times as many LEOs die by suicide as die directly in the line of duty (Burr, 2020; Hilliard, 2019; Officer.com, 2020; Perine, 2021). A recent study even noted that LEOs have a higher suicide risk than any other profession (Hilliard, 2019). Only 5% of the 18,000+ LEAs in the United States have formal suicide prevention programs (Hilliard, 2019).

Police Officers in Need of Mental Health Counseling and Intervention

Based on many studies (e.g., Jetelina, et al., 2020; National Alliance on Mental Illness, n.d.), approximately one quarter of all law enforcement officers engage in hazardous alcohol consumption, about 10% suffer from anxiety disorder or suicidal thoughts, and at least 14% suffer from post-traumatic stress disorder or depression – all far in excess of the analogous values for the general public. Some 25% of all law enforcement officers in the United States have considered committing suicide (American Police Officers Alliance, 2019).

Police officers, in the main, absorb risk and stress at work on virtually every shift (Purba & Demou, 2019). The stress can include assaults, seeing dead and injured persons, dealing with people at their worst moments, interacting with abused children and sexual assault victims, and so on (Fair, 2020). Some officers leave home for their shift at times wondering if they will return home again. No officer can accurately predict what risks will be encountered in the next traffic stop or domestic disturbance call. That stress accumulates as instances of trauma – perhaps accompanied by strife at home – become compound traumas, or even post-traumatic stress disorder, over time, because the last trauma has not abated by the time the next trauma occurs (Carrier, 2020; Eliasson, 2021; Lees, Elliott, Gunning, Newton, Rai & Lal, 2019; Papazoglou & Tuttle, 2018; Police Executive Officer Forum, 2019).

Police officers' job duties, in addition to risk and uncertainty with each call for service, also yield additional stress – financial stress from low pay, sleep deprivation stress from shift work (Brown, Martin, Nagaria, Verceles, Jobe, & Wickwire, 2020), missed family holidays and vacations due to compelled overtime and assigned workdays, vigilance from constant observation from supervisors and the public with cell phone cameras at the ready, and performance stress related to policies and procedures manuals that purport to guide action but leave little room for the flexibility some calls require (Ayres, 1990).

Moreover, officers in recent years have absorbed far more job duties than they have been adequately trained to absorb – mental health calls, terrorism-related incidents (Johnson, 2017; Paton & Violanti, 2008), pandemic and post-pandemic response and protocols (Drew & Martin, 2020), crisis interventions, and increasingly well-armed criminals with extensive digital equipment and methods. Some officers have been doxed (Kranick & Stelter, 2015) and exposed in social media and in the press. Others are singled out for vitriolic press coverage. Finally, officers are more frequently than in the past the subjects of civilian complaints, civilian review boards, civil suits, and even criminal charges for actions on duty.

In that quagmire of stress, trauma, exposure, and uncertainty (Sherwood, Hegarty, Vallieres, Hyland, Murphy, Fitzgerald, & Reid, 2019; van der Velden, Rademaker, Vermetten, Portengen, Yzermans, & Grievink, 2013; Violanti, 2018; Violanti et al., 2017), some officers suffer extensive mental health challenges from trauma and post-traumatic stress syndrome to depression and hyper-vigilance. However, many officers feel they cannot seek counseling or psychological/psychiatric intervention without compromising their reputations, career prospects, and even authority to wear the badge and carry a service weapon.[2] Still other officers do not want to appear weak – the picture some officers think they betray by seeking mental health assistance. Furthermore, for some officers, as trauma compounds, that serves as a moral injury, weakening officers' moral compass and ethical resolve (Lentz, Smith-McDonald, Malloy, Carleton, & Brémault-Phillips, 2021). Finally, although most law enforcement agencies report that they offer mental health support services, for many agencies that may merely be a Chief or Deputy Chief with a ready ear.

That leaves us with officers suffering mental health issues with limited prospects for treatment and intervention. Officers with a uniform, badge, and arrest powers, who are actively suffering from acute or chronic emotional and psychological challenges, are quite likely to make poor decisions yielding costly mistakes – sometimes tragic ones. The consequences and aftermath of allowing a cadre of stressed officers to serve in uniform are quantified in the next section.

The Consequences of Allowing Mental Health-Compromised Officers to Serve on Duty

The consequences of allowing mentally unhealthy officers to serve befall not just the officer and the agency but the communities they serve and the individuals they encounter on the job.

As but one example, in 2019, 228 officers died by suicide, the highest number in history to that point (Blue H.E.L.P., n.d.). In 2019, while 228 officers died by suicide, just 132 died in the line of duty (Blue H.E.L.P., n.d.; Officer.com, 2020). Ten New York City Police Department police officers died by suicide in 2019 alone (Barr, 2020). Suicide is police officers' greatest risk from within (at least twice the rate in the general population) exacerbated by the stigma that prevents so many officers from seeking the help they desperately need (Blue H.E.L.P., n.d.; Karaffa, 2016; Redman, 2018). Three responding officers committed suicide shortly after the insurrection at the United States Capitol Building on January 6, 2021 (Hermann, 2021). Blue H.E.L.P. (Honor, Educate, Lead, Prevent), an officer suicide prevention group, reports that officer suicides nationwide were 149 (2016), 174 (2017), 182 (2018), 239 (2019), 173 (2020), and 69 (2021, through June 30, 2021 – that is, an annualized estimate of 138) (Blue H.E.L.P., 2021). Those numbers indicate a substantial suicide problem (NBC News, 2019; Violanti, Robinson, & Shen, 2013) in the United States if not notable recent growth in the number of officer suicides. Note that officer suicide is a global problem and not confined to the United States alone (Preidt, 2020). Note also that suicide rates are very high, as well, for corrections officers (Violanti, 2017), firefighters (Ruderman Family Foundation, n.d.), and other first responders (Vigil, Grant, Perez, Blust, Chikani, & Vadeboncoeur, 2018).

Furthermore, officer stress is also acutely felt by the officer's family members (Arredondo, Shumway, Kimball, Dersch, Morelock, & Bryan, 2002), as indicated by high rates of divorce, domestic abuse (Bond, 2014; Goodmark, 2015), and financial stress (McCartney, 2020) among officers' families. Officers absorb stress on the job then come home with that stress still on board, only to confront unpaid bills and domestic strife while they are unable to share their war stories with their family members or friends. That unresolved stress and their mutual reliance exacerbates the tendency of police officers to socialize predominantly or only with fellow officers, whom they deem the only people who "understand" (McCartney & Parent, 2021).

Officer mental health challenges can also adversely affect the communities the officers serve and the people they encounter on the job. While explaining that mental stress can also be a life-saving characteristic for officers in the field, heightening awareness and accelerating responses, Verhage, Noppe, Feys, & Ledegen (2018) exhaustively combed the literature for adverse on-the-job performance corollaries that can result from officers with mental health issues. They found the following *risks to the public* flowing from officer mental health challenges:

- impaired officer decision-making
- physical performance decline if stress is prolonged
- cognitive reaction time increase
- auditory exclusion
- tunnel vision and selective attention
- deteriorating verbal/social abilities
- impaired short-, moderate-, and long-term memory
- vasoconstriction and some reduced ability to use extremities
- distorted understanding of surroundings and events
- headaches, tiredness, sleep difficulties
- post-traumatic stress syndrome and disorder
- flashbacks, irritability, hyper-vigilance
- avoidance
- heightened amygdala activity and concomitant reduction of prefrontal cortex activity
- heightened awareness and over-estimation of the degree of threats
- impulse management challenges
- impaired decision-making based on a clipped subset of available information
- a perception that a threat is physically closer to the officer than in actuality, thereby increasing the apparent (but perhaps not the actual) risk and artificially and unnecessarily reducing the amount of time the officer takes to assess the actual threat and decide the appropriate, justified, and reasonable response
- motor skill deterioration with more time required for each action to be taken
- deterioration of perceptive accuracy regarding non-threat-related information

Officers under stress are more inclined to shoot overall, more likely to shoot sooner, and more likely to shoot subjects intending to surrender. They experience a decline in shooting accuracy from over 90% hits in the absence of stress to 36–54% under stress. Officers under stress can be predisposed toward alcohol and drug dependence that may worsen these operational risks flowing from officer stress. Some argue that unrelenting officer mental health issues can also lead to a sort of impaired conscience that can adversely impact officers' decision-making.

These stress-triggered challenges can adversely affect officers' abilities to safely, logically, reasonably, and lawfully perform their job duties and can thereby put the public at enhanced risk (Graves & Lynn, 2020). Thus, managing officer risk and long-term stress and trauma-related psychological and emotional declines can help both the officer and the public.

Solutions

To protect officer mental health and thereby protect public safety based on the threat posed to the public when police officer mental health issues and stress are unaddressed, we must strive to remove the obstacles, ease the path, and provide mental health funding and resources for police officers at risk (Beshears, 2017; Henderson, Steinkopf, Straud, Vincent, Crouch, Guszowski, & van Hasselt, n.d.).

Reduce the stigma. Law enforcement officers, like soldiers, work in a male-dominated and some would say toxic masculine workplace, where toughness, masculinity, aggressiveness, and competitiveness are often expected if not celebrated (Cooper, 2009; Levant & Pryor, 2020; Rawski & Workman-Stark, 2018). Many officers believe that an admission of mental health issues will result in confiscation of their badges and guns and the end of their law enforcement careers (Karaffa, 2016; Karaffa & Tochkov, 2013; Wheeler, Fisher, Jamiel, Lynn, & Hill, 2021). Furthermore, given that many officers and soldiers consider seeking mental health intervention and counselling to be an admission of weakness, many officers are loath to seek help and perceive stigma associated with submitting to counselling services, known as "self-stigma" (Karaffa, 2016). External and internal stigmas may not just be "perceived." Indeed, with 22% of female and 12% of male officers reporting in confidential surveys that they suffer from significant depression, and 35% of all officers in confidential surveys reporting they suffer post-traumatic stress disorder symptoms, both self-stigma and public stigma (Karaffa, 2016) routinely appear to prevent officers from seeking and obtaining the mental health services they require (Violanti, et al., 2017).

Effective mental health treatment requires a subject willing to both seek it and cooperate with it, but stigma-driven reticence prevents too many officers from improving their mental health. Many officers are afraid to seek help because they have been socialized to believe that failure to quietly manage stress and trauma could adversely affect their careers or that admitting mental health challenges to other officers may lead those other officers to withhold trust from the officer in need of help. The relatively monolithic police culture presupposes officers are all the same: tough, courageous, and able to "handle" the stress of the job. In one study (Karaffa & Tochkov, 2013), more than one-half of the officer respondents indicated they would want to seek mental health help if they found themselves worried or upset for an extended period, but less than one-quarter indicated that other officers would seek mental health help in those circumstances. Non-reporting and under-reporting of mental health symptoms (Marshall, Milligan, Saville, Petrie, Bryant, Mitchell, & Harvey, 2021) both expose a need for more mental health screening for officers and more stigma reduction.

Re-write policy statements and state statutes to support and not penalize officer counselling. Procedures and policies manuals in some law enforcement agencies may be ambivalent toward or implicitly or explicitly adverse to officers seeking mental health care. At a minimum, officers could read the procedures and policies or infer from the organizational culture that seeking mental health treatment could sabotage their careers. Thus, procedures and policies manuals should be modified to reflect a very positive approach to officers seeking such services to remove that impediment to counseling and treatment. Perhaps this should include a policy that provides confidential psychological referrals (Price, 2017) and a written policy guaranteeing that when officers seek psychological help, their gun and badge are not automatically taken from them (Rappleye & Siegel, 2019).

Provide sufficient resources to fund mental health services and policy changes. In 2017, Congress passed the Law Enforcement Mental Health and Wellness Act (2017) supporting enhanced resources for providing mental health services to state, local, tribal, and federal law enforcement officers. The Act was signed into law in 2018 (34 U.S.C. §§ 10491–10487 (2018)). It called for research and reporting to Congress regarding expanding peer mentoring programs, mandating that officer mental health services be private, and the efficacy of crisis lines and periodic mental health checkups for officers. The first report to Congress (DOJ-COPS, 2019) required by the Act supported application of several existing veteran and active-duty military mental health services approaches to law enforcement officers, including a public service campaign regarding officer mental health, developing more resources to support community-based psychology clinicians to serve officers, embedding mental health professionals and services within law enforcement agencies, supporting family services for officers, suicide prevention activities (Ramchand, Saunders, Osilla, Ebener, Kotzias, Thornton, Strang, & Cahill, 2019), crisis lines for officers, using retired officers as peer mentors, legislated protections for officers seeking help, ensuring privacy of those officers seeking help, enhancing stress management skills through training, and mental health checks for officers following critical incidents and intermittently on a schedule. The Act was another step in the right direction after many police departments had already expended resources to create related officer mental health approaches and tools. That work continues across the country although stigma still dampens its success.

However, officer mental health funding is far more than a congressional challenge. Instead, adequate officer mental health-related funding is a function of the local budgets of thousands of counties, cities, tribes, and other jurisdictions across the United States (Lucia & Halloran, 2020; Thoen, Dodson, Manzo, Piña-Watson, & Trejos-Castillo, 2020). In tough budget times and economic downturns, there is a risk that the deliberative bodies that set budgets for police departments and sheriff's offices are even more likely to scrimp on this essential need. We all need to support enhanced funding for officer mental health in our local areas.

Other approaches to manage officer mental health. Some agencies have created family support programs and resources to help officers' families cope and help the family to help the officer cope with stress, trauma, and mental health stressors related to the officers' work (CopsAlive.com, 2010; IACP, n.d.). Other agencies have begun to offer financial counselling and assistance for officers struggling with the low pay of law enforcement work and the high costs of providing for their families (DOJ-COPS, 2020). Many agencies have begun providing peer support groups (Milliard, 2020; Toone & Wallentine, 2020) and arranged for prepaid counselors to help their officers (Redman, 2018). A small number of law enforcement agencies have tried to reduce or eliminate required rotating shift work (Ma, Andrew, Fekedulegn, Gu, Hartley, Charles, Violanti, & Burchfiel, 2015) and mandatory overtime requirements that contribute to officer mental health stress and challenges. Some agencies provide downtime and debriefing opportunities for officers as resources and not in a pejorative manner. Some departments have created officer wellness programs with other agencies ensuring some measure of officer privacy by offering those services through external, third-party counselors. Finally, just 5% of the 18,000-plus law enforcement agencies in the United States have formal officer suicide prevention programs, although they appear to be very successful at reducing officer suicides up to 22 years following initiation of the program (Mishara & Fortin, 2021). We can and must do better.

We cannot afford to ignore law enforcement officer wellness concerns, which can harm the officer, the officer's family, and the members of the public with whom the officer interacts, nor can we allow mental health intervention stigma to linger and thereby prevent struggling officers from seeking help. We cannot afford to address officer mental health "on the cheap." Solutions require a commitment to offering and adequate funding to support a broad array of stress reduction and management approaches and programs, mental health services, and suicide prevention programming (McDevitt & McDevitt, 2020).

Problems

Problem One

Imagine you are the elected county sheriff and you have decided to dedicate substantial department resources to officer mental health and suicide prevention in your department. The county board of commissioners supported this officer health initiative with up to $1 million of county funds per year for five years. You believe you have created a broad and holistic program of mental health, stress reduction, and stress management for your officers and their families, and suicide prevention for your officers. Identify the key features of your program and explain why you deem each to be essential to help you manage and reduce mental health issues among your sworn officers and their families.

Problem Two

Imagine you are the same elected county sheriff that developed the broad and holistic mental health and suicide prevention program discussed in your answer to Problem One, above. However, you are concerned that you may encounter weak officer buy-in and program involvement due to the adverse impacts of self-stigma, public stigma, and officer stigma on officer willingness to report mental health issues and seek counseling to alleviate stress. You want to (A) lay out the full program for your officers and (B) do all you can to garner officer support and buy-in while minimizing stigma when addressing all your officers in the squad room at the start of each of the three shifts tomorrow. Draft your squad room remarks to your officers addressing your concerns A and B, above.

Problem Three

As a research analyst with the Congressional Research Service, a non-partisan group that serves both houses of Congress by providing detailed research and input on proposed and enacted federal legislation, you have been asked to put together a ten-point plan identifying the ten most important features/programs Congress should add to its next bills supporting law enforcement officer mental health. Identify your ten most important features/programs for officer mental health and explain why you assigned each to a spot in the top ten.

Problem Four

You are a chief of police serving a large city in the Midwest. Over the preceding five years, you have sensed that your officers are under an increasing degree of stress driven by several high-profile excessive force complaints and difficulty hiring sufficient officers to fill all the open positions. Along with your senior administrators, you wish to devise a way to augment, manage, and schedule your sworn officer workforce to (A) adequately protect and serve while (B) fully covering all shifts around the clock. You believe rotating shift work and long shifts both increase your officers' mental and physical stress. How would you schedule your sworn officers to optimize A and B while minimizing mental and physical stress on your officers? Explain why you settled on that schedule to achieve A and B.

Problem Five

There is obvious crossover, at times, between mental health issues suffered by peace officers and mental health issues plaguing some civilians in our communities. Consider and propose at least three ways a law enforcement agency may capitalize on that crossover by designing training, community outreach, or problem-oriented policing approaches that "kill two birds with one stone."

Notes

1 Chuck MacLean was the principal author of this chapter.
2 See Solutions section subtitled, "Reduce the Stigma."

References

American Police Officers Alliance (2019, September 19). Mental health statistics: Police officers. Available at https://americanpoliceofficersalliance.com/mental-health-statistics-police-officers/.

Arredondo, R., Shumway, S. T., Kimball, T. G., Dersch, C. A., Morelock, C. N., & Bryan, L. (2002, December). *Law enforcement and corrections family support: Final report of the development and evaluation of a stress management program for officers and their spouses*. Available at https://www.ojp.gov/pdffiles1/nij/grants/197900.pdf.

Ayres, R. M. (1990). *Preventing law enforcement stress: The organization's role*. United States Department of Justice, National Institute of Justice. Available at https://www.ojp.gov/pdffiles1/Digitization/141934NCJRS.pdf.

Barr, L. (2020, January 2). Record number of US police officers died by suicide in 2019, advocacy group says. *ABC News*. Available at https://abcnews.go.com/Politics/record-number-us-police-officers-died-suicide-2019/story?id=68031484.

Beshears, M. (2017, March 30). How police can reduce and manage stress. *Police1*. Available at https://www.police1.com/stress/articles/how-police-can-reduce-and-manage-stress-AThewNlseDwMYCcB/.

Blue H.E.L.P. (n.d.). Website, available at www.bluehelp.org.

Blue H.E.L.P. (2021, June 30). *Suicides by year*. Available at https://bluehelp.org/.

Bond, M. (2014, April 25). Married to the badge: Stress in the law enforcement marriage. *MultiBriefs*. Available at http://exclusive.multibriefs.com/content/married-to-the-badge-stress-in-the-law-enforcement-marriage/law-enforcement-defense-security.

Bond, M. (2014, May 22). Children of the badge: The impact of stress on law enforcement children. *MultiBriefs*. Available at https://exclusive.multibriefs.com/content/children-of-the-badge-the-impact-of-stress-on-law-enforcement-children/law-enforcement-defense-security.

Brown, J. P., Martin, D., Nagaria, Z., Verceles, A. C., Jobe, S. L., & Wickwire, E. M. (2020). Mental health consequences of shift work: An updated review. *Current Psychiatry Reports*, 22, article 7. doi:10-1007/s11920-020-1131-z.

Burr, L. (2020, January 2). Record number of US police officers died by suicide in 2019, advocacy group says. *ABC News*. Available at https://abcnews.go.com/Politics/record-number-us-police-officers-died-suicide-2019/story?id=68031484#:~:text=with%20news%20about-,Record%20number%20of%20US%20police%20officers%20died%20by%20suicide%20in,228%20from%20172%20in%202018.&text=In%202019%2C%20228%20current%20or,announced%20on%20Thursday.

Carrier, A. C. (2020, August). *The experiences of police officers exposed to daily trauma as a course of their employment: A phenomenological study*, Dissertation (Sam Houston State University). Available at https://shsu-ir.tdl.org/bitstream/handle/20.500.11875/2853/CARRIER-DISSERTATION-2020.pdf?sequence=1.

Cooper, F. R. (2009). "Who's the man?": Masculinities studies, Terry stops, and police training. *Columbia Journal of Gender and Law*, 18(3), 671–742. Available at https://scholars.law.unlv.edu/cgi/viewcontent.cgi?article=2146&context=facpub.

CopsAlive.com (2010, February 15). *Family support groups for law enforcement agencies*. Available at https://www.copsalive.com/family-support-groups-for-law-enforcement-agencies/.

DOJ-COPS, see United States Department of Justice Community Oriented Policing Services.

Drew, J. M. & Martin, S. (2020, July). Mental health and well-being of police in a health pandemic: Critical issues for police leaders in a post-COVID-19 environment. *Journal of Community Safety and Well-Being*, 5(2), 31–36. Available at https://journalcswb.ca/index.php/cswb/article/view/133/257.

Eliasson, M. N. (2021). *Police officers: Invisible victims in the line of duty*. IGI Global.

Fair, T. (2020, August 24). The impact of policing on law enforcement mental health. *The Center for Community Solutions*. Available at https://www.communitysolutions.com/impact-policing-law-enforcement-mental-health/.

Goodmark, L. (2015). Hands up at home: Militarized masculinity and police officers who commit intimate partner abuse. *Brigham Young University Law Review, 2015*(5), 1183–1246. Available at https://digitalcommons.law.byu.edu/cgi/viewcontent.cgi?article=3002&context=lawreview.

Graves, J. S. & Lynn, M. M. (2020, Fall). Psychiatric disorders arising from cumulative stress in police officers offer clues for decreasing excessive use of force. *Journal of Colorado Policing*, 5(2), 12–22. Available at https://www.colochiefs.org/assets/JOCP%20Vol%205%20Iss%202%20Fall%202020%20final.pdf.

Henderson, S., Steinkopf, B., Straud, C., Vincent, N., Crouch, A., Guskowski, K., & van Hasselt, V. (n.d.). Mental health of law enforcement officers: Current strategies and issues in prevention and intervention. Available at https://adaa.org/sites/default/files/Henderson_100.pdf.

Hermann, P. (2021, February 12). Two officers who helped fight the Capitol mob died by suicide. Many more are hurting. *The Washington Post*. Available at https://www.washingtonpost.com/local/public-safety/police-officer-suicides-capitol-riot/2021/02/11/94804ee2-665c-11eb-886d-5264d4ceb46d_story.html.

Hilliard, J. (2019, September 14). New study shows police at highest risk for suicide of any profession. *Addiction Center*. Available at https://www.addictioncenter.com/news/2019/09/police-at-highest-risk-for-suicide-than-any-profession/.

IACP. See International Association of Chiefs of Police.

International Association of Chiefs of Police ("IACP") (n.d.). Law enforcement family resources. Available at https://www.theiacp.org/ICPRlawenforcementfamily.

Jetelina, K. K., Molsberry, R. J., Gonzalez, J. R., Beauchamp, A. M., & Hall, T. (2020, October 7). Prevalence of mental illness and mental health care use among police officers. *JAMA Network Open*. doi:10.1001/jamanetworkopen.2020.19658. Available at https://jamanetwork.com/journals/jamanetworkopen/fullarticle/2771400.

Johnson, O. (2017, April 17). How terroristic attacks affect responding police officers. *Gov1*. Available at https://www.gov1.com/emergency-management/articles/how-terrorist-attacks-affect-responding-police-officers-A7mmML3C2HIM7Znb/.

Karaffa, K. M. (2016). *Stigma, pluralistic ignorance, and attitudes toward seeking mental health services among police officers*. Dissertation (Oklahoma State University). Available at https://shareok.org/bitstream/handle/11244/48822/Karaffa_okstate_0664D_14483.pdf?sequence=1.

Karaffa, K. M. & Tochkov, K. (2013). Attitudes toward seeking mental health treatment among law enforcement officers. *Applied Psychology in Criminal Justice*, 9(2), 75–99. http://dev.cjcenter.org/_files/apcj/apcjspring%202013karaffa.pdf_1383836355.pdf.

Kranick, L. & Stelter, L. (2015, September 1). When officers become the target: How to protect yourself from doxing. *American Military University Edge*. Available at https://amuedge.com/when-officers-become-the-target-how-to-protect-yourself-from-doxing/.

Law Enforcement Mental Health and Wellness Act (2017). 115th Congress, 1st Session, HR 2228. Available at https://www.govinfo.gov/content/pkg/BILLS-115hr2228enr/pdf/BILLS-115hr2228enr.pdf.

Lees, T., Elliott, J. L., Gunning, S., Newton, P. J., Rai, T., & Lal, S. (2019). A systematic review of the current evidence regarding interventions for anxiety, PTSD, sleepiness and fatigue in the law enforcement workplace. *Industrial Health*, 57(6), 655–667. Available at https://www.ncbi.nlm.nih.gov/pmc/articles/PMC6885597/pdf/indhealth-57-655.pdf.

Lentz, L. M., Smith-MacDonald, L., Malloy, D., Carleton, R. N., & Brémault-Phillips, S. (2021, March 31). Compromised conscience: A scoping review of moral injury among firefighters, paramedics, and police officers. *Frontiers in Psychology*, 12, 639781. doi:10.3389/fpsyg.2021.639781. Available at https://www.frontiersin.org/articles/10.3389/fpsyg.2021.639781/full.

Levant, R. F. & Pryor, S. (2020, September 10). The role of masculinity in reforming police departments. Oxford University Press blogpost. Available at https://blog.oup.com/2020/09/the-role-of-masculinity-in-reforming-police-departments/.

Lucia, D. J. & Halloran, M. J. (2020). An investigation of the efficacy of programs to prevent stress in law enforcement officers: A program manager's perspective. *Journal of Police and Criminal Psychology*, 35, 35–47. Available at https://www.researchgate.net/publication/334781678_An_Investigation_of_the_Efficacy_of_Programs_to_Prevent_Stress_in_Law_Enforcement_Officers_a_Program_manager%27s_Perspective

Ma, C. C., Andrew, M. E., Fekedulegn, D., Gu, J. D., Hartley, T. A., Charles, L. E., Violanti, J. M., & Burchfiel, C. M. (2015). Shift work and occupational stress in police officers. *Safety and Health at Work*, 6, 25–29. Available at https://www.ncbi.nlm.nih.gov/pmc/articles/PMC4372186/pdf/main.pdf.

Marshall, R. E., Milligan-Saville, J., Petrie, K., Bryant, R. A., Mitchell, P. B., & Harvey, S. B. (2021). Mental health screening amongst police officers: Factors associated with under-reporting of symptoms. *BMC Psychiatry*, 21, 135. doi:10.1186/s12888-021-03125-1. Available at https://bmcpsychiatry.biomedcentral.com/track/pdf/10.1186/s12888-021-03125-1.pdf.

McCartney, R. (2020, June 22). Police critic says officers need more money and less stress, along with greater accountability. *The Washington Post.* Available at https://www.washingtonpost.com/local/police-critic-says-officers-need-more-money-and-less-stress-along-with-greater-accountability/2020/06/21/dee93ebe-b23c-11ea-8f56-63f38c990077_story.html.

McCartney, S. & Parent, R. (2021). Socialization of police, chapter 8.2 in *Ethics in Law Enforcement.* Open Text British Columbia. Available at https://opentextbc.ca/ethicsinlawenforcement/chapter/8-2-socialization-of-police/.

McDevitt, D. & McDevitt, M. F. (2020). Behind the shield; Promoting mental health for law enforcement personnel. *Nursing*, 50(6), 62–65. doi:10.1097/01.NURSE.0000662332.48712.6d. Available at https://journals.lww.com/nursing/fulltext/2020/06000/behind_the_shield__promoting_mental_health_for_law.18.aspx.

Milliard, B. (2020). Utilization and impact of peer-support programs on police officers' mental health. *Frontiers in Psychology*, 11, article 1686. doi:10.3389/fpsyg.2020.01686. Available at https://www.ncbi.nlm.nih.gov/pmc/articles/PMC7381167/pdf/fpsyg-11-01686.pdf.

Mishara, B. L., & Fortin, L.-F. (2021, forthcoming in print). Long-term effects of a comprehensive police suicide prevention program: 22-year follow-up. *Crisis: The Journal of Crisis Intervention and Suicide Prevention.* Advance online publication. doi:10.1027/0227-5910/a000774. Available at https://econtent.hogrefe.com/doi/full/10.1027/0227-5910/a000774?rfr_dat=cr_pub++0pubmed&url_ver=Z39.88-2003&rfr_id=ori%3Arid%3Acrossref.org.

National Alliance on Mental Illness ("NAMI") (n.d.). Law enforcement. Available at https://www.nami.org/Advocacy/Crisis-Intervention/Law-Enforcement?gclid=CjwKCAiA4rGCBhAQEiwAelVti0gd3QIIoK7k-QjWY3Oy4tMiviDzUarz-Yx_GdaOxFTIIOtUQ5Kw4BoCK9EQAvD_BwE.

NBC News (2019, June 7). *Police departments seeing tragic rise in officer suicides* (video: 5:00). Available at https://www.nbcnews.com/now/video/police-departments-seeing-tragic-rise-in-officer-suicides-114433093693.

Officer.com (2020, January 3). Report: 228 U.S. law enforcement officers died by suicide in 2019: Law enforcement officer deaths by suicide once again exceeded line-of-duty deaths.

Available at https://www.officer.com/command-hq/supplies-services/public-awareness/news/21119956/report-228-us-law-enforcement-officers-died-by-suicide-in-2019.

Papazoglou, K. & Tuttle, B. M. (2018). Fighting police trauma: Practical approaches to addressing psychological needs of officers. *Sage Open*, 8(3) doi:10.1177/2158244018794794. Available at https://journals.sagepub.com/doi/full/10.1177/2158244018794794.

Paton, D. & Violanti, J. M. (2008, Spring). Law enforcement response to terrorism: The role of the resilient police organization. *International Journal of Emergency Mental Health*, 10(2), 125–135.

Perine, T. (2021, May 26). The law enforcement suicide data collection: The FBI's new data collection on officer suicide and attempted suicide. *Police Chief Online*. Available at https://www.policechiefmagazine.org/the-le-suicide-data-collection/.

Police Executive Officer Forum (2019, October). *An occupational risk: What every police agency should do to prevent suicide among its officers*. Available at https://www.policeforum.org/assets/PreventOfficerSuicide.pdf.

Preidt, R. (2020, May 22). Mental health is big issue for police officers around the world: Study. *U.S. News & World Report*. Available at https://www.usnews.com/news/health-news/articles/2020-05-22/mental-health-is-big-issue-for-police-officers-around-the-world-study#:~:text=Previous%20studies%20have%20suggested%20that,police%20officers%20in%2024%20countries.

Price, M. (2017). Psychiatric disability in law enforcement officers. *Behavioral Sciences & the Law*, 35(2), 113–123.

Purba, A., & Demou, E. (2019). The relationship between organisational stressors and mental wellbeing within police officers: A systematic review. *BMC Public Health*. doi:10.1186/s12889-019-7609-0. Available at https://bmcpublichealth.biomedcentral.com/articles/10.1186/s12889-019-7609-0.

Ramchand, R., Saunders, J., Osilla, K. C., Ebener, P., Kotzias, V., Thornton, E., Strang, L., & Cahill, M. (2019). Suicide prevention in U.S. law enforcement agencies: A national survey of current practices. *Journal of Police and Criminal Psychology*, 34, 55–66.

Rappleye, H., & Siegel, E. R. (2019, September 10). How this police department is fighting for its officers' mental health after suicides. *NBC News*. Available at https://www.nbcnews.com/news/us-news/police-department-grapples-officer-health-wake-suicides-n1051696.

Rawski, S. L. & Workman-Stark, A. L. (2018). Masculinity contest cultures in policing organizations and recommendations for training interventions. *Journal of Social Issues*, 74 (3), 607–627.

Redman, J. (2018, January 23). Why do cops avoid counselling? Eight myths about law enforcement officers and mental health treatment. *Counseling Today*. Available at https://ct.counseling.org/2018/01/why-do-cops-avoid-counseling-eight-myths-about-law-enforcement-officers-and-mental-health-treatment/.

Ruderman Family Foundation (n.d.). Study: Police officers and firefighters are more likely to die by suicide than in line of duty. Available at https://rudermanfoundation.org/white_papers/police-officers-and-firefighters-are-more-likely-to-die-by-suicide-than-in-line-of-duty/.

Sherwood, L., Hegarty, S., Vallieres, F., Hyland, P., Murphy, J., Fitzgerald, G., & Reid, T. (2019). Identifying the key risk factors for adverse psychological outcomes among police officers: A systematic literature review. *Journal of Traumatic Stress*, 32(5), 688–700.

Thoen, M. A., Dodson, L. E., Manzo, G., Piña-Watson, B., & Trejos-Castillo, E. (2020). Agency-offered and officer-utilized suicide prevention and wellness programs: A national study. *Psychological Services*, 17(2), 129–140. Preprint available at https://www.academia.edu/42556589/Psychological_Services_Agency_Offered_and_Officer_Utilized_Suicide_Prevention_and_Wellness_Programs_A_National_Study.

Toone, B. & Wallentine, K. (2020, June 24). Therapeutic considerations in police peer support. *Lexipol*. Available at https://www.lexipol.com/resources/blog/therapeutic-considerations-in-police-peer-support/.

United States Code, title 34, §§ 10491–10487 (2018).

United States Department of Justice Community Oriented Policing Services ("DOJ-COPS") (2019, March). *Law Enforcement Mental Health and Wellness Act: Report to Congress*. Available at https://cops.usdoj.gov/RIC/Publications/cops-p370-pub.pdf?utm_medium=email&utm_source=govdelivery.

United States Department of Justice Community Oriented Policing Services ("DOJ-COPS") (2020, January). Reduce stress about money: The importance of financial counselling. *Community Policing Dispatch*, 13(1). Available at https://cops.usdoj.gov/html/dispatch/01-2020/reduce_stress.html.

United States Department of Justice Community Oriented Policing Services ("DOJ-COPS") (2021). *Law Enforcement Officer Suicide: 2020 Report to Congress*. Available at https://cops.usdoj.gov/RIC/Publications/cops-p429-pub.pdf.

van der Velden, P. G., Rademaker, A. R., Vermetten, E., Portengen, M-A, Yzermans, J. C., & Grievink, L. (2013). Police officers: A high-risk group for the development of mental health disturbances? A cohort study. *BMJ Open*. doi:10.1136/bmjopen-2012-001720. Available at https://bmjopen.bmj.com/content/bmjopen/3/1/e001720.full.pdf.

Verhage, A., Noppe, J., Feys, Y., & Ledegen, E. (2018). Force, stress, and decision-making within the Belgian police: The impact of stressful situations on police decision-making. *Journal of Police and Criminal Psychology*, 33, 345–357.

Vigil, N. H., Grant, A. R., Perez, O., Blust, R. N., Chikani, V., & Vadeboncoeur, T. F. (2018). Death by suicide – The EMS profession compared to the general public. *Prehospital Emergency Care*, 23(3), 340–345. Available at https://cdn.ymaws.com/www.nemsma.org/resource/collection/04CCA6A7-1F85-44B1-B2EC-28D168114BD2/Death_by_Suicide_The_EMS_Profession_Compared_t.pdf.

Violanti, J. M. (2017). Suicide behind the wall: A national analysis of corrections officer suicide. *Suicidology Online*, 8(1), 58–64.

Violanti, J. M. (2018). Police officer suicide. *Criminology and Criminal Justice*. Available at https://oxfordre.com/criminology/view/10.1093/acrefore/9780190264079.001.0001/acrefore-9780190264079-e-87?rskey=uz9NXL.

Violanti, J. M., Charles, L. E., McCanlies, E., Hartley, T. A., Baughman, P., Andrew, A. E., Fekedulegn, D., Mam, C. C., Mnatsakanova, A., & Burchfiel, C. M. (2017). Police stressors and health: A state-of-the-art review. *Policing*, 40(4), 642–656. Available at https://www.ncbi.nlm.nih.gov/pmc/articles/PMC6400077/.

Violanti, J. M., Robinson, C. F., & Shen, R. (2013). Law enforcement suicide: A national analysis. *International Journal of Emergency Mental Health and Human Resilience*, 15(4), 289–297. Available at https://pubmed.ncbi.nlm.nih.gov/24707591/.

Wheeler, C., Fisher, A., Jamiel, A., Lynn, T.J., & Hill, W. T. (2021). Stigmatizing attitudes toward police officers seeking psychological services. *Journal of Police and Criminal Psychology*, 36, 1–7. doi:10.1007/s11896-018-9293-x.

PART II
Attorneys and Courts

This part of the book discusses the roles of attorneys and courts in ensuring that the criminal justice system is conducted in a fair, impartial, and reliable manner. The chapters in this part will require you to propose solutions that address the infirmities and inequities in particular areas of the criminal justice system along three dimensions: cash bail and unequal justice (chapter 4); ineffective assistance of defense counsel (chapter 5), and prosecutorial misconduct, consequences, remedies, and immunity (chapter 6). Each chapter provides the factual backdrop for the issue addressed, proposes a number of solutions, then calls on you to devise the wisest course of action.

Furthermore, as stated in the Preface, this book is intended not merely to help you acquire knowledge, but to require you to offer workable solutions that make a positive difference in people's lives. Put differently, it is not sufficient to merely complain about a problem. Transformative thinkers offer solutions that make a different in people's lives.

DOI: 10.4324/9781003163411-5

4

BAIL, BAIL BONDS, CASH BAIL, AND UNEQUAL JUSTICE[1]

Bail is an amount of money set by a judge that must be posted by a criminal defendant to secure his pretrial release. Sometimes that cash bail may be accompanied by conditions (remain law abiding, make all court appearances, have no contact with the alleged victim, etc.). Bail and release conditions are used to ensure the defendant will appear at future hearings and to protect the public from the defendant committing new criminal acts while awaiting resolution of the current criminal charges. The former usually rests on the defendant's history of failures to appear and ties to the community; the latter usually rests on the defendant's criminal history and the severity of the instant offense. Sometimes judges set both a lower conditional bail (subject to specified conditions) and a higher but unconditional bail (subject only to re-appearing for future proceedings). The United States Constitution and most state constitutions require that bail be set at a "reasonable" and not excessive amount. Some state constitutions require bail for all criminal cases and other state constitutions permit no-bail detentions in particularly serious cases and circumstances. The issues addressed in this chapter revolve around justice, equity, and fair treatment in bail setting and enforcement for defendants of all races, ethnicities, and abilities to pay.

Incredibly, between 60% and 70% of all inmates in local jails have not been convicted of the crime for which they are in jail. With a median felony bail in America of about $10,000, those arrestees, who are presumed innocent but unable to make bail, will languish in jail, weaken their families, perhaps lose their jobs or housing or become ill or injured in crowded jails, and have a difficult time contacting and consulting with their attorneys to prepare their defense. Something must be done and soon.

DOI: 10.4324/9781003163411-6

Chapter Highlights

✓Case Spotlight: Kalief Browder's pretrial limbo

✓Excessive bail is expressly precluded by the Eighth Amendment to the United States Constitution.

✓Bail is arguably set to ensure the defendant's reappearance at future court hearings and to protect public safety.

✓When bail is set at a level the defendant cannot post, that defendant remains incarcerated pretrial, before conviction, although presumed innocent, and faces a far more difficult path to meet with defense counsel and staff and to prepare a defense.

✓When bail is set at an unaffordable level, there are immediate costs and losses borne by the defendant, the defendant's family, their neighborhood, and beyond.

✓Bail is disparately applied across races and abilities to pay.

✓Bail schedules are tables of preset bail amounts by type of offense. They are inherently unequal because they are usually based on severity of the instant offense alone without regard to ability to post bail or the defendant's history of appearance or failure to appear.

✓Bail set at $5,000 for two similarly situated defendants who committed the same criminal offense with the same criminal history and same history of appearance for prior court hearings sounds fair enough – but if one of those defendants is well-to-do and the other has no available resources or assets to pledge to secure bail, one will be free pending trial or other resolution and the other will be held in jail, away from family, friends, job, home, and defense counsel.

✓The bail bond system is particularly prone to inequity – poor defendants pay a bondsman a non-refundable premium (often 10%) to post bail on the defendants' behalf while wealthy defendants post cash bail and are refunded the entire posted bail without the necessity of paying any non-refundable bail bond.

✓"Unequal justice" as used here refers to the dichotomized justice system that provides one set of procedures, due process, and outcomes for members of some groups but denies those benefits to similarly situated members of other groups.

Case Spotlight: Kalief Browder's Pretrial Limbo

In 2010, sixteen-year-old Kalief Browder was arrested for allegedly having stolen a backpack in New York. Bail was set at $3,000, a level Kalief could not afford, so he was placed at Riker's Island, New York City's largest jail facility. Kalief waited at Riker's for more than 1,000 days, two years of that in solitary confinement, for a trial that never came. Eventually, after the complainant left the country, and after 31 separate court hearings in his case, and multiple attempted suicides, the charge against Kalief was dismissed. He had lost his freedom and his childhood and never fully recovered. Kalief later committed suicide by hanging himself at home. [Case facts drawn from Gonnerman (2014, 2015).]

Culminating in 2015, the year Kalief died, pretrial inmates at Riker's Island waited 593 days, on average, for their trials to begin (King, 2015). These inmates

FIGURE 4.1 Riker's Island

were presumed innocent, but warehoused, on average, for over a year and a half. Pretrial detention is an affront to justice and to defendants' rights enshrined in the United States Constitution. The judges presiding over and the lawyers operating within a criminal justice system that would yield such long pretrial delays are violating their oaths – to justice and to the Constitution.

It is past time to be creative, be courageous, and create bail and pretrial release practices that respect human rights.

An Introduction to Bail and Bail Bonds

Bail, when it is not simply read off a published bail schedule, is typically set based on reappearance risk and risk to public safety. In assessing those risks, the presiding judge should consider ties to the community, employment status, prior failures to appear, prior bail or probation violations, criminal history, and the severity of the instant offense.

As empirical studies have almost universally found, that approach inures to the detriment of communities of color, who tend to have prior records, be more transient, have less steady employment, and the like (Arnold, Dobbie, & Yang, 2018; Assefa, 2018). For those administering that bail system, it may seem neutral and fair, but decades of disparate treatment of communities of color have left them with high static bail markers (e.g., convictions, arrests, prior failures to appear for court), yielding higher bail settings. Finally, when two defendants charged with similar crimes are assessed the same bail amount, say $10,000, the well-to-do defendant can simply post cash bail, which will be returned in full to the defendant when the case concludes. The less wealthy defendant cannot post a $10,000 cash bail, so is obliged to either sit in jail in lieu of bail or post a bail bond for which a non-refundable ~10% premium (in this scenario, a $1,000 premium) must be paid to a bail bondsman to post the bail on the defendant's behalf. That less wealthy defendant will not receive any part of that $1,000 bond premium back when that case concludes. The benefit flows to the wealthy defendant; the inequity flows to the less wealthy defendant. Since wealth is disparately distributed along race lines, African-Americans are disparately harmed by the cash bail system.

The solution has several features here. First, the bail schedule system must be eliminated or leavened by consideration of the defendant's ability to pay. Second, bail must always be set based not solely on reappearance risk and risk to public safety as presently defined but should be based on more dynamic and relevant factors, including the defendant's ability to pay. Finally, the cash bail system must be eliminated or modified to provide less of a windfall to wealthy defendants and more equity to defendants with fewer resources.

Poor arrestees "are presumed innocent under the law, yet they will suffer the harms of incarceration unless they have enough money to pay bail and buy their freedom. This two-tier system criminalizes poverty and is a structural linchpin of mass incarceration and racial inequality. It affects entire communities, devastates families for generations, and guts the presumption of innocence" (Bail Project Inc., 2020, p. 3). As Vermont Senator Bernie Sanders has explained, the current cash bail system creates a "modern-day debtors prison" (Carlisle, 2018).

Pretrial detention in lieu of bail is a growth industry driven by judges' bail decisions and a bail bond industry eager to maximize profits. Between 1970 and 2015 alone, pretrial detention in the United States increased 433% (Harriot, 2018). Those people are not serving time; they are waiting for justice (Vera Institute, n.d.) from a glacially slow court system. Sadly, the "number of Americans sitting in jail without a conviction is larger than most other countries' entire incarcerated population … and 75 percent of pretrial detainees have been charged with only drug or property crimes" (Mathews & Curiel, 2019).

Disparities in Bail and Pretrial Release

Like most segments of the American criminal justice system, the bail system is ripe with racial and wealth-driven disparities. Black defendants are more likely to receive higher bail and more restrictive release conditions (Assefa, 2018). Bail decisions are often made very quickly during overbooked arraignment calendars in court. Implicit biases can drive those bail decisions since bail is often decided in minutes and on very little information regarding dangerousness and reappearance risk (Assefa, 2018). Some commentators have found that when bail is set quickly, racial stereotypes can affect the perceived public safety risk because, for example, some judges may harbor beliefs that Black offenders are "more dangerous" (Arnold, Dobbie, & Yang, 2018).

Disparities flow based on comparative wealth of arrestees, as well, in a cash bail system that some have labelled the "criminalization of poverty" (Mathews & Curiel, 2019). The American economy does not share its blessings equally across all races. Persons of color are more likely to be unable to post bail (May, 2018). Thus, when a Black arrestee is also a poor arrestee, as the next section explains, the scourge of race-based bail ripples through all steps of the criminal justice process as many, eager to return to their jobs and families, may be tempted to plead guilty just to get it over with for "time served" (Donnelly & MacDonald, 2018). Thus, unaffordable cash bail for poor (and, too often, Black) arrestees leads to more convictions, longer sentences, and criminal histories that can haunt them for the rest of their lives.

The Toll Bail Exacts on Defendants, Families, Communities, and the Public Purse

Unaffordable cash bail heightens racial disparities, drains wealth from poor individuals, families, and communities, and does not support public safety (Minneapolis Foundation, 2019). Instead, pretrial bail holds exact a toll on poor arrestees and arrestees of color and on their families, their communities, and the public purse (Arnold, Dobbie, & Yang, 2018). Poor arrestees of color held on unaffordable pretrial bail are:

- three-to-four times more likely to plead guilty (Freethink, 2020) just to get on with their lives, thus making it more difficult for them to be gainfully employed in the future
- more likely to receive a harsh sentence if they face new charges in the future, since they will have higher criminal history scores driving future sentences higher still
- prone to exhibit greater recidivism, unemployment, and homelessness due to the added criminal history and time away from family and work (Freethink, 2020)
- less likely to retain custody of their children (Freethink, 2020)
- less likely to be able to cooperate and consult with their defense attorneys to mount a vigorous defense (Gold & Wright, 2020)
- less able to successfully reenter society and reintegrate after serving the sentence (Huebner, Lentz, & Gibson, 2020)
- held in sometimes overcrowded and dangerous jail facilities (Appleman, 2012)
- more likely to suffer physical, mental, and emotional struggles while in jail (Petteruti & Walsh, 2008; Zeng, 2021)
- more likely to lose their employment or suffer adverse employment consequences (Wiseman, 2014)
- more likely to have their children placed in foster care or with other family members (Petteruti & Walsh, 2008)

The percentage of all jail inmates who are being held pretrial (that is, are being held in jail without having been convicted of the crime for which they are in jail) is increasing slightly and has exceeded 60% of all local jail inmates since at least 2004.

Finally, pretrial delay can seem interminable as those who cannot afford to post bail must wait in jail for each hearing. One can only imagine the cost, loss, and anguish suffered by those pretrial defendants, presumed innocent, yet condemned by unaffordable bail to languish in jail waiting for justice instead of expeditiously receiving it (see Figure 4.3).

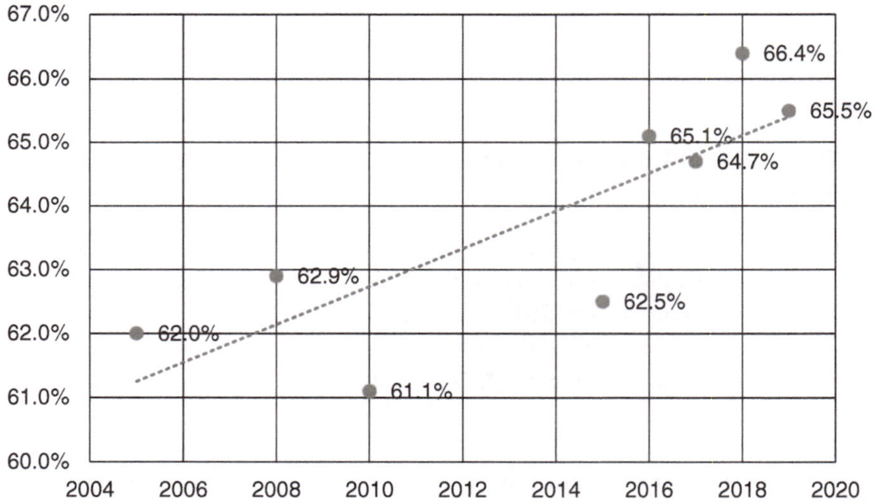

FIGURE 4.2 Percentage of All Inmates in Local Jails Who Are Being Held Pretrial

Bail, especially cash bail, does not ensure reappearance for future court appearances (Barno, Neverez Martinez, & Williams, 2020), but it certainly disproportionately harms the poor and arrestees of color (Edelman, 2021; Hernandez, 2021).

The Constitutional Bottom Line for Bail Reform

> No person shall be … deprived of life, liberty, or property, without due process of law … (U.S. Const. amend. V).
>
> [N]or shall any state deprive any person of life, liberty, or property, without due process of law … (U.S. Const. amend. XIV, § 1).
>
> Excessive bail shall not be required, nor excessive fines imposed, nor cruel and unusual punishments inflicted (U.S. Const. amend. VIII).
>
> Prior to conviction, the accused is shielded by the presumption of innocence, the "bedrock[,] axiomatic and elementary principle whose enforcement lies at the foundation of the administration of our criminal law" (*Betterman v. Montana*, 136 S. Ct. 1609, 1614 (2016) (quoting *Reed v. Ross*, 468 U.S. 1, 4 (1984)).
>
> No state shall … deny to any person within its jurisdiction the equal protection of the laws (U.S. Const. amend. XIV, § 1).

Those constitutional and related principles circumscribe (or should circumscribe) the jurisprudential crucible within which we must evaluate bail practices in the United States today. After all, criminal defendants are presumed innocent, yet about two-thirds of the inmates in American jails are not serving time after a conviction but are simply in jail because they are unable to afford to pay bail or secure a bail bond. That begs the following italicized questions.

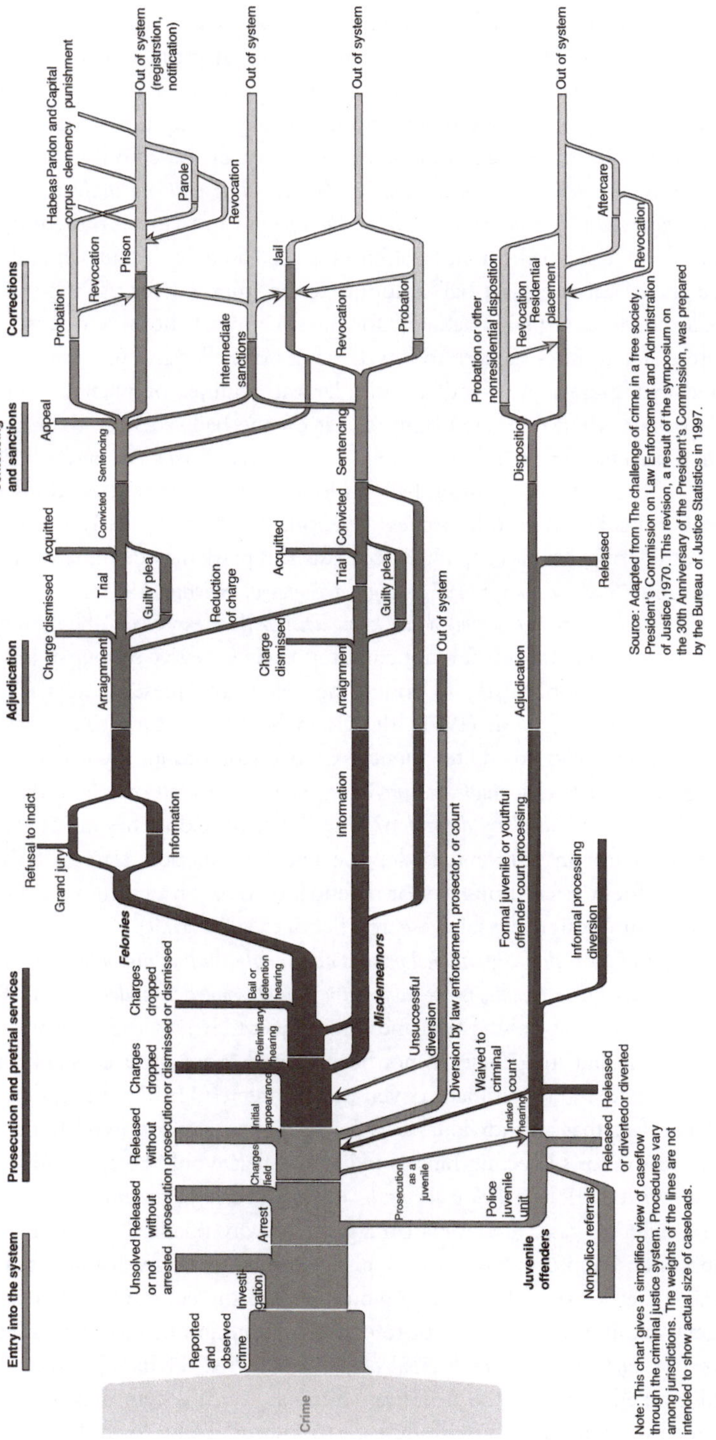

FIGURE 4.3 The Criminal Justice Process – step-by-step

Is pretrial detention in lieu of bail consistent with the presumption of innocence? When identical defendants – one rich and one poor – are assigned the same bail amount that the rich defendant can afford to post but the poor one cannot, is the poor defendant, incarcerated pretrial, really presumed innocent – that presumption should abide for all defendants equally and should not be doled out unequally based on wealth.

When bail is set solely based on a published bail schedule with no individualized assessment of this defendant, is that consistent with due process? In many jurisdictions and for many minor offenses, bail for new offenses is set based on a bail schedule, a pre-published list of offenses and bail amounts to be imposed for each listed offense. Those bail schedules arguably account for the severity of the new offense category but ignore characteristics specific to the particular offender and particular offense. It is assumed that there is no need to consider the equities or what bail amount is justifiable or fair when one need only read it off the bail schedule then impose it.

Is pretrial detention in the absence of conviction consistent with due process? Extended pretrial detention in lieu of posting bail has long been recognized as consistent with procedural and substantive due process (Carroll, 2020), particularly if the bail was set after considering on an individualized basis the particular defendant's flight and re-offense risks (*Stack v. Boyle*, 1951; *United States v. Salerno*, 1987).

Under the Eighth Amendment, how do we know when bail is "excessive"? The United States Supreme Court has held that bail is not constitutionally excessive so long as it is not "set higher than … reasonably likely to ensure the defendant's presence at trial" (*Stack v. Boyle, 1951*). In *Stack v. Boyle* (1951), the Court held that setting bail at $50,000 for indigent defendants who posed little flight risk was unconstitutionally excessive.

Is setting bail at a level so high the presiding judge has reason to believe the defendant could not afford it "excessive" by definition? The Supreme Court has never found cash bail approaches unconstitutional under the equal protection clause of the Fourteenth Amendment even though poor defendants have a much more difficult time posting cash bail (Congressional Research Service, 2019, p. 7).

If the bail system treats similarly situated persons dissimilarly, such as disparate results depending on one's race, ethnicity, or wealth, is everyone being equally protected under the law? Race has been treated as a suspect classification and thus subject to strict scrutiny review of equal protection claims, but indigency has not been treated as a suspect class and thus need only be supported by a legitimate governmental interest. In dissent, Justice Stevens argued, "The fact that an individual may be unable to pay for a bail bond … is an insufficient reason for subjecting him to indignities that would be appropriate punishment for convicted felons" (*Bell v. Wolfish*, 1979, Stevens, J., dissenting). However, in dissent in a different case, Justice Harlan argued, "Every financial exaction which the State imposes on a uniform basis is more easily satisfied by the well-to-do than by the indigent … [Y]et I take it that no one would dispute the constitutional power of the State to levy a uniform sales tax … or to establish minimum bail for various categories of offenses" (*Douglas v. People of the State of California,* 1963, Harlan, J., dissenting).

The distributed nature of the American criminal justice system makes it very difficult to conceive of and much more difficult to institute bail reform that applies in all jurisdictions, all court systems, and all cases. Nonetheless, parts of the system have labored for years on a series of efforts striving to rationalize bail and make it fairer and less prone to unintended disparities and equal protection concerns. The next section briefly discusses a few notable efforts in the recent history of American bail reform.

The Bail Reform Process in Recent Years

Huebner, Lentz, and Gibson (2020, p. 1261) discussed some of the efforts over the 2010s, "to reduce the use of jails, reform and eliminate money bail, and to improve conditions of confinement." More recently, in what some call the third wave of bail reform seeking to eliminate wealth-based discrimination (Van Brunt & Bowman, 2019), almost every state has considered or adopted legislation to address bail reform, admittedly often through the lens of the COVID-19 pandemic (Sawyer, 2019). Many of those approaches can be boiled down to Prather's (2016) catch phrase: "Time to be right on crime not tough on crime." Some of those efforts led to remarkable improvements in local bail systems, but in spite of that lofty phrase, some of those efforts failed – some quite remarkably.

> In response to the COVID-19 pandemic, California eliminated cash bail for most low-level offenses. This allowed thousands of defendants to await trial at home rather than in crowded jails during a pandemic. Washington, D.C., New Jersey, and Harris County, Texas (which includes Houston, the third-largest jail system in the country) have reformed their pretrial systems by essentially ending cash bail. Washington, D.C. and New Jersey have released approximately 95 percent of defendants pretrial. Nearly 90 percent of them appear at their trial dates. States and localities could eliminate cash bail for certain misdemeanors, nonviolent felonies, and other minor offenses, and explore different ways for defendants to reassure judges they will make their court appearances.
>
> *(Shah & Seervai, 2020)*

California's bail reform efforts have been panned by some as COVID-driven and not lasting or as a simple trade of cash bail in exchange for pretrial risk assessment algorithms – deemed by many to be much worse (May, 2018).

In 2017, New Jersey's Criminal Justice Reform Act virtually eliminated the state's previous cash bail system. The Act led to some quick gains but did not materially impact over-incarceration or racial disparities. The New Jersey Judiciary's annual report (New Jersey Judiciary, 2019) on the state's 2017 bail reform law quantified the key impacts traced to the Act:

- The state's pretrial jail population had dropped 43.9 percent since the end of 2015
- 6,200 fewer arrestees were incarcerated pretrial in 2018 (compared to 2012)
- In 2018, money bail was set for just 102 out of 44,383 total defendants
- Court appearance rates were high before and after the Act went into effect
- New offenses committed by defendants on pretrial release under bail reform did not increase compared to the pre-act era
- Nearly 82% of defendants were released within 24 hours of arrest

Other commentators have noted, though, that although New Jersey's jail population dropped 44% between the end of 2015 and 2018, arguably as a result of eliminating cash bail, Black men, who were 54% of New Jersey's jail population in 2015, were still 54% of New Jersey's inmates in 2018 (Mathews & Curiel, 2019).

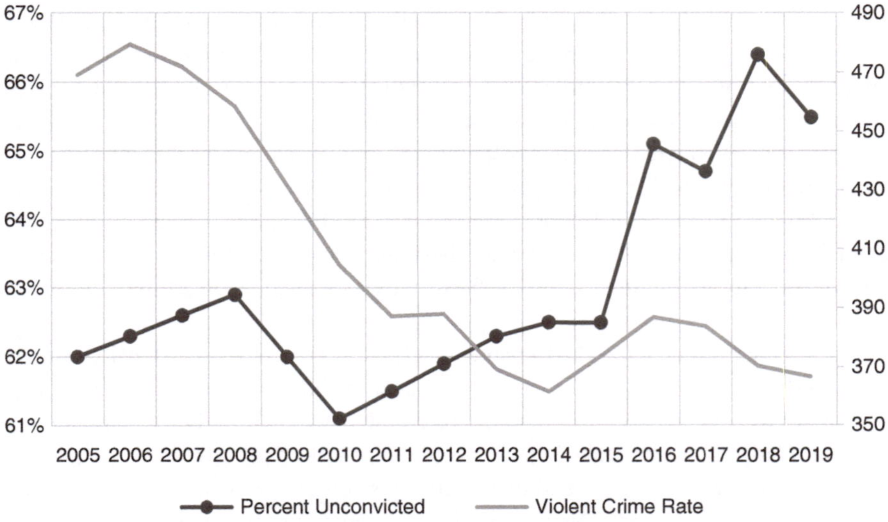

FIGURE 4.4 Percent of Jail Inmates Who Were Not Convicted Versus Violent Crime Rate

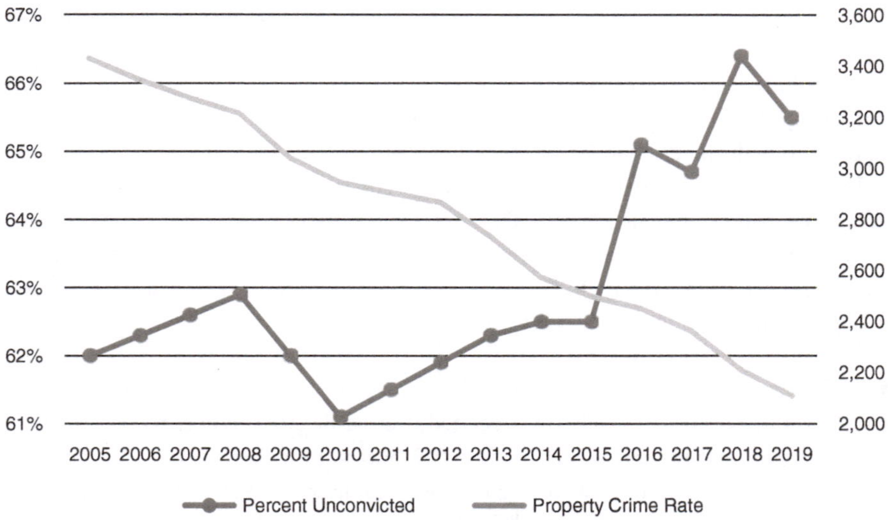

FIGURE 4.5 Percent of Jail Inmates Who Were Not Convicted Versus Property Crime Rate

Bail reform, like the other challenges discussed in this volume, can be approached in a step-wise and evolutionary manner or with far more revolutionary strategies and tactics. Those two approaches are discussed sequentially in the following two sections.

Some Common *Evolutionary* Bail Reform Themes

Bail reform addressed in an evolutionary sense requires many small steps that together can improve the justice and due process achieved in the bail system. These evolutionary approaches can be tailored to virtually any jurisdiction ready to make a change for the better.

Evolutionary Approach #1: Eliminate Cash Bail

Once one acknowledges the disparate impact of cash bail systems on the poor and defendants of color, particularly when those impacts then ripple through the rest of the criminal justice system in higher rates of guilty pleas, convictions, aggravated sentences, and in longer terms of incarceration (Donnelly & MacDonald, 2018), eliminating cash bail seems an attractive option. Unaffordable cash bail does not ensure reappearance or protect public safety, but it certainly harms poor individuals, families, and communities. Of course, there will be opposition, such as the Massachusetts Special Commission on Bail Reform (2019, p. 13): "The Commission does not recommend the elimination of cash bail or substantially altering conditions of release at this time." Although the follow-through was not flawless, several jurisdictions that have ended – or largely ended – cash bail have saved incarceration dollars while helping defendants move on with their lives, provide for their families, and prepare their own defenses. If a jurisdiction does not completely end cash bail, they should at least make bail holds the last resort (Bail Project Inc., 2020); release on recognizance ("ROR" or "ROPR") releases should be the norm and bail the exception (Hopkins, Bains, & Doyle, 2019).

Corollary to Evolutionary Approach #1: Cash Bail Should Not Be Merely Replaced by Increased Release Conditions

Commentators have demonstrated quite conclusively that ending cash bail and replacing bail with enhanced release conditions merely replicates racial and wealth-based disparities from cash bail systems. Release conditions can be Draconian and expensive, leaving poor defendants and defendants of color unable to meet those stringent conditions and leading them to end up back in jail, thus disproportionately harming marginal defendants even in the absence of cash bail (Carroll, 2021; Hopkins, Bains, & Doyle, 2019). Other commentators argue, however, that ending cash bail and replacing it with pretrial release conditions, services, day reporting, random alcohol and drug testing, and electric home monitoring can work if those are free to the releasee (Hopkins, Bains, & Doyle, 2019). Some bemoan that California's attempt to end cash bail and replace it with risk assessment algorithms yielded a worse result for poor defendants and defendants of color (May, 2018), but Hopkins, Bains, and Doyle (2019) explain that so long as the release conditions, supervision, and monitoring are free and do not exceed the government's legitimate interest in requiring them, pretrial release conditions could be a far wiser path than continuing the cash bail system.

Evolutionary Approach #2: Bail Should Only Be Set After an Adversarial, Individualized Hearing with Defense Counsel

Procedural due process requires notice, an opportunity to be heard, and an individualized decision by a neutral magistrate (*Mullane v. Central Hanover Bank & Trust Co.*, 1950). Setting bail in a formulaic sense by reference to a published bail schedule provides no individualized bail assessment at all. Bail set in cattle call hearings with dozens of defendants appearing one after the other for bail setting that lasts only a few minutes forces the judge to base the bail decision not on an effective individualized basis, but on the basis of knee-jerk assessments or stereotypes (Assefa, 2018) and frequently happen without a defense counsel present. Using a slightly more quantitative approach, such as by reference to a pretrial risk assessment algorithm, has the benefit of being – to a degree, at least – an individualized assessment, but when static measures (criminal history, prior failures to appear, and the like) predominate in the algorithm, it measures the risk of a person who is not the defendant presently before the court. It would certainly be a best practice in an individualized hearing for the presiding judge to inquire after and take into account each arrestee's ability to pay (Freethink, 2020).

Evolutionary Approach #3: Secure Community Involvement in Risk Assessment and Bail Process

If one conceives of the criminal justice system as both a creation of and servant to the community, it only makes sense to solicit input and ideas from the community on what they would like to see in terms of risk assessment, cash bail modifications, release conditions, and the like. That is particularly salient for those of us who recognize that ill-conceived approaches to bail and pretrial conditions can harm the entire community and not just the defendants and their families. On a related note, there should be ongoing updates to the communities served by regularly publishing judges' bail setting practices and track records (Assefa, 2018).

Evolutionary Approach #4: Improve and Validate Pretrial Risk Algorithms to Reduce/Remove Disparities

Research has found that pretrial risk assessment algorithms can be designed to reduce or remove disparities if the algorithms are specified so they ignore input data that might contain such disparities (Carlisle, 2018). As one example, past convictions are particularly prone to being grounded in past discrimination in investigation, trial, plea bargaining, and sentencing; thus, a pretrial risk assessment algorithm designed to give great weight to past convictions in assessing future risk will automatically carry with it the discrimination implicitly and deeply hidden within those conviction records.

That said, many commentators agree that well-designed pretrial risk assessment ("PRA") algorithms are usually better than cash bail (e.g., Barno, Neverez Martinez, & Williams, 2020). In one meta-study, PRA tools usually showed excellent predictive validity, although slightly less so for defendants of color (Desmarais, Zottola, Duhart Clark, & Lowder, 2021). Careful design and validation of PRAs can yield good estimates of flight and re-offense risk if they are validated locally and not just globally (Hamilton, 2021) and if online PRAs are protected from glitches and hacking (Gipson Rankin, 2021).

Evolutionary Approach #5: Make It Easier to Appear in Court

It is often very difficult for poor defendants and defendants with jobs and young children to appear in court. Their prior failures to appear for court dates may have largely flowed from necessity not intransigence. Bail Project Inc. (2020) has proposed a series of outstanding ideas to make it easier for defendants to appear in court, including (1) providing free or subsidized transportation; (2) offering subsidized childcare; (3) granting a grace period for failures to appear; (4) converting more hearings to either optional or remote via Zoom or other remote technology; and (5) institutionalizing a process of regular and augmented court appearance reminders. All those options are low cost and could contribute to reducing pretrial incarceration and its evils.

Some *Revolutionary* Bail Reform Themes

For some, taking an evolutionary approach to bail reform would be too little, too late, because individuals, families, and communities are suffering now and there are many more revolutionary approaches that should be adopted or at least tried in some jurisdictions.

Revolutionary Approach #1: Mandate Citations in Lieu of Arrest

For all but the most serious felonies, jurisdictions could mandate issuance of citations (Bail Project Inc., 2020; Freethink, 2020). For the most serious felonies, a prompt, particularized bail hearing with defense counsel present within twenty-four hours of arrest should be the gold standard or the guarantee.

Revolutionary Approach #2: Decriminalization to Reduce Pretrial Detention Volume

The voices in favor of decriminalization of marijuana for personal use have grown louder in recent years. That decriminalization, the arguments go, would save dollars on investigation and incarceration, avoid adverse criminal records, and free up court calendars and jail space for those suspected or convicted of more serious crimes, among other benefits. The United States already has the highest incarceration rate of any country in the world (Equal Justice Initiative, 2019) and as we have been reminded in this chapter, two-thirds of the people in our local jails have not been convicted and are being held pretrial in lieu of posting bail. Decriminalization of other minor offenses would reduce jail overcrowding and certainly would reduce the pretrial jail population (Bail Project Inc., 2020). We could start by decriminalizing recreational use of marijuana in those jurisdictions where it remains illegal, then move to decriminalize quality of life crimes (Mathews & Curiel, 2019), then add property crimes where money damages would be a sufficient resolution, and on from there.

Revolutionary Approach #3: Eliminate Pretrial Risk Assessment Algorithms

Research has demonstrated that many pretrial risk assessment algorithms, as presently designed and applied, merely continue, and in some cases exacerbate, wealth-based and race disparities endemic in cash bail systems (Bail Project Inc., 2020; Covert, 2020). Static questions about home ownership, duration at current residence, employment status, prior failures to appear for court, and cellphone ownership can disadvantage poor defendants and arrestees of color (Freethink, 2020). This approach assumes that revolutionary changes are needed now and not mere tinkering with algorithms or other pretrial risk assessment tools.

Revolutionary Approach #4: Invest in Social Services and Other Community Resources to Reduce Crime

Supporters of this revolutionary approach explain that in America's slave era, slave patrols chased down escaped slaves, took them into custody, placed them in handcuffs, and incarcerated them. That sounds familiar in many communities and neighborhoods, where parents of children of color feel obliged to have "the talk" with their children about the need to be compliant and very, very careful of law enforcement officers – today's slave patrols. We need not incarcerate a generation or a community. Instead, we can and should invest in social services, educational and employment opportunities, health services, childcare, and the like, to invest our way out of the incarceration problem in the United States (Bail Project Inc., 2020).

Revolutionary Approach #5: Make Bail Decisions Susceptible to Immediate Appellate Review

Even a few days in jail on excessive bail improvidently set can impose deep costs in the forms of lost jobs, housing, and freedom, adversely affecting defendants, families, and communities. Perhaps there should be an immediate "appellate" or *de novo* review option where a magistrate other than and superior to the initial bail-setting judge can conduct a real, individualized hearing, fully argued, with defense counsel present, with required written opinions, and which could accelerate relief from excessive bail and help initial bail-setting judges get it "right" the first time (Weldon, 2018).

Unequal Justice

Today, we look back at the criminal justice system in the United States as it was 20 years ago with derision and wonder "what they were thinking?". Twenty years from now, those who follow us will look back at our criminal justice system today and wonder what *we* were thinking. The time to fix our criminal justice system is now.

"W]e have to reform a system of criminal justice that continues to treat people better if they are rich and guilty than if they are poor and innocent" (Stevenson, 2014, p.381). The refrain is clear by now. Rich defendants can afford bail, private counsel, and better arguments yielding better plea deals, more dismissed cases, and a greater quantum of justice. Conversely, poor defendants are held in lieu of bail they cannot afford to pay, saddled by criminal records that reflect a lifetime of disparate treatment, they are appointed counsel or public defenders, and simply receive less justice. The American criminal justice system ought not to be doling out justice to the highest bidder.

The United States criminal justice system also confers different and lower levels of justice to persons of color than to White persons along virtually all dimensions of the criminal process, from (A) suspicion and investigation, to (B) arrests and citations, to (C) bail and release conditions, to (D) charging and plea negotiations, to (E) convictions and sentencing, and beyond.

We can and must do better. The Pledge of Allegiance promises that the United States guarantees "liberty and justice for all." The lintel of the United States Supreme Court building in Washington DC proclaims "EQUAL JUSTICE UNDER LAW," but liberty is unequally distributed in the United States based on wealth and race. Justice is a fleeting concept benefiting and protecting some groups while brutally harming other groups. The words of the Pledge and emblazoned at the Supreme Court cannot be treated as relics or worse, as merely aspirational. They are guideposts and commitments that we are not now fully honoring. We hope that those who read this book and think through the problems and challenges will join us in that quest to evolve the U.S. criminal justice system to a higher form that delivers on its promises. Perhaps evolution will suffice; perhaps revolution is required.

Exercises

Exercise One

You are working with a special interest group seeking legislation to end the cash bail system in your state. Assemble a list of talking points persuasively arguing: (A) why the cash bail system is unjust and perpetuates wealth-based and racial disparities; (B) why the "parade of horribles" the opposition may offer to explain that cash bail is the only workable approach is inaccurate and misleading; and (C) in detail, what should replace the current cash bail system and how that will simultaneously protect defendants' rights, victims' interests, public safety, the public purse, due process, and justice, while buoying communities of color and poor neighborhoods that are being irreparably harmed by the cash bail system. Number and write the talking points and explain and argue persuasively the rationale for each.

Exercise Two

You are a defense attorney now representing Thaddeus Williams, who has been held in pretrial custody on felony theft for allegedly stealing $702 worth of groceries to feed his wife and three children. Williams is long-term under-employed but is a hard worker when employed. He has no prior criminal history and thus no prior failures to appear for court and no prior probation violations. Williams has never been on probation for anything and never been convicted of anything in his life. The judge at the Arraignment set bail at $1,404 – cash only – with conditions and $3,510 – cash or bail bond – without conditions based on a bail schedule providing that standard conditional bail for felony theft is two times the value of the allegedly stolen property and standard unconditional bail for felony theft is five times the value. At the Arraignment, Williams was not represented by counsel (you had not yet been appointed to represent Williams) and Williams did not offer any statement regarding bail. Williams is unable to post $1,404 cash bail with conditions and unable and unwilling, even if he was able to pay the 20% bail bond premium ($702) the bail bondsman requires, to cover the unconditional bail amount. Williams has lived in the same house since he was fourteen years old – he is now 34. His three children are 11, 13, and 15 years old. Prepare a thorough written bail argument to present at the bail review hearing you requested.

Exercise Three

You are a legislative intern working with State Senator Vicki Smith, who would like to draft a bill to abolish cash bail. Senator Smith has asked you to review the New Jersey, California, and Harris County, Texas bail reform successes and failures and write a six-page white paper describing each of the three bail reform approaches in some level of detail and taking a stand as to which was most successful, and which would be easiest to adopt and emulate in your jurisdiction. Draft that white paper.

Exercise Four

Prepare a six-page paper addressing the "unequal justice" section of this chapter. With three of the pages, write a defense for the arguments espoused in the "unequal justice" section. With the remaining three pages, write a critique of the arguments espoused there and offer an argument for status quo as the appropriate goal for the United States criminal justice system, since it is so "evolved, fair, and just."

Exercise Five

You work as a prisoner advocate in a community where the local bench has adopted and slavishly follows a bail schedule for all crimes below the felony level, applying the same bail amount for the same offense without regard to the individual circumstances of the arrestee (such as prior failures to appear, prior convictions, ability to pay bail or bond, and family and other obligations). Draft an extended letter to the editor explaining to the readership of the local newspaper that bail schedules, particularly when followed so slavishly, are unequal justice that inures to the detriment of those who can least afford bail.

Note

1 Chuck MacLean was the principal author of this chapter.

References

American Civil Liberties Union (and others) (2018). The use of pretrial "risk assessment" instruments: A shared statement of civil rights concerns. Available at http://civilrightsdocs.info/pdf/criminal-justice/Pretrial-Risk-Assessment-Full.pdf.

Appleman, L. I. (2012). Justice in the shadowlands: Pretrial detention, punishment, & the Sixth Amendment. *Washington & Lee Law Review*, 69(3), 1297–1369.

Arnold, D., Dobbie, W., & Yang, C. S. (2018, May). Racial bias in bail decisions. *The Quarterly Journal of Economics*, 133(4), 1885–1932. doi:10-1093/qje/qjy012.

Assefa, L. S. (2018). Assessing dangerousness amidst racial stereotypes: An analysis of the role of racial bias in bond decisions and ideas for reform. *Journal of Criminal Law & Criminology*, 108(4), 653–678.

Bail Project, Inc. (2020). *After cash bail: A framework for reimagining pretrial justice*. Available at https://bailproject.org/wp-content/uploads/2020/02/the_bail_project_policy_framework_2020.pdf.

Bell v. Wolfish, 441 U.S. 520 (1979).

Betterman v. Montana, 578 U.S. __, 136 S. Ct. 1609, 1614 (2016). Available at https://supreme.justia.com/cases/federal/us/578/14-1457/.

Carlisle, M. (2018, September 21). The bail-reform tool that activists want abolished: The worry that algorithms used to determine a person's flight risk will only perpetuate racial discrimination. *The Atlantic*. Available at https://www.theatlantic.com/politics/archive/2018/09/the-bail-reform-tool-that-activists-want-abolished/570913/.

Barno, M., Neverez Martinez, D., & Williams, K. R. (2020). Exploring alternatives to cash bail: An evaluation of Orange County's Pretrial assessment and Release Supervision (PARS) program. *American Journal of Criminal Justice*, 45, 363–378. Available at https://escholarship.org/uc/item/3qz81051.

Carroll, J. (2020). The due process of bail. *Wake Forest Law Review*, 55(4), 757–793. Preprint available at https://papers.ssrn.com/sol3/papers.cfm?abstract_id=3772533.

Carroll, J. E. (2021). Beyond bail. *Florida Law Review*, 73, 143–197.

Congressional Research Service (2019, February 26). U.S. constitutional limits on state money-bail practices for criminal defendants. Available at https://fas.org/sgp/crs/misc/R45533.pdf.

Covert, B. (2020, July 12). A bail reform tool intended to curb mass incarceration has only replicated biases in the criminal justice system. *The Intercept*. Available at https://theintercept.com/2020/07/12/risk-assessment-tools-bail-reform/.

Desmarais, S. L., Zottola, S. A., Duhart Clarke, S. E., & Lowder, E. M. (2021). Predictive validity of pretrial risk assessments: A systematic review of the literature. *Criminal Justice and Behavior*, 48(4), 398–420.

DisasterCenter.com (n.d.). United States Crime Rates, 1960–2019. Available at https://www.disastercenter.com/crime/uscrime.htm.

DOC-BJS. See United States Department of Justice, Bureau of Justice Statistics.

Donnelly, E. A., & MacDonald, J. M. (2018, Fall). The downstream effects of bail and pretrial detention on racial disparities in incarceration. *Journal of Criminal Law and Criminology*, 108(4), 775–813.

Douglas v. People of the State of California, 372 U.S. 353 (1963).

Doyle, C., Bains, C., & Hopkins, B. (2019, February). *Bail reform: A guide for state and local policymakers*. Harvard Law School Criminal Justice Policy Program. Available at https://university.pretrial.org/HigherLogic/System/DownloadDocumentFile.ashx?DocumentFileKey=9a804d1d-f9be-e0f0-b7cd-cf487ec70339&forceDialog=0.

Edelman, P. (2021). Criminalization of poverty: Fines, fees, money bail and much more, chapter 32 in Borden, S. L. *The Routledge companion to media and poverty*. London and New York: Routledge/Taylor & Francis Group.

Equal Justice Initiative (2019, April 26). United States still has highest incarceration rate in the world. Available at https://eji.org/news/united-states-still-has-highest-incarceration-rate-world/.

Freethink (2020, August 8). *How cash bail keeps the poor in jail* (video, 6:28). Available at https://youtu.be/nnXmH5iC9Ms.

Gipson Rankin, S. M. (2021). Technological tethered: Potential impact of untrustworthy artificial intelligence in criminal justice risk assessment instruments. *Washington & Lee Law Review*, 78, 647–724.

Gold, R. M. & Wright, R. F. (2020). The political patterns of bail reform. *Wake Forest Law Review*, 55(4), 743–756.

Gonnerman, J. (2014, September 29). Before the law: A boy was accused of taking a backpack. The courts took the next three years of his life. *The New Yorker*. Available at https://www.newyorker.com/magazine/2014/10/06/before-the-law.

Gonnerman, J. (2015, June 7). Kalief Browder, 1993–2015. *The New Yorker*. Available at https://www.newyorker.com/news/news-desk/kalief-browder-1993-2015?mbid=social_twitter.

Hamilton, M. (2021, Spring). Evaluating algorithmic risk assessment. *New Criminal Law Review*, 24, 155–211.

Harriot, M. (2018, December 20). Money bail might be the most racist, immoral part of America's criminal injustice system. *The Root*. Available at https://www.theroot.com/money-bail-might-be-the-most-racist-immoral-part-of-am-1831241786.

Hernandez, A. (2021). An absolute deprivation of liberty: Why indigents' wealth-based discrimination claims brought under the Equal Protection Clause should be subject to intermediate scrutiny. *Golden Gate University Law Review*, 51, 103–126. Available at https://digitalcommons.law.ggu.edu/ggulrev/vol51/iss2/4.

Hopkins, B., Bains, C., & Doyle, C. (2019). Principles of pretrial release: Reforming bail without repeating its harms. *Journal of Criminal Law & Criminology*, 108(4), 679–700.

Huebner, B. M., Lentz, T. S., & Gibson, M. (2020). Systematic case review strategies: An application for jail population reduction. *Justice Quarterly*, 37(7), 1261–1276.

Hunter, L. (2020, March 16). What you need to know about ending cash bail. Center for American Progress. Available at https://www.americanprogress.org/issues/criminal-justice/reports/2020/03/16/481543/ending-cash-bail/.

King, S. (2015, June 17). The average inmate at Riker's Island now waiting a ridiculous 593 days for their trial to begin. *Dailykos.com*. Available at https://www.dailykos.com/stories/2015/6/17/1394091/-The-average-inmate-at-Riker-s-Island-is-now-waiting-a-ridiculous-593-days-for-their-trial-to-begin.

Massachusetts Special Commission on Bail Reform (2019, December 31). *Final report of the Special Commission to evaluate policies and procedures related to the current bail system*. Available at https://malegislature.gov/Bills/191/SD2718.pdf and https://d279m997dpfwgl.cloudfront.net/wp/2020/01/0102_bail-reform-report.pdf.

Mathews, J., & Curiel, F. (2019, November 30). Criminal justice debt problems. *American Bar Association*. Available at https://www.americanbar.org/groups/crsj/publications/human_rights_magazine_home/economic-justice/criminal-justice-debt-problems/.

May, K. T. (2018, August 31). How the bail system in the US became such a mess: And how it can be fixed. *Ideas.ted.com*. Available at https://ideas.ted.com/how-the-bail-system-in-the-us-became-such-a-mess-and-how-it-can-be-fixed/.

Minneapolis Foundation (2019, October). *Pretrial justice: A report on the cash bail system*. Available at https://www.minneapolisfoundation.org/wp-content/uploads/2019/10/Report_Pretrial_Final.pdf.

Mullane v. Central Hanover Bank & Trust Co., 339 U.S. 306 (1950).

New Jersey Judiciary (2019, April). *Criminal justice reform: Report to the Governor and the Legislature*, 2018. Available at https://www.njcourts.gov/courts/assets/criminal/2018cjrannual.pdf?c=dSE.

Oprysko, C. (2020, January 31). 2020 candidates' views on cash bail reform. *Politico*. Available at https://www.politico.com/2020-election/candidates-views-on-the-issues/criminal-justice-reform/cash-bail-reform/.

Petteruti, A., & Walsh, N. (2008, April). Jailing communities: The impact of jail expansion and effective public safety strategies. Justice Policy Institute. Available at https://justicepolicy.org/wp-content/uploads/justicepolicy/documents/08-04_rep_jailingcommunities_ac.pdf.

Phelps, M. S. (2016). Possibilities and contestation in twenty-first-century US criminal justice downsizing. *Annual Review of Law and Social Science*, 12(1), 153–170. doi:10.1146/annurev-lawsocsci-110615-085046.

Prather, S. (2020, September 15). Ramsey County looks to reform cash bail system. *Minneapolis Star Tribune*. Available at https://www.startribune.com/ramsey-county-looks-to-reform-cash-bail-system/572422902/#:~:text=Ramsey%20County%20leaders%20plan%20to,in%20the%20criminal%20justice%20system.

Pretrial Justice Institute (2021, January 20). *What's happening in pretrial justice: Q4*, 2000.

Reed v. Ross, 468 U.S. 1, 4 (1984). Available at https://supreme.justia.com/cases/federal/us/468/1/.

St. Louis, S. (2020). Neighborhood context and the pretrial process: Do defendants face adverse outcomes due to their home address? *Criminal Justice Policy Review*, 31(9), 1340–1365.

Sawyer, W. (2019, October 9). How race impacts who is detained pretrial. *Prison Policy Initiative*. Available at https://www.prisonpolicy.org/blog/2019/10/09/pretrial_race/.

Selby, D. (2019, September 9). Bail reform: 6 myths and misconceptions about cash bail, busted. *Global Citizen*. Available at https://www.globalcitizen.org/en/content/cash-bail-reform-myths-criminal-justice/.

Shah, A., & Seervai, S. (2020, June 17). How the cash bail system endangers the health of Black Americans. *The Commonwealth Fund*. Available at https://www.commonwealthfund.org/blog/2020/how-cash-bail-system-endangers-health-black-americans.

Stack v. Boyle, 342 U.S. 1 (1951).

Stevenson, B. (2014). *Just mercy: A story of justice and redemption*. New York NY: Spiegel & Gbau.

United States v. Salerno, 481 U.S. 739 (1987).

United States Constitution, Eighth Amendment (U.S. Const. amend. VIII). Available at https://www.govinfo.gov/content/pkg/GPO-CONAN-2002/pdf/GPO-CONAN-2002-9-9.pdf.

United States Constitution, Fifth Amendment (U.S. Const. amend. V). Available at https://www.govinfo.gov/content/pkg/GPO-CONAN-1992/pdf/GPO-CONAN-1992-10-6.pdf.

United States Constitution, Fourteenth Amendment (U.S. Const. amend. XIV). Available at https://www.govinfo.gov/content/pkg/GPO-CONAN-1992/pdf/GPO-CONAN-1992-10-15.pdf.

United States Department of Justice, Bureau of Justice Statistics ("DOJ-BJS") (n.d.). Criminal justice system flowchart. Available at https://bjs.ojp.gov/media/image/45506.

United States Department of Justice, Federal Bureau of Investigations ("FBI") (n.d.). Uniform Crime Reports, Crime in the United States, 2019. Available at https://ucr.fbi.gov/crime-in-the-u.s/2019/crime-in-the-u.s.-2019/topic-pages/tables/table-1.

Van Brunt, A. & Bowman, L. E. (2019). Toward a just model of pretrial release: A history of bail reform and a prescription for what's next. *Journal of Criminal Law and Criminology*, 108(4), 701–774.

Vera Institute (n.d.). Bail and pretrial. Available at https://www.vera.org/ending-mass-incarceration/reducing-the-use-of-jails/bail.

Weldon, D. (2018). More appealing: Reforming bail review in state courts. *Columbia Law Review*, 118, 2401–2445.

Wiseman, S. R. (2014). Pretrial detention and the right to be monitored. *Yale Law Journal*, 123(5), 1344–1404.

Zeng, Z. (2021, March). Jail inmates in 2019. United States Department of Justice, Bureau of Justice Statistics. Available at https://bjs.ojp.gov/content/pub/pdf/ji19.pdf.

5

INEFFECTIVE ASSISTANCE OF DEFENSE COUNSEL[1]

The Sixth Amendment to the United States Constitution guarantees that every defendant in a criminal trial shall have the right to the assistance of counsel. Furthermore, the United States Supreme Court has held that the right to counsel implies the right to effective assistance of counsel, which means that counsel's performance before and during trial must be reasonably competent. Unfortunately, however, the Sixth Amendment right to counsel has proved illusory for many criminal defendants, most of whom are indigent and thus represented by court-appointed public defenders. Sadly, the minimal resources that states provide to public defenders, coupled with public defenders' overwhelming caseloads, has often made it impossible for counsel to represent indigent defendants competently and effectively. To make matters worse, in *Strickland v. Washington*, the United States Supreme Court has made it almost impossible for indigent defendants to show on appeal that their counsel's performance violated the Sixth Amendment. Specifically, the Court held that indigent defendants must prove that counsel's performance was negligent and prejudicial, namely, that had counsel's performance been effective, the outcome of the trial would have been different. The prejudice prong made it nearly impossible for defendants to succeed on an ineffective assistance of counsel claim, as appellate courts routinely refused to second-guess jury verdicts and thus upheld guilty verdicts where counsel was drunk, on drugs, or sleeping during trial. In fact, from 1984 to 2000, not a single claim of ineffective assistance of counsel succeeded on appeal, which led to upholding guilty verdicts where counsel's performance was grossly negligent. For these reasons, the criminal justice system for indigent defendants was decidedly unjust. The solution is to reject *Strickland*, particularly the prejudice prong, and hold that the Sixth Amendment is violated where counsel's performance was negligent and where such negligence deprived the defendant of a fair trial.

DOI: 10.4324/9781003163411-7

Chapter Highlights

- The Sixth Amendment to the United States Constitution provides that all criminal defendants are guaranteed a right to counsel during criminal proceedings.
- In *Gideon v. Wainwright,* the United States Supreme Court held that in criminal cases the state must provide counsel to defendants who cannot afford attorneys.
- Unfortunately, limited resources allocated to public defenders, coupled with public defenders' overwhelming caseloads, often leave indigent criminal defendants vulnerable to incompetent and ineffective representation.
- In *Strickland v. Washington*, the United States Supreme Court made it exceedingly difficult to demonstrate that counsel's performance was constitutionally ineffective because the Court required proof that counsel's performance was negligent, *and* that the outcome of the trial would have been different but for such negligence (the "prejudice" prong).
- Poor defendants have often received substandard legal representation – even in capital cases – yet had no meaningful remedy. This has created a system in which the wealthy received more favorable outcomes at trials than the poor.
- The *Strickland* standard should be revised. Instead of the outcome-determinative prejudice prong, the Court should hold that ineffective assistance of counsel exists where the defendant's counsel was negligent, and that negligence deprived the defendant of a fair trial.

Introduction

John is accused of murdering his wife Julia when he discovered that she was having an affair with his best friend. After a thorough investigation, the evidence suggests that John and Julia were engaged in a heated argument on the night of the murder, during which Julia stated that she wanted to divorce John immediately. John, who was legally intoxicated and suffered from bi-polar disorder, lost his temper and killed Julia via strangulation. Thereafter, John attempted to cover up the murder by claiming to law enforcement officers that an intruder had unlawfully entered the house and attacked Julia. The evidence, however, showed that there was no unlawful entry, and that John's DNA was found on Julia's neck. Ultimately, John voluntarily confessed to the murder. He was charged with first-degree murder and faced life imprisonment.

John was indigent and therefore a public defender was appointed to represent John, who claimed that the confession was coerced, and that Julia's death was an accident.

Unfortunately, John's attorney did not move to suppress the confession and did not meaningfully investigate whether Julia's death was an accident. In fact, during the trial, John's attorney often fell asleep and appeared intoxicated. In addition, John's attorney failed to meaningfully cross-examine the prosecution's witnesses and advised John not to testify in his defense. As a result, the jury convicted John and he was sentenced to life imprisonment.

On appeal, the court ruled that, although John's counsel was negligent and incompetently represented John, the evidence against John was so strong that no reasonable juror would have voted to acquit John. As such, John's appeal was denied.

Do you agree with the appellate court's ruling? After all, if John is guilty, why should the court care about whether counsel's performance was negligent if it would not have changed the outcome? Explain your reasoning and, in so doing, identify the criteria or standards upon which you would rely to determine whether counsel's performance violated the Sixth Amendment to the United States Constitution.

Discussion

The Sixth Amendment to the United States Constitution provides as follows:

> In all criminal prosecutions, the accused shall enjoy the right to a speedy and public trial, by an impartial jury of the State and district wherein the crime shall have been committed, which district shall have been previously ascertained by law, and to be informed of the nature and cause of the accusation; to be confronted with the witnesses against him; to have compulsory process for obtaining witnesses in his favor, and to have the Assistance of Counsel for his defense.
>
> *(U.S. Const. amend. VI)*

Importantly, in *Gideon v. Wainwright* (1963), the United States Supreme Court held that, in criminal prosecutions, the state must provide attorneys for indigent defendants who cannot afford representation. Furthermore, the right to counsel applies during the plea bargaining, pretrial, trial, and appellate phases (*Missouri v. Frye*, 2012). On its face, the Court's rulings appeared to safeguard equality, due process, and justice by ensuring that all individuals, regardless of socioeconomic status, were provided with legal representation. However, the right to effective assistance of counsel only has meaning if there is a legal remedy available to defendants whose counsel fails to provide minimally competent representation.

Unfortunately, however, the promise underlying *Gideon* proved to be illusory, as unfairness and inequality continue to plague the criminal justice system. This is due to the Supreme Court's decision in *Strickland v. Washington* (1984), which made it difficult, if not nearly impossible, for defendants, indigent or otherwise, to demonstrate that they were denied the effective assistance of counsel under the Sixth Amendment.

The United States Supreme Court's Standard for Determining Whether Counsel's Performance Violates the Sixth Amendment

In *Strickland v. Washington,* the United States Supreme Court established the standard to determine whether counsel's performance was ineffective and thus violated the Sixth Amendment (1984). The Court held that defendants must prove that: (1) counsel's performance was negligent; and (2) counsel's negligent performance prejudiced the defendant. The Court held that the "prejudice" prong was only satisfied if a defendant could demonstrate that, but for counsel's negligence, *the outcome of the trial would have been different* (*Strickland v. Washington*, 1984).

The Court's decision in *Strickland* had predictably disastrous consequences. To begin with, regarding the negligence prong, the courts are very deferential to counsel's performance – or strategic decisions – thus rendering it difficult to satisfy *Strickland's* first prong:

> A fair assessment of attorney performance requires that every effort be made to eliminate the distorting effects of hindsight, to reconstruct the circumstances of counsel's challenged conduct, and to evaluate the conduct from counsel's perspective at the time. Because of the difficulties inherent in making the evaluation, a court must indulge a strong presumption that counsel's conduct falls within the wide range of reasonable professional assistance; that is, the defendant must overcome the presumption that, under the circumstances, the challenged action "might be considered sound trial strategy".
>
> (Strickland v. Washington, *1984)*

In other words, counsel's decisions during trial or sentencing, however ill-advised, are often considered "strategic" decisions, thus not a basis to demonstrate ineffective assistance of counsel. But what is a "strategic" decision? The Court provided no answer and thus no guidance. Instead, it created a broad category that almost any court, endeavoring to uphold a conviction could use as a safety valve – even if counsel's performance was obviously defective, it could be considered "strategic" based on a judge's subjective predilections. In fact, the *Strickland* Court went so far as to hold that there exists a *strong presumption* that counsel's conduct was the product of "strategic" decision-making and thus reasonable, which diminished substantially the appellate courts' and defendants' ability to satisfy the negligence prong. Put simply, the Court was stacking the proverbial deck against poor defendants whose defense counsel provided ineffective assistance.

The most pernicious aspect of *Strickland* is the "prejudice" prong. Even if a defendant managed to satisfy the negligence prong, the "prejudice" prong emerged as an almost insurmountable obstacle. Specifically, the *Strickland* Court stated that a "defendant must show that there is a reasonable probability that, but for counsel's unprofessional errors, the result of the proceeding would have been different" (*Strickland v. Washington*, 1984, p. 694). How could a defendant possibly show that a jury would have returned a not guilty verdict if counsel had been more effective? And how would an appellate court assess the facts and evidence to make such a determination? After all, appellate judges don't have a crystal ball and they cannot magically transport themselves into the minds of the jurors. Put simply, the concept of "prejudice" was itself prejudicial – against the poorest and most vulnerable defendants. That is what made *Strickland* so unjust and implausible – the Court made it nearly impossible to prove that counsel's performance violated the Sixth Amendment.

The Prejudice Prong Makes it Nearly Impossible to Establish a Sixth Amendment Violation

Not surprisingly, from 1984 to 2000, the Court did not find a *single* instance of constitutionally ineffective assistance of counsel and during these sixteen years, criminal defendants, particularly those who were poor, often received shockingly substandard representation that no reasonable interpretation of the Sixth Amendment would countenance and that no one with common sense would support. To be sure, *Strickland* created a standard that "is a very low one" that "was not intended to impose rigorous standards on criminal defense attorneys," and that promoted the "tolerance of abysmal lawyering" (Cooley, 2005). Indeed, and alarmingly, the Court tolerated lawyering so poor that in some instances, a defendant was, for all intents and purposes, subject to a kangaroo court.

> Lawyers have been found to be *drunk or drugged, mentally ill, or asleep while representing a defendant.* In addition, several recent studies of capital trials reveal that lawyers who represented death row inmates at trial were subsequently disbarred, suspended, or otherwise disciplined at a rate three to forty-six times the average for the relevant states ... For those attorneys whose clients were executed, the rate of disciplinary sanctions was almost forty times that of the bar as a whole.
>
> *(Benson-Amram, 2004, pp. 431–433)*

As one commentator explains, the prejudice standard is "nearly impossible to meet" (Reissman, 2002, pp. 47–48).

For example, in *Bellamy v. Cogdell*, the defendant, who was charged with second-degree murder and criminal possession of a weapon, sought post-conviction relief on the grounds that, pursuant to *Strickland*, he had been denied the Sixth Amendment right to counsel (1992). Specifically, in the month before trial, the defendant's attorney "was observed as having suffered from a certain amount of disorientation," and was subsequently diagnosed with "a variety of physiological ailments, including a ... condition 'characterized by peripheral motor weakness'" (*Bellamy v. Cogdell*, 1992, p. 303). In fact, due to physical and emotional stress, the defendant's lawyer was "virtually incapacitated," and had an "inability to concentrate" (*Bellamy v. Cogdell*, 1992, p. 304). Not surprisingly, the defendant was convicted and, two months later, the defendant's counsel was suspended from the practice of law (*Bellamy v. Cogdell*, 1992, p. 304).

Amazingly, however, the Second Circuit Court of Appeals held that counsel's performance did not violate *Strickland* because it did not "approach the type of fraudulent behavior" that was typically present in cases where counsel was deemed constitutionally ineffective (*Bellamy v. Cogdell*, 1992, p. 307). Based upon these facts, which did not relate whatsoever to counsel's actual performance at trial, the court found that "it cannot be said that [counsel's] conduct approached the egregious deceptive behavior of counsel" sufficient to constitute a Sixth Amendment violation (*Bellamy v. Cogdell*, 1992, p. 308).

What's more, defense attorneys who were actively using drugs have not been deemed ineffective under *Strickland*, thus further weakening the Sixth Amendment's guarantees. For example, in *Berry v. King* (1985), the defendant was charged and convicted of first-degree murder and alleged that his attorney's drug use prevented him from receiving effective assistance of counsel at trial or sentencing. Specifically, the defendant argued that counsel did not adequately prepare for trial and performed poorly during trial, and at sentencing introduced no evidence whatsoever to mitigate the defendant's culpability. The Fifth Circuit Court of appeals found that the attorney's performance did not violate the Sixth Amendment right to counsel, stating that "under *Strickland* the fact that an attorney used drugs is not, in and of itself, relevant to an ineffective assistance claim" (*Berry v. King*, 1985, p. 454).

Furthermore, in *State v. Coates* (1990), the Montana Supreme Court held that "cocaine abuse, which [had] become public knowledge," did not constitute ineffective assistance of counsel (*State v. Coates*, 1990, pp. 1185–1186). In so holding, the court stated that "cocaine abuse is irrelevant to the issue of ineffective assistance of counsel" (*State v. Coates*, 1990, p. 1187). As the saying goes, you cannot make this stuff up. Likewise, in *Burnett v. Collins* (1993), the Fifth Circuit Court of Appeals held that counsel was not ineffective even though the defendant "could smell alcohol on his … breath; and after trial, his counsel entered a facility for treatment of alcohol abuse" (*Burnett v. Collins*, 1993, p. 930). Similarly, in *People v. Garrison* (1989), the Supreme Court of California held that counsel was not constitutionally ineffective despite being an alcoholic and appearing drunk during the trial. In so holding, the Court stated as follows:

> Although it is uncontested that Beardsley [defense counsel] was an alcoholic at the time of trial and that he has since died of the disease, defendant has failed to prove that Beardsley's performance was deficient. His reliance on a per se rule of deficiency for alcoholic attorneys is contrary to settled law … It is undisputed that Beardsley was an alcoholic at the time of his representation and that he consumed large amounts of alcohol each day of the trial. The declarations in the petition and traverse indicate that Beardsley drank in the morning, during court recesses, and throughout the evening. Although these declarations confirm that Beardsley was an alcoholic, they do not address whether Beardsley's addiction adversely affected his courtroom performance to such an extent that defendant was denied effective assistance of counsel. Statements made by the bailiff … Hector Delgadillo, declare that he was in close contact with Beardsley throughout the trial [and] that Beardsley always smelled of alcohol … [In addition], on the second day of jury selection, Beardsley was arrested for driving to the courthouse with a. 27 blood-alcohol content … The judge stated that Beardsley's courtroom behavior had not given him any reason to believe that Beardsley should not continue and told defendant, "I personally can assure you that you probably have one of the finest defense counsel in this county …" Our review of the facts indicate that Beardsley did a fine job in this case.
>
> *(People v. Garrison, 1989, pp. 440–441)*

One can only wonder what these courts would have required before they deemed an attorney ineffective under the Sixth Amendment.

Additionally, at least one court has held that counsel was not constitutionally ineffective even though he slept during portions of the trial. In *United States v. Muyet* (1998), for example, the court held that, despite falling asleep during portions of the trial, counsel's performance did not "fall below prevailing professional norms" (*United States v. Muyet*, 1998, p. 561). In *Burdine v. Johnson* (2001) the Fifth Circuit stated that "we decline to adopt a per se rule that any *dozing by defense counsel* during trial merits a presumption of prejudice" (p. 349).

To make matters worse, appellate courts have declined to deem counsel constitutionally ineffective even where defense counsel suffered from a severe mental illness. For example, in *Smith v. Ylst* (1987), the defendant argued on appeal that his counsel's suspicious behavior during trial was due to a mental illness that caused counsel to have a "paranoid psychotic reaction," and believe "that his client was the target of a murder conspiracy involving the victim's relatives and lover." Counsel "also repeatedly expressed concern that people were going to try to kill him" (*Smith v. Ylst*, 1987, p. 874). Despite these facts, the appellate court held that counsel's performance had not violated *Strickland* and thus upheld the conviction.

Finally, the courts' reticence to find that counsel performance was ineffective under *Strickland* extends to cases in which the defendant receives the death penalty. Indeed, "[i]n many instances, appellate courts have found that an appointed lawyer was completely unqualified to handle a capital case." The courts found no violation under *Strickland,* which rendered the Sixth Amendment right to counsel more illusory than real (Benson-Amram, 2004, p. 433).

Amazingly, in *none* of these cases – despite drunk, drugged, sleeping, and severely mentally ill lawyers, and even where a defendant faced the death penalty – did the appellate courts find that counsel's performance violated the Sixth Amendment right to effective assistance of counsel. This fact demonstrates that the Court's decision in *Strickland* had achieved the objective of making it nearly impossible for a defendant to show that counsel's performance violated the Sixth Amendment. As scholars have emphasized, *Strickland* utterly fails to protect a defendant's Sixth Amendment right to counsel:

> *Strickland* has proven to be inadequate in protecting a capital defendant's Sixth Amendment right to effective assistance of counsel … [I]t is almost as difficult to prove ineffectiveness now as it was prior to *Strickland*. Courts have been unwilling to find that an attorney's performance was deficient *even in the most egregious cases* or they have often held that the defendant was not prejudiced by counsel's representation.
>
> *(Williams, 2005, p. 139)*

The message is clear: *Strickland* eviscerated, rather than protected, the Sixth Amendment right to counsel and the defect can be traced to the prejudice prong.

> A central reason that Strickland has been so heavily criticized for creating an "almost insurmountable hurdle" for defendants claiming ineffective assistance is the extreme difficulty in establishing the second prong—that the defendant was treated with actual prejudice because of counsel's deficient conduct. Strickland stated that a defendant must show that there is a "reasonable probability that, but for counsel's unprofessional errors, the result of the proceeding would have been different." The Court then defines a reasonable probability as "sufficient to undermine confidence in the outcome." Requiring a defendant to bear the burden of demonstrating a "reasonable probability" that the result of the proceeding would have been different but for counsel's ineffective assistance is merely a deceptive way of saying that the defendant must prove that he would have been acquitted. In other words, he must prove his innocence rather than forcing the state to prove his guilt. Strickland allows appellate courts to bypass the first prong of evaluating counsel's performance and simply analyze the difficult-to-meet prejudice requirement, because if a defendant cannot effectively prove his innocence, his counsel's performance is irrelevant.
>
> *(Fogelman, 2002, p. 78)*[2]

To be sure, it is not sufficient for courts merely to say that, despite counsel's negligent performance, the verdict would have remained unchanged. After all, on one hand, appellate courts express reluctance – appropriately so – to review a trial court's factual findings and only reverse such findings under an "abuse of discretion" standard. Yet, at the same time, appellate courts are willing to unhesitatingly and affirmatively hold despite evidence that, for example, trial counsel was on drugs, an alcoholic, or sleeping during the trial, that the outcome would not have changed even if counsel had performed effectively. How can appellate courts possibly know this? How can appellate courts know the verdict that twelve people would have reached had defense counsel presented more effective evidence or cross-examined the prosecution's witnesses more effectively? What criteria, other than its own subjective assessment of the evidence, do appellate courts use to make this determination with any reasonable degree of certainty? None. That is the problem. The appellate courts are not being deferential in this instance; rather, they are affirmatively holding that a jury would not have reached a different conclusion if counsel had effectively represented the defendant. This is nothing more than conjecture. As one commentator explained:

> [I]t is often very difficult to tell whether a defendant convicted after a trial in which he was ineffectively represented would have fared better if his lawyer had been competent. Seemingly impregnable cases can sometimes be dismantled by good defense counsel … The difficulties of estimating prejudice after the fact are exacerbated by the possibility that evidence of injury to the defendant may be missing from the record precisely because of the incompetence of defense counsel. In view of all these impediments … it seems to me

senseless to impose on a defendant whose lawyer has been shown to have been incompetent the burden of demonstrating prejudice.

(Strickland v. Washington, 1984, p. 710 (Marshall, J., dissenting))

One need only examine the O. J. Simpson trial – specifically, the performance of his counsel at that trial – to understand the impact of an attorney's performance on a trial's outcome, even where the evidence overwhelmingly suggests the defendant's guilt. In the O. J. Simpson case, the evidence was so overwhelming that he murdered his former wife, Nicole Brown Simpson, and Ronald Goldman that few believed that Simpson could possibly obtain a not guilty verdict. After all, Simpson had a history of abusing Nicole Brown Simpson. O. J. Simpson's blood and shoeprints were found at the crime scene. Nicole Brown Simpson's and Ronald Goldman's blood was found inside O. J. Simpson's Ford Bronco *and* inside his home.

Nevertheless, famed defense attorney Johnny Cochran, along with top-notch defense attorneys Barry Scheck, F. Lee Bailey, Robert Shapiro, and Peter Neufeld, managed to obtain a not guilty verdict. In fact, after an eleven-month trial and scores of witnesses, the jury deliberated for only four hours before returning a not guilty verdict.

Now, imagine if O. J. Simpson was poor and was appointed a public defender. Do you think that the result would have been different? Of course. He would have been found guilty and spent the rest of life in jail. If his attorney had been on drugs, intoxicated, or fallen asleep during the trial, would O. J. Simpson have had a viable claim for ineffective assistance of counsel? No. If O. J. Simpson's attorney suffered from a severe mental illness, would that have mattered? No.

Put simply, in the Simpson case, the difference between a guilty and not guilty verdict was *money*. Essentially, *Strickland* enshrined into the criminal law a system of "haves" and "have nots." In this system, the wealthy, who can afford the highest-priced attorneys, are more likely to achieve "justice," while indigent defendants, who cannot afford any attorney, are most likely to face injustice. It is quite a common tale in the United States: the poor get substandard or, at best, mediocre representation, while the wealthy hire the best attorneys who provide the gold standard of legal representation. What's worst is that in the vast majority of cases, the poor have no legal remedy. In fact, as stated above, from 1984 to 2000, the United States Supreme Court found not a *single* case of ineffective assistance of counsel.

That is the legacy of *Strickland*. It is a legacy of injustice and inequality because it makes it near-impossible to demonstrate that counsel's performance violated the Sixth Amendment. Put simply, *Strickland* is a failure as a matter of law and justice.

The consequences are severe both to the procedural and substantive aspects of justice. After all, the failure to represent a defendant effectively can – and does – threaten to result in the incarceration, even execution, of innocent individuals. Not surprisingly, as Table 5.1 illustrates, over one thousand defendants have been exonerated in the United States and it is not unreasonable to suggest that counsel's negligent representation, among other factors, played a role in these injustices.

TABLE 5.1 U.S. States with the Most Exonerations

State	*Exonerations*
Texas	363
Illinois	303
New York	281
California	205
Michigan	99
Ohio	83
Florida	78
Pennsylvania	78
Massachusetts	69
Louisiana	63

McCarthy, 2019

The facts regarding exonerations, however, do not necessarily end the inquiry. After all, maybe the Court was correct in *Strickland* to make it so difficult to succeed on an ineffective assistance of counsel claim. Most defendants are guilty of the crimes with which they are charged. In many cases, the evidence of a defendant's guilt, whether through a confession or witness testimony, is overwhelming. Thus, even assuming that a defendant's counsel was grossly negligent and, for example, fell asleep during the trial, was addicted to cocaine, or was suffering from schizophrenia, why should that matter if the defendant is guilty? Imagine telling a victim's family that the person who murdered their son or daughter is being released on a technicality even though the defendant confessed to the crime. In other words, *Strickland* serves the salutatory purpose of ensuring that, in most instances, the guilty remain imprisoned.

This argument lacks merit for one simple reason: *process matters*. In the United States, it does not matter how guilty or culpable a defendant may appear. The foundation of justice is *due process* and *equal protection of the laws*. If the apparent, or even admitted, guilt of an offender mattered more than the process to which that offender – and all offenders – were due, criminal courts would transform into kangaroo courts. No society dedicated to fairness, equality, and due process could possibly support dispensing with fair procedures – or providing no legal remedy for the violation of such procedures, particularly when enshrined in the Constitution – simply to reach a desired outcome. This "ends justified the means" approach deprives even those who are guilty of the most heinous crimes the fundamental guarantee on which liberty is based: due process of law. It diminishes, degrades, and denies constitutional rights to those who we subjectively deem unworthy of their protections. That is a recipe for inequality of the most unconstitutional and undemocratic kind.

This is why *Strickland* is fundamentally unjust. It dispenses with the commitment to *due process* to facilitate desired *outcomes*, turning a blind eye to abjectly terrible legal representation and creates a tiered system of justice that favors the wealthy and marginalizes the poor. Such an approach is antithetical to justice.

> In *Strickland*, the Supreme Court was confronted for the first time with the task of determining the standard to be used for assessing the effectiveness of counsel in a criminal case. The Court had the opportunity to render an opinion that could have benefitted untold numbers of indigents represented by court appointed private attorneys or public defenders. The competency of defense counsel had long been of concern and the Court's decision was eagerly awaited by those associations of attorneys most involved with providing and assessing defense services … [Unfortunately], the *Strickland* Court's clear diminution of the import of effective counsel … has led to a situation in the state and federal courts of this country wherein defense counsel are routinely denied the time and resources with which to challenge the prosecutor's case … The Court has reduced the Sixth Amendment to one of form over substance.
>
> *(Klein, 1999, pp. 1477–1478)*

In so doing, *Strickland* ensured that justice was conditioned often on an offender's wealth rather than basic right to due process. The time has arrived to end this charade. *Strickland* should be overruled.

Exercises

Before discussing the solution to rectify *Strickland's* deleterious effects, consider the problems below. In so doing, decide whether counsel was ineffective under the Sixth Amendment and identify the factors that support such a determination and address all relevant counterarguments. In addition, develop a legal standard by which to reliably and fairly determine whether counsel was ineffective under the Sixth Amendment.

Exercise One

Jonathan, who is thirty years old, suffers from anxiety, depression, and narcissistic personality disorder. In addition, Jonathan was sexually abused as a child and has struggled to maintain healthy relationships throughout his life.

Recently, Jonathan's relationship to his girlfriend of five years, Rebecca, ended. Jonathan proposed marriage to Rebecca, but Rebecca declined, at which point she informed Jonathan that she had been having an affair with his best friend Brian. Understandably, Jonathan was very hurt and upset as he struggled with the end of their relationship and the realization that Brian betrayed him and their friendship.

One evening, as Brian was dining at his favorite restaurant with his sister and discussing the unexpected end of his relationship, he witnessed Rebecca and Brian enter the restaurant. At this moment, Jonathan lost his composure and sprinted to his car, where he retrieved a handgun. Jonathan proceeded into the restaurant and fired two shots. The first struck Rebecca in the head, killing her instantly. The second shot, which was aimed at Brian, missed and struck an elderly man who was dining at a nearby table in the chest. He died hours later.

After Jonathan was arrested, he confessed to the crime and explained that he simply snapped after being traumatized for days.

Jonathan was charged with two counts of first-degree murder, which carried a sentence upon conviction of life imprisonment without parole. Some attorneys in the prosecutor's office believe that Jonathan should have been charged with voluntary manslaughter because they claimed that the crimes resulted from the "hear of passion" rather than premeditation. However, the prosecutor, who was facing re-election, wanted to appear "tough on crime" and thus charged Jonathan with first-degree murder.

Because Jonathan could not afford an attorney, the court appointed a public defender, who had recently graduated from law school, to represent Jonathan. After several lengthy and often contentious conversations, the prosecution agreed to reduce the charges to second-degree murder for both crimes, each of which carried forty-five years' imprisonment. However, under the plea agreement, the prosecutor agreed to recommend that the sentences be served concurrently, thus resulting in a total sentence of forty-five years' imprisonment. At the public defender's urging, Jonathan accepted the deal and pled guilty to both crimes. Additionally, the public defender urged Jonathan to express remorse at the sentencing hearing to ensure that the judge would agree with the prosecutor's recommendation. Apart from that, the public defender conducted no investigation into Jonathan's background and thus was unaware of the mental illnesses from which Jonathan suffered.

At the sentencing hearing, Jonathan expressed remorse and begged for the court's mercy. However, the judge was not persuaded. Claiming that Jonathan's actions were "abhorrent and showed a complete disregard for human life," the judge imposed the sentences consecutively, resulting in a total sentence of ninety years.

***

Did Jonathan's counsel's performance violate the Sixth Amendment? In analyzing this question, address all relevant counterarguments.

Exercise Two

Christina is eighteen years old and a freshman at an elite university in the northeast. Unfortunately, shortly after enrolling at the university, Christina began to abuse alcohol and was frequently seen intoxicated at parties and even in some classes. When her friends attempted to discuss Christina's drinking habits with her, she insisted that she did not have a drinking problem and rejected her friends' suggestions to seek psychological counseling.

One week later, Christina was driving to her parents' home for the weekend, and, during the drive, Christina consumed a significant amount of alcohol. When she was approximately thirty minutes from home and driving normally, a law enforcement officer, who was recently reprimanded for not issuing a sufficient number of citations to motorists, decided to stop Christina. The officer had neither probable cause nor reasonable suspicion to believe that Christina had violated any law.

When the officer stopped Christina, she immediately objected, claiming that the officer had no reason whatsoever to initiate the stop. As she was speaking, the officer smelled alcohol on Christina's breath and asked her to step out of her vehicle. A breathalyzer test revealed that Christina's blood alcohol was nearly twice the legal limit. The officer arrested Christina and, after placing her in the squad car, briefly searched her vehicle. In doing so, the officer discovered two grams of cocaine in the passenger compartment. Christina was subsequently charged with driving while under the influence of alcohol and possession of cocaine.

After being arrested, and after receiving *Miranda* warnings, Christina admitted voluntarily to being intoxicated and stated that she had recently purchased the cocaine to help her study for the university's upcoming midterm examinations.

Christina's parents hired and paid for an outstanding criminal defense attorney to represent Christina, who informed the attorney that the officer had no reason whatsoever to stop her vehicle, thus constituting a Fourth Amendment violation and rendering the search unlawful and the evidence inadmissible. Christina's attorney agreed and expressed confidence that the charges would be dismissed.

A few days before the trial, however, Christina's parents contacted the attorney and adamantly objected to the attorney's plan to seek dismissal of the charges. "My daughter has a serious problem," Christina's mother said. "This is our only chance to teach her a lesson and get her into some type of rehabilitation program."

Moved by Christina's mom's concern, the attorney decided not to file a motion to dismiss the charge. Instead, the attorney negotiated a deal with the prosecutor whereby Christina would plead guilty to the driving while intoxicated and drug possession charges in exchange for receiving no term of imprisonment and being eligible to participate in a diversion program that provided substance abuse treatment for first-time offenders.

Christina reluctantly accepted the deal, yet questioned why the attorney made no attempt to dismiss the charges. The attorney responded by saying, "Your parents are paying the bill, not you." After Christina pled guilty, she was accepted into the diversionary program, which required her to attend weekly "life skills" classes, submit to a weekly drug test, and surrender her license for six months. Christina's university placed her on probation and informed her that any additional violations of the law would result in her immediate expulsion from the university.

***

Did Christina's counsel's performance violate the Sixth Amendment? In analyzing this question, address all relevant counterarguments.

Exercise Three

David lives in a neighborhood that is inhabited primarily by married couples with children. Recently, however, several children have been victims of disturbing sexual assaults by a perpetrator that the children describe as "really tall and skinny." David is 6.3' and weighs 175 pounds.

One evening, David's neighbors and friends, Jake and Julia, who recently celebrated their daughter Kimberly's tenth birthday, asked David if he would watch Kimberly while they dined at a local restaurant and attended a movie with a few of their friends. David agreed and he spent most of the evening playing board games with Kimberly and watching movies that were suitable for Kimberly's age. While watching a particularly funny scene in one of the movies, David and Kimberly began innocently tickling each other and their uproarious laughter attracted the attention of a married couple that was walking by the apartment with their dog and their nine-year-old daughter Emily, who had recently been a victim of sexual assault. As they glanced into the windows, Emily screamed, "That's him! That is the man who touched me and hurt me!"

The couple immediately contacted law enforcement officers, who arrived at the scene within minutes and, upon hearing Emily's allegations, arrested David and took him into custody. Additionally, upon questioning by one of the law enforcement officers, Kimberly stated that David had been "touching and tickling me a lot " shortly before they arrived. David adamantly and repeatedly claimed that he was innocent, and that this was a case of mistaken identity. Based on Emily's and Kimberly's statements, however, David was charged with the first-degree sexual assault of Emily and a third-degree misdemeanor for improperly touching Kimberly.

Given that he was indigent, the court appointed a public defender, Jeremy Kelvin, to represent David, who continued to vigorously protest his innocence.

During the trial, Jeremy gave an impassioned opening statement, arguing that there was no physical evidence connecting David to the alleged sexual assaults of Emily and Kimberly, and that Emily and Kimberly's testimony, given their age and susceptibility to coercion by their parents and psychologists, would be inherently unreliable. However, when Emily and Kimberly testified, Jeremy refused to cross examine them, believing that doing so would alienate the jury. Additionally, Jeremy refused to allow David to testify in his defense, despite David repeatedly demanding that he be allowed to tell his story to the jury. In fact, Jeremy decided not to put on any defense whatsoever, telling David that the prosecution's case "doesn't come close to establishing that you sexually assaulted Emily and Kimberly beyond a reasonable doubt."

After two hours of deliberations, the jury returned a guilty verdict, and David was sentenced to twelve years imprisonment.

***

Did David's counsel's performance violate the Sixth Amendment? In analyzing this question, address all relevant counterarguments.

Exercise Four

For over twenty-five years, Miranda Davis had been a high school teacher at Spirit High School, where she taught English and Social Studies. Miranda was widely popular among the students, who admired her real-world teaching style, authenticity, and availability outside of the classroom.

Recently, Spirit High School had hired a new principal, Dr. Dan Carmine, who was a fairly well-known educator who championed groundbreaking and innovative teaching methods that are intended to maximize students' performance and give students more authority over the material covered in a given class. Specifically, Dr. Carmine provided the students with a survey containing the courses in Spirit High School's required curriculum and asked the students to identify the topics they would like to cover in each course, and the skills that they believed were most important to acquire in each course. Based on the survey responses, Dr. Carmine required teachers in the required courses to adjust their syllabi and assessments to accommodate the students' desires.

Miranda strongly objected to this approach, claiming that it was tantamount to the "inmates running the asylum," and "held teachers hostage to the whims of students who were insufficiently knowledgeable to dictate the content covered and skills acquired in these courses."

Dr. Carmine did not react kindly to Miranda's criticism. In fact, shortly after Dr. Carmine became aware of these comments, he scheduled a meeting with Miranda. In that meeting, he informed Miranda that she would "obey" and "do things his way, or else." Appalled by Dr. Carmine's threats, Miranda refused to comply with the new curriculum and informed him that forcing her to adopt his "ill advised" curriculum infringed on her academic freedom.

The next day, Dr. Carmine fired Miranda, which caused significant objections from the students. In response, Dr. Carmine held a school-wide meeting in Spirit High School's auditorium, where he informed the students that Miranda was fired for "being insubordinate" and "refusing to comply with requirements of our new student-centered curriculum." In addition, Dr. Carmine stated that, "Ms. Davis is also being investigated for having inappropriate sexual relations with a student at Spirit High School." The students were shocked.

The truth is that Dr. Carmine fabricated this story to provide support for his decision to fire Miranda.

After the meeting, several students contacted Miranda via her cell phone to inform her of Dr. Carmine's statements. Already dejected from being terminated from a job that had been her life's passion, Miranda became enraged. "I'm not going to let him get away with this!" Miranda screamed as she hung up the phone, grabbed a loaded revolver from her closet, and drove to Spirit High School.

Upon arriving, Miranda raced into Dr. Carmine's office, where she confronted him about the false allegations. "Just covering my tracks," Dr. Carmine said, chuckling. "You made your bed. Now you have to lie in it, not pun intended."

Miranda could no longer control herself. She grabbed the revolver out of her purse and pointed it at Dr. Carmine, stating, "Now I'm going to fire you, no pun intended." Dr. Carmine panicked, begged for Miranda to put the gun down, and assured her that she would be re-hired at Spirit High School. Miranda decided to believe Dr. Carmine and end this confrontation. As she was placing the gun back into her purse, however, it accidentally went off, striking Dr. Carmine's secretary in the head and killing her instantly. Dr. Carmine, who had a severe heart condition, was so traumatized by the situation that he suffered a massive heart attack and later died at Spirit Hospital. Finally, after the gun went off, the Vice Principal, Glen Forrester, who was seated in an adjacent room, charged at Miranda with a knife. Fearing for her life, Miranda fired at Mr. Forrester, but the bullet missed and struck Donna Buford, a senior at Spirit High School who had been enrolled in Miranda's classes and who was at the principal's office to meet Spirit High School's college admissions counselor. The bullet struck Donna in the leg, which severed her femoral artery and led to her death a few hours later. Fortunately, Spirit High School's college admissions counselor, Ms. Amy Chandler, witnessed Miranda fire the gun at Mr. Forrester and accidentally strike Donna.

Prosecutors subsequently arrested Miranda and interrogated her at Spirit Police Headquarters. At the beginning of the interrogation, Miranda requested that she be accompanied by an attorney before answering any questions, which under Spirit Supreme Court's recent decision, required investigators to cease the interrogation until a public defender arrived.

However, the investigators failed to comply with this requirement. Instead, they threatened to deprive Miranda of food and sleep until she confessed to intentionally murdering Dr. Carmine, his secretary, and Donna. Additionally, the investigators told Miranda that the judge would "go really easy" on her if she cooperated. Finally, one investigator told Miranda that the public defender wouldn't arrive for at least two days, during which time "anything can happen to you and no one would know."

Scared and alone, Miranda signed a written confession in which she acknowledged responsibility for all three murders and admitted "brandishing a gun with the intent, at one point during the confrontation, to kill Dr. Carmine." Miranda was charged with first-degree murder for the death of the secretary, second-degree murder for the death of Dr. Carmine, and involuntary manslaughter for the death of Donna.

The public defender, Mr. James Dugan, visited Miranda at Spirit Prison the next day and listened to her account of the events. "But you signed a confession," Mr. Dugan said. "It doesn't look good." As he said these words, Miranda detected the smell of alcohol on his breath. "Look, this was all an accident!" Miranda said. "I never meant to harm anyone, and I only fired at Forrester because he was charging me with a knife! Also, the investigators threatened me and forced me to confess!" By the time Miranda finished speaking, Mr. Dugan had passed out on the floor.

Before the trial, Mr. Dugan failed to file a motion to exclude the confession from evidence even though it was obtained in violation of the Spirit Supreme Court's recent decision. Furthermore, during the trial, Miranda explained to Mr. Dugan that Ms. Chandler did not see the portion of the incident resulting in Dr. Carmine and his secretary's death. As such, Mr. Dugan cross-examined Ms. Chandler, who admitted that she had only heard a sound of a gunshot at first and did not witness the deaths of either Dr. Carmine or his secretary, but assumed that Miranda had been responsible for their deaths. Although this admission was significant, it did not change the fact that Miranda had confessed to killing Dr. Carmine and his secretary – a confession that was never challenged in pretrial proceedings.

Also, when the prosecution's case rested, Miranda insisted that Mr. Dugan allow her to testify so that she could provide a full and accurate accounting of the events that transpired at Spirit High School.

"It's too risky," Mr. Dugan said, his breath again smelling of alcohol. "You confessed, Miranda. Whatever you say, the prosecutor will simply read from your confession and destroy your credibility." Miranda reluctantly agreed not to testify but expressed shock that Mr. Dugan appeared to be intoxicated during portions of the trial.

After a few hours of deliberation, the jury convicted Miranda on all counts, and she was sentenced to sixty years imprisonment which, given that Miranda was forty-eight years old, meant that she would spend the rest of her life in prison.

***

Did Miranda's counsel's performance violate the Sixth Amendment? In analyzing this question, address all relevant counterarguments.

Exercise Five

Anthony Marceau and Aurora Davis have been married for nearly ten years. During this time, their marriage has been extremely volatile. Sadly, Anthony struggles with schizophrenia and severe anxiety, and recently became addicted to painkillers during a lengthy recovery from a back surgery. However, Anthony has vehemently denied that he is addicted to the painkillers, and recently Anthony decided to stop taking his psychiatric medication, believing that he no longer suffered from schizophrenia or severe anxiety. Unfortunately, a few weeks after stopping his medication, Anthony's behavior changed drastically. Specifically, he has often verbally abused Aurora and, on two occasions, was physically abusive. Anthony's mental health and substance abuse issues have placed a great strain on his marriage and caused Aurora to consider filing for a divorce.

Before making this decision, Aurora decided to schedule an appointment with a psychologist, as she was struggling to cope with the stress in her marriage and undecided about whether it was worth saving. Aurora met with Dr. Paul Santoro, a clinical psychologist who was well-regarded by his peers.

When Aurora met with Dr. Santoro, an immediate connection developed between them, and after several sessions, Dr. Santoro asked Aurora if she would accompany him to dinner. Aurora said yes and they ate together at Soulmate Garden, one of the most popular restaurants in the area. After dinner, Aurora went with Dr. Santoro to his home, where they had sexual intercourse. Over the next several weeks, the affair continued, and Aurora decided to leave Anthony.

Ultimately, Aurora knew she would have to tell Anthony the truth. Thus, one evening, Aurora approached Anthony while he was watching television and told him that she wanted a divorce. Anthony became extremely angry and began screaming at Aurora, asking her why she wanted a divorce. Aurora stated that the marriage just wasn't working because of his denial about his mental health issues and substance abuse, and because she had met someone that she loved and believed was her soulmate. Anthony flew into a rage and demanded to know who this person was. Aurora admitted that it was Dr. Santoro. Upon hearing this, Anthony began to cry. He called his best friend, Chris Morrison, who agreed that Anthony could stay at his apartment indefinitely, or until Aurora moved out of their house.

A few days after Anthony moved in with Chris, his anxiety worsened substantially, and he began to experience hallucinations. Additionally, Anthony began to hear voices commanding him to kill Dr. Santoro and avenge the loss of his relationship. These voices continued on a near-daily basis until, approximately two weeks later, Anthony decided to act. On a Friday morning at 9:30 a.m., after Chris had left for work, Anthony stole a gun from Chris's bedroom closet, got into his car, and drove to Dr. Santoro's office. During this time, Anthony kept hearing voices telling him to kill Dr. Santoro.

When he arrived at Dr. Santoro's office, Anthony burst into the reception area wielding a gun and demanding to know where Dr. Santoro could be found. The receptionist, who was scared for her life, pointed to a conference room that was approximately fifty feet away. Anthony sprinted into the conference room and, upon seeing Dr. Santoro, began firing uncontrollably. One of the bullets from Anthony's gun struck Dr. Santoro in the head, killing him instantly. Shocked that he had just killed another human being, Anthony panicked and ran out of the conference room toward the exit. Before he reached the exit, Anthony saw Aurora racing into the office, having apparently heard the gunshots.

"You're the one who did this," Anthony said to Aurora with a sinister smile. "'Til death do us part." After saying these words, Anthony shot Aurora in the chest with the last bullet in his gun. Aurora died shortly thereafter. Seconds later, Anthony approached the receptionist, who had already called law enforcement officers for assistance, and pulled the trigger. Fortunately, Anthony had no bullets in his gun and thus the receptionist was unharmed. At that time, law enforcement officers burst into Dr. Santoro's office. Anthony was immediately restrained and arrested.

About an hour later, at Soulmate Police Headquarters, Anthony was seen by detectives talking to himself and apparently acknowledging invisible voices. Seizing on this opportunity, two detectives entered the interrogation room where Anthony was placed and said, "We hear the voices too. They told us that you must tell the truth or burn in hell." Petrified and intimidated, Anthony told the detectives that he was diagnosed with schizophrenia many years ago, had stopped taking his medication, and was suffering withdrawals because he had lost his supply of painkillers. Anthony also stated that he snapped after discovering that Aurora had been having an affair with Dr. Santora and that Aurora wanted a divorce. Anthony admitted to shooting Dr. Santoro and Aurora, and to attempting to shoot the receptionist.

> "You've been through so much," one of the detectives said with a smirk. "We're here to help you and make sure that you never get hurt again. So, we just want you to sign a written statement that says all the things you just described. Then, we can help you."

Anthony signed a written confession a few months later. He was subsequently charged with two counts of first-degree murder and one count of attempted first-degree murder. If convicted, Anthony faced the death penalty. Because he was indigent, the court appointed a public defender, Shelly Gordon, to represent Anthony. Shelly had graduated from law school a year earlier and had recently passed the bar exam after having failed on his first attempt.

Before trial, Shelly did not file a motion to suppress the confession, believing that, although Anthony was under some duress, he was not coerced into signing the confession. Moreover, given the confession, coupled with the fact that the receptionist would testify for the prosecution, Shelly believed that Anthony would be convicted at trial. Therefore, Shelly negotiated a deal with the prosecutor whereby Anthony would plead guilty to two counts of voluntary manslaughter for the deaths of Dr. Santoro and Aurora, and the attempted first-degree murder charge would be dropped. The prosecution intended to recommend a sentence of twenty-five to thirty-five years' imprisonment.

Anthony objected to the plea bargain, claiming that the voices told him that he would be found not guilty and become President of the United States. Despite having serious concerns about Anthony's mental health, Shelly did not request a psychiatric examination to determine if Anthony was competent to stand trial, and did not investigate the viability of an insanity defense if the case went to trial. Instead, Shelly convinced Antony to accept the plea bargain, which Anthony did reluctantly.

The judge accepted the plea and before sentencing, offered Shelly the opportunity to offer evidence on Anthony's behalf that might impact Anthony's culpability and the resulting sentence. Shelly spoke for approximately thirty minutes, during which time he argued that Aurora's affair, and the impending dissolution of their marriage, caused Anthony to snap. "He suffered a broken heart," Shelly stated. "And we all know how much love hurts." Anthony did not mention Anthony's mental health issues.

The judge was not convinced and sentenced Anthony to thirty-five years' imprisonment.

***

Did Anthony's counsel's performance violate the Sixth Amendment? In analyzing this question, address all relevant counterarguments.

Solutions

It is not sufficient to merely identify the problems with *Strickland* and lament the injustices that it causes. Rather, whether a student, lawyer, or legislator, the goal is to develop a workable solution. Below are proposed solutions.

Develop Compliance Requirements that Defense Attorneys Must Follow to Ensure a Minimum Acceptable Level of Competency

Legislatures, courts, or the drafters of the relevant rules governing ethical conduct in each state can create a checklist that identifies the minimum standards by which to measure attorney competence. Failure to comport with one or more of these requirement will create a rebuttable presumption that counsel's performance violated the Sixth Amendment. However, the Supreme Court specifically rejected this approach in *Strickland,* holding:

> The Sixth Amendment refers simply to "counsel," not specifying particular requirements of effective assistance … In any case presenting an ineffectiveness claim, the performance inquiry must be whether counsel's assistance was reasonable considering all the circumstances. Prevailing norms of practice as reflected in the American Bar Association Standards and the like … are guides to determining what is reasonable, but they are only guides. No particular set of detailed rules for counsel's conduct can satisfactorily take account of the variety of circumstances faced by defense counsel or the range of legitimate decisions regarding how best to represent a criminal defendant. Any such set of rules would interfere with the constitutionally protected independence of counsel and restrict the wide latitude counsel must have in making tactical decisions … Indeed, the existence of detailed guidelines for representation could distract counsel from the overriding mission of vigorous advocacy of the defendant's cause. Moreover, the purpose of the effective assistance guarantee of the Sixth Amendment is not to improve the quality of legal representation … [but] simply to ensure that criminal defendants receive a fair trial.
>
> *(Strickland v. Washington, 1984, pp. 688–689)*

The Court's language, however, missed the mark. Although it is unadvisable to micromanage counsel's performance and establish a rigid set of procedures, certain benchmarks can be adopted to ensure a minimum level of competence consistent with the Sixth Amendment. This might include, but not be limited to, the following requirements:

- Filing all relevant pretrial motions that a reasonably competent attorney would file under the circumstances
- Conducting a comprehensive assessment into the defendant's medical and mental health history
- Investigating the defendant's personal background
- Providing competent advice concerning the acceptance of a plea bargain
- Ensuring that all legal and evidentiary arguments are consistent with and demonstrate an awareness of governing state or federal law
- Preserving material issues for appellate review by proffering timely objections
- Presenting all relevant mitigating evidence at the sentencing phase
- Competently advising the defendant regarding issues for appeal and the likelihood of success on the merits

Furthermore, judges can and should be more active during the trial phase to enforce compliance with these requirements and thus maximize the likelihood that the trial will be conducted fairly and in accordance with the Sixth Amendment (Lamparello, 2010).

Revisit the Strickland *Standard and Replace the Prejudice Prong*

There is a more fundamental problem with *Strickland* that has rendered the Sixth Amendment guarantee illusory in many instances: the prejudice prong. Simply put, the prejudice prong should be eliminated, *Strickland* should be overruled, and a new legal test should be developed. As discussed below, counsel should be found constitutionally defective under the Sixth Amendment if: (1) counsel's performance is negligent, given the totality of the circumstances; and (2) counsel performance *deprived the defendant of a fair trial and thus violated the defendant's right to due process of law*. This approach would ensure that convictions obtained through tainted processes would not withstand constitutional scrutiny, and it would recognize that the "prejudice" prong is nothing more than a thinly veiled mechanism to render the right to counsel illusory for many criminal defendants. Put simply, a verdict obtained through illegitimate means, such as where defense counsel is sleeping at trial or intoxicated, is never reliable.

Still, remember one important counterargument. If the defendant is guilty, why should we set him or her free merely because counsel was ineffective, and the resulting trial was tainted? After all, addressing the injustice occasioned by ineffective assistance of counsel can lead to a more profound injustice – the release of inmates who have committed horrible crimes. How would you reconcile these competing considerations?

***

Consider the arguments in favor of and against these proposals. In so doing, develop specific legal standards to determine whether, and under what circumstances, a defendant has been deprived of ineffective assistance of counsel under the Sixth Amendment. When drafting these standards, consider factors including, but not limited to, the criteria upon which counsel would be deemed negligent, the impact of evidence suggesting the defendant's guilt on whether the Sixth Amendment was violated, and whether judges should be required to identify instances of ineffective assistance of counsel at the trial stage and thus remedy defects as they occur. Additionally, provide context-specific examples of when the Sixth Amendment right to counsel would and would not be violated, while explaining the rationale undergirding the distinction between compliance with or a violation of the Sixth Amendment.

Notes

1 Adam Lamparello was the principal author of this chapter.

2 Matthew J. Fogelman, "Justice asleep is justice denied: Why dozing defense attorneys demean the Sixth Amendment and should be deemed per se prejudicial," 26 J. LEGAL PROF. 67, 78 (2002).

References

Bellamy v. Cogdell, 974 F.2d 302 (2d Cir. 1992) (en banc). Available at https://scholar.google.com/scholar_case?case=6633167354716134048&hl=en&as_sdt=6&as_vis=1&oi=scholarr.

Benson-Amram, G. (2004). Protecting the integrity of the court: Trial court responsibility for preventing ineffective assistance of counsel in criminal cases. *New York University Review of Law & Social Change*, 29, 425–458. Available at https://socialchangenyu.com/wp-content/uploads/2017/12/GALIA-BENSON-AMRAM_RLSC_29.2.pdf.

Berry v. King, 765 F.2d 451 (5th Cir. 1985). Available at https://casetext.com/case/berry-v-king-3.

Burdine v. Johnson, 262 F.3d 336 (5th Cir. 2001). Available at https://casetext.com/case/burdine-v-johnson?q=burdine%20v.%20johnson&PHONE_NUMBER_GROUP=P&sort=relevance&p=1&type=case.

Burnett v. Collins, 982 F.2d 922 (5th Cir. 1993).

Cooley, C. M. (2005). Mapping the monster's mental health and social history: Why capital defense attorneys and public defender death penalty units require the services of mitigation specialists. *Oklahoma City University Law Review*, 30, 23–119.

Fogelman, M. J. (2002). Justice asleep is justice denied: Why dozing defense attorneys demean the Sixth Amendment and should be deemed per se prejudicial. *Journal of the Legal Profession*, 26, 67–100.

Gideon v. Wainwright, 372 U.S. 335 (1963). Available at https://supreme.justia.com/cases/federal/us/372/335/.

Klein, R. (1999). Symposium—A generation later: The constitutionalization of ineffective assistance of counsel. *Maryland Law Review*, 58, 1433–1479. Available at https://digitalcommons.tourolaw.edu/cgi/viewcontent.cgi?article=1216&context=scholarlyworks.

Lamparello, A. (2010). Establishing guidelines for attorney representation of criminal defendants at the sentencing phase of capital trials. *Maine Law Review*, 62, 98–153. Available at https://digitalcommons.mainelaw.maine.edu/mlr/vol62/iss1/5/.

McCarthy, N. (2019, July 23). *The U.S. states with the most exonerations*. Available at https://www.statista.com/chart/18772/number-of-exonerations-for-wrongful-convictions/.

Missouri v. Frye, 566 U.S. 134 (2012). Available at https://supreme.justia.com/cases/federal/us/566/134/.

People v. Garrison, 765 P.2d 419 (Cal. 1989). Available at https://scocal.stanford.edu/opinion/people-v-garrison-23510.

Reissmann, K. (2002). "Our system is broken": A study of the crisis facing the death-eligible defendant. *Northern Illinois University Law Review*, 23, 43–79. Available at https://commons.lib.niu.edu/handle/10843/21782.

Smith v. Ylst, 826 F.2d 872 (9th Cir. 1987).

State v. Coates, 786 P.2d 1182 (Mont. 1990). Available at https://case-law.vlex.com/vid/786-p-2d-1182-619267534.

Strickland v. Washington, 466 U.S. 668 (1984). Available at https://supreme.justia.com/cases/federal/us/466/668/.

United States Constitution, Sixth Amendment (U.S. Const. amend. VI). Available at https://www.govinfo.gov/content/pkg/GPO-CONAN-REV-2016/pdf/GPO-CONAN-REV-2016-10-7.pdf.

United States v. Muyet, 994 F. Supp. 550 (S.D.N.Y. 1998). Available at https://law.justia.com/cases/federal/district-courts/FSupp/994/550/1530711/.

Williams, K. (2005). Ensuring the capital defendant's right to competent counsel: It's time for some standards! *Wayne Law Review*, 51, 129–161.

6

PROSECUTORIAL MISCONDUCT, CONSEQUENCES, REMEDIES, AND IMMUNITY[1]

Prosecutors exercise tremendous power in criminal cases. Prosecutors decide (1) whether to bring charges against a suspect, (2) what charges to bring, (3) when to bring those charges, (4) what bail and release conditions to seek, (5) what evidence to disclose, (6) whether to extend diversion options to the accused, (7) what plea bargains to extend and which to accept, (8) which cases to dismiss and what tradeoffs to exact for many of those dismissals, (9) which cases to try and which to settle, (10) which defendants and witnesses will be granted use immunity, (11) what sentence to seek upon conviction, and so on. The Catch-22 is that no one else has the power to effectively monitor prosecutors' decisions, so many occur without witnesses or record in the prosecutors' offices. Even state supreme courts and bar associations rarely act against a prosecutor's law license for quite egregious ethical and legal lapses, even those intentionally committed. Furthermore, the United States Supreme Court has rendered prosecutors virtually immune from civil actions against the prosecutors personally and their offices. That leaves the criminal justice system with little power to rein in errant prosecutors.

Prosecutors also are prone to become caught up in the adversary nature of trial work where win–loss percentages and front-page stories can sometimes trump doing the "right thing," morally, ethically, and legally. Beyond the drive to win, lead prosecutors in most jurisdictions must stand for reelection before an electorate uninformed about what really transpires in the local courthouse or prosecutor's office. That leads some prosecutors to pander to the preferences of the majority of voters rather than adhering to the ethical and legal requirements of their powerful positions.

This chapter addresses prosecutorial misconduct and error and proposes a number of reforms that could better level the criminal justice playing field, prevent prosecutor overreach, hold prosecutors to account for violating ethics and legal requirements, compensate those harmed by prosecutor misconduct, and adequately

DOI: 10.4324/9781003163411-8

inform the voters so they can select ethical and responsible prosecutors committed to ensuring procedural justice for all. As with other areas of the criminal justice system, it is very difficult to craft effective nationwide solutions, because most prosecution offices are stand-alone affairs with procedural and policy perspectives guided by the elected or appointed prosecutor with only limited control exercised by legal precedent, ethics rules, and attorney licensing boards or courts.

Chapter Highlights

- Case Spotlight: Andre Hatchett
- Lead prosecutors are usually elected officials and the elected prosecutors, in turn, appoint their assistant prosecutors.
- Prosecutors are variously known as prosecuting attorneys, district attorneys, and county attorneys, among other labels.
- Prosecutors, by most accounts, wield the most power in the courthouse.
- Prosecutors should be guided by ethics rules and principles but those are aspirational only.
- Prosecutors can contribute to, cause, or prevent much misconduct that occurs in criminal investigations and prosecutions.
- Prosecutors are rarely disciplined for ethical missteps and prosecutorial misconduct.
- Prosecutors are free of most meaningful oversight by the public, federal and state constitutions, and the courts. The United States Supreme Court has rendered prosecutors almost judgment proof.
- Qualified immunity and harmless error stand out as two principles that serve as barriers to greater oversight over prosecutorial overreach and misconduct.

Case Spotlight: Andre Hatchett – 25 Years in Prison for Nothing

After the brutal murder of Neda Mae Carter in 1991 in Brooklyn, New York, Andre Hatchett, a man with special needs and a friend of the victim, was interviewed and eventually arrested. Two eyewitnesses, who saw the crime from about 30–40 feet away on a dark and rainy night, eventually and somewhat reluctantly identified Hatchett from a live lineup as the killer. Hatchett, who was recovering from unrelated serious injuries at the time of the crime, could scarcely have committed the brutal crime, but was arrested and charged nonetheless. Prosecutors only called one of the two eyewitnesses during the trial and Hatchett was convicted.

After Hatchett had spent years in prison for the murder, the Innocence Project, working with the Brooklyn District Attorney's Conviction Integrity Unit, dug deeply into the case files. They found Hatchett had been represented by an abjectly ineffective defense counsel and found the prosecutors had withheld from the defense that the main eyewitness – the one who had testified at the trial – had initially identified a different person as the murderer and had been expecting favorable treatment on the eyewitness's own pending criminal case as a result of his "cooperation" in the Hatchett trial.

Prosecutors must disclose to the defense all evidence in their custody or control that may be favorable to the defense in the case-in-chief, for impeachment, or at the sentencing phase (*Brady v. Maryland*, 1963). Withholding *Brady* material impedes the defendant in preparing a defense, and if it materially prejudices the defendant, or precludes the defendant from exercising with impunity a constitutional right by denying that defendant due process.

After the *Brady* violation was discovered, it was presented to a trial court judge, who exonerated Hatchett, vacated his conviction, and ordered him released from prison. Hatchett was released from prison in 2016. Fifty years old on the day he was released from prison, Hatchett had spent half his life in prison for a murder he had not committed. [Case facts drawn from Innocence Project (n.d.)]

Prosecutors Defined

Perhaps the most famous description of prosecutors was delivered in 1940 by then-United States Attorney General Robert H. Jackson – excerpted here:

> The prosecutor has more control over life, liberty, and reputation than any other person in America. His discretion is tremendous. He can have citizens investigated and, if he is that kind of person, he can have this done to the tune of public statements and veiled or unveiled intimations. Or the prosecutor may choose a more subtle course and simply have a citizen's friends interviewed. The prosecutor can order arrests, present cases to the grand jury in secret session, and on the basis of his one-sided presentation of the facts, can cause the citizen to be indicted and held for trial. He may dismiss the case before trial, in which case the defense never has a chance to be heard. Or he may go on with a public trial. If he obtains a conviction, the prosecutor can still make recommendations as to sentence, as to whether the prisoner should get probation or a suspended sentence, and after he is put away, as to whether he is a fit subject for parole. While the prosecutor at his best is one of the most beneficent forces in our society, when he acts from malice or other base motives, he is one of the worst … .
>
> If the prosecutor is obliged to choose his cases, it follows that he can choose his defendants. Therein is the most dangerous power of the prosecutor: that he will pick people that he thinks he should get, rather than pick cases that need to be prosecuted … .
>
> The qualities of a good prosecutor are as elusive and as impossible to define as those which mark a gentleman. And those who need to be told would not understand it anyway. A sensitiveness to fair play and sportsmanship is perhaps the best protection against the abuse of power, and the citizen's safety lies in the prosecutor who tempers zeal with human kindness, who seeks truth and not victims, who serves the law and not factional purposes, and who approaches his task with humility.
>
> *(Jackson, 1940, pp. 18–20)*

The prosecutor has the power to select the defendants, the crimes, the timing, the bail and conditions to seek, the arguments to proffer, the plea offers to extend and those to reject, the cases to divert, the informants to trust, the sentences to seek, the witnesses to call, the witnesses to be granted use immunity, and the appeals to bring. By most accounts, the prosecutor is the most powerful person in the courthouse. The lives, reputations, and freedom of suspects are held in the palm of the prosecutor's hand. When prosecutorial power is wielded fairly and justly, justice can prevail, but when prosecutorial power is exercised spitefully, unequally, for self-aggrandizement, or with other impermissible motives, justice does not stand a chance.

The Prosecutor's Role and Ethics/Professional Conduct Codes

Prosecutors are quasi-judicial officers whose role is to serve as an administrator of justice, seeking justice and not merely convictions, re-election, or optimum win–loss records. Those principles and related rules guiding prosecutor behavior are codified in the American Bar Association ("ABA") Criminal Justice Standards for the Prosecution Function, Fourth Edition ("ABA Standards") (2017), Rule 3.8 of the ABA Model Rules of Professional Conduct (adopted in whole or in large part in most jurisdictions) ("ABA Model Rules") (1983 and as amended thereafter), and, to a lesser extent, the National District Attorneys Association's ("NDAA") National Prosecution Standards (2009). As quasi-judicial officers and administrators of justice, prosecutors differ from other categories of attorneys because their obligation is to seek justice and not just court victories. As the ABA Standards (2017) provide:

> The prosecutor is an administrator of justice, a zealous advocate, and an officer of the court. The prosecutor's office should exercise sound discretion and independent judgment in the performance of the prosecution function. ABA Standard 3–1.2(a).
>
> The prosecutor should seek to protect the innocent and convict the guilty, consider the interests of victims and witnesses, and respect the constitutional and legal rights of all persons, including suspects and defendants … . ABA Standard 3–1.2(b).
>
> The prosecutor should not manifest or exercise, by words or conduct, bias or prejudice based upon race, sex, religion, national origin, disability, age, sexual orientation, gender identity, or socioeconomic status. A prosecutor should not use other improper considerations, such as partisan or political or personal considerations, in exercising prosecutorial discretion … . ABA Standard 3–1.6(a).
>
> The prosecutor should not permit the prosecutor's professional judgment or obligations to be affected by the prosecutor's personal, political, financial, professional, business, property, or other interests or relationships. A prosecutor should not allow interests in personal advancement or aggrandizement to affect judgments regarding what is in the best interests of justice in any case. ABA Standard 3–1.7(f).

> When a prosecutor reasonably believes that another person associated with the prosecutor's office intends or is about to engage in misconduct, the prosecutor should attempt to dissuade the person. If such attempt fails or is not possible, and the prosecutor reasonably believes that misconduct is ongoing, will occur, or has occurred, the prosecutor should promptly refer the matter to higher authority in the prosecutor's office including, if warranted by the seriousness of the matter, to the chief prosecutor. ABA Standard 3–1.12(b).
>
> If … the chief prosecutor permits, fails to address, or insists upon an action or omission that is clearly a violation of law, the prosecutor should take further remedial action, including revealing information necessary to address, remedy, or prevent the violation to appropriate judicial, regulatory, or other government officials not in the prosecutor's office. ABA Standard 3–1.12(c).
>
> After charges are filed if not before, the prosecutor should diligently seek to identify all information in the possession of the prosecution or its agents that tends to negate the guilt of the accused, mitigate the offense charged, impeach the government's witnesses or evidence, or reduce the likely punishment of the accused if convicted. ABA Standard 3–5.4(a).
>
> A prosecutor should seek or file criminal charges only if the prosecutor reasonably believes that the charges are supported by probable cause, that admissible evidence will be sufficient to support conviction beyond a reasonable doubt, and that the decision to charge is in the interests of justice. ABA Standard 3–4.3(a)
>
> After criminal charges are filed, a prosecutor should maintain them only if the prosecutor continues to reasonably believe that probable cause exists and that admissible evidence will be sufficient to support conviction beyond a reasonable doubt. ABA Standard 3–4.3(b).
>
> If a prosecutor has significant doubt about the guilt of the accused or the quality, truthfulness, or sufficiency of the evidence in any criminal case assigned to the prosecutor, the prosecutor should disclose those doubts to supervisory staff. The prosecutor's office should then determine whether it is appropriate to proceed with the case. ABA Standard 3–4.3(c).
>
> A prosecutor's office should not file or maintain charges if it believes the defendant is innocent, no matter what the state of the evidence. ABA Standard 3–4.3(d).
>
> The prosecutor should not offer evidence that the prosecutor does not reasonably believe to be true, whether by documents, tangible evidence, or the testimony of witnesses … . ABA Standard 3–6.6(a).

Although the ABA and NDAA standards are aspirational (ABA Standard 3–1.1(c)) and not required or prescriptive, many courts have referred to the ABA Standards, particularly, when determining what qualifies as prosecutorial error and misconduct. Rule 3.8 of the ABA Model Rules provides: "A prosecutor has the responsibility of a minister of justice and not simply that of an advocate. This responsibility carries with it specific obligations to see that the defendant is accorded procedural justice, that guilt is decided upon the basis of sufficient evidence, and that special precautions are taken to prevent and to rectify the conviction of innocent persons." ABA Model Rule 3.8 applies and is required and prescriptive in all jurisdictions that have adopted it. Each federal prosecutor is bound to adhere to the version of Rule 3.8 that has been adopted in the state(s) in which the federal prosecutor serves.

Prosecutorial Error and Prosecutorial Misconduct

Criminal investigations, prosecution, and trials are human endeavors, each fraught with errors that accompany all human endeavors. Prosecutors, in particular, often have the last clear chance to prevent or blunt the impact of errors during the investigation, the prosecution, and the trial (Hatch & Gerstein, 2020; Innocence Project, 2018). So, the question ought not focus on whether there was error – there is error in every investigation and in every criminal case. Instead, the inquiry must focus on whether the type and degree of error in an individual case were sufficient to have adversely affected the defendant's substantial constitutional or statutory rights, especially the suspect's or defendant's constitutional guarantee of due process, and thus sufficient error to justify or require reversal of the conviction. Errors that do not rise to the level of reversible error are deemed harmless errors. Reversible errors must, in most situations, have been objected to during the trial by the party (the defendant in a criminal case) injured by the error (Brown, 2020). However, in particularly egregious cases of prosecutorial misconduct, the error can be deemed plain error or fundamental error and thus eligible for appellate review in most jurisdictions even if not objected to in the lower court (Ramirez, 2016).

Appellate courts considering claims of trial error usually start from the presumption that the trial was without reversible error, then transfer the burden to the defendant to produce sufficient evidence that there was error (either individual instances of error or in the aggregate) and that in the absence of that error, the result would (or may) have been different. The precise standard can differ from situation to situation and from jurisdiction to jurisdiction. Error that denies the defendant a fundamental right – such as to remain silent or be represented by counsel at a critical stage in adversarial criminal proceedings – need not also show prejudice, which is presumed. Prosecutorial misconduct is most often heavily dependent on the facts in each individual case and other evidence adduced at trial.

Some commentators and advocates argue prosecutorial misconduct has become an epidemic, a torrent that threatens to swamp due process and procedural justice (Womack, 2019). Others, in response, argue that the epidemic or torrent is merely an artifact that convicted defendants will add any colorable claim to an appellate court brief and often assert prosecutorial misconduct that is merely harmless error (Harker, 2018; Kepple, 2018; MacLean, Berles, & Lamparello, 2015). Since prosecutorial misconduct is thereby incorporated in such a large share of defense appeals, they argue, the courts and observers have been misled into believing that it has become an epidemic or torrent.

Categories of Prosecutorial Error and Misconduct

Before discussing the key categories of prosecutorial misconduct and error, two principles should be underscored. First, individual instances of misconduct or error alone can be enough to garner reversal of an improvidently obtained conviction, but isolated errors can also be aggregated to determine the total adverse impact on a defendant's statutory and constitutional rights. Second, error must be judged in light of the entire record and not by review of the error(s) alone. Thus, a very strong case can render otherwise serious prosecutorial misconduct harmless error, because the misconduct in all probability had no impact on the outcome of the case and even without the error having been committed, the verdict or result would have been the same. Finally, although scrupulous and ethical prosecutors can prevent most governmental misconduct in criminal cases, prosecutorial misconduct can and does contribute to wrongful convictions (Gross, Possley, Roll, & Stephens, 2020). With those reminders in place, and with recognition that prosecutorial misconduct can occur in many forms (National Association of Criminal Defense Lawyers, 2019), the remainder of this section addresses key categories of prosecutorial error or misconduct that could yield reversal of a conviction using the Caldwell (2017) prosecutorial misconduct categories as a base.

Improper Voir Dire, *Sandpapering the Jury, and* Batson *Violations*

Before trial begins, the parties select the jury in a process known as jury selection or *voir dire*. In state courts, that is the attorneys' opportunity to question and observe the prospective jurors to determine which prospective jurors should be stricken from the jury and which should be selected to serve on the trial (that is, the petit) jury. In federal courts, judges usually conduct the *voir dire*, but the attorneys exercise the strikes. Strikes are of two types: cause strikes when the prospective juror is deemed not qualified to serve on the jury, and peremptory strikes (Federal Rules of Criminal Procedure, Rule 24(b), c(4)) where each side can strike a fixed number of prospective jurors without the need to prove they are not qualified to serve. In many circumstances, a prosecutor may peremptorily strike from jury service persons who are a certain race, ethnicity, or gender (*Batson v. Kentucky*, 1986; *J.E.B. v. Alabama ex rel. T.B.*, 1994). That can be deemed improper. Peremptorily striking jurors for such impermissible reasons in some cases can be deemed to violate both the struck jurors' right to serve on a jury and the defendant's constitutional right to due process and a fair trial. Peremptory strikes based on actual or perceived religious affiliation are recognized as potentially unconstitutional in ten states so far but not by the United States Supreme Court. Note there is a move afoot to add actual or perceived gender identity and sexual orientation to the current race, ethnicity, and gender *Batson* categories (Wojcik, 2019).

Some prosecutors may be tempted to use the *voir dire* process to predispose or "sandpaper" the jury – that is, to begin arguing the case before it has even begun or to begin to convince the jurors to vote in favor of conviction before the jury has been sworn in. That is improper. This prosecutor misuse of *voir dire* is very uncommon in federal court, where most questions posed to prospective jurors are posed by the presiding judge and not by the prosecutor or defense attorney.

Brady *Violations*

As clarified in *Brady v. Maryland* (1963), prosecutors must disclose to the defense in advance of trial all evidence that may be favorable to the defense – often labelled exculpatory evidence, although *Brady* material need not be fully exculpatory to fall within the rule and may simply be evidence relevant to seeking a lesser sentence or evidence relating to impeachment of a trial witness. Withholding *Brady* material, if it materially prejudices the defendant, denies that defendant due process under the Fifth and Fourteenth Amendments to the United States Constitution.

Commenting on the Defendant's Invocation of the Right to Remain Silent

The Fifth Amendment to the United States Constitution guarantees to all the right to remain silent and guarantees for each criminal defendant the right to remain silent at trial: "No person shall be … compelled in any criminal case to be a witness against himself …" (U.S. Constitution, amend. V). As a result, criminal defendants cannot be called to the witness stand in their own cases and are free to testify or decline to testify in their own defense. That constitutional protection against compelled self-incrimination loses its meaning and power if the prosecutor at trial were free to use the defendant's silence against him with impunity. The prosecutor can do that in many ways. The prosecutor could directly argue to the jury, "An innocent person would have testified before you in this trial," or could more indirectly argue that "the state's evidence is not contradicted by the defendant, so there is no reasonable doubt," or "the defendant never took the stand to challenge any of the State's evidence, so the prosecution's evidence in this trial is uncontroverted." All of those variants are improper arguments that can violate the defendant's constitutional right to be free of compelled self-incrimination under the Fifth Amendment (*Doyle v. Ohio*, 1976). A prosecutor arguing during trial that a defendant's failure to confess is an admission of guilt or arguing at a sentencing hearing that the defendant's silence evidences lack of remorse are also improper. All of these comments on the defendant's exercise of the right to remain silent are prosecutorial misconduct and can lead to a mistrial.

Misstating the Law

At a jury trial, the jury determines the facts but the law is given by the judge through a set of jury instructions read to the jury. The prosecutor is free to comment on the law and argue its applicability to the facts adduced in the case, but a prosecutor cannot misstate the law or present the law to the jury in ways that are inconsistent with the judge's jury instructions. When a prosecutor misstates the law, the jurors can become confused and could base their verdict on matters other than the facts and the law provided by the judge. A prompt curative judicial instruction or effective counter-argument by the defense can usually attenuate the taint of a prosecutor's misstatement of the law. In the absence of attenuation, prosecutors misstating the law can amount to prosecutorial misconduct, because prosecutors, as quasi-judicial officers and ministers of justice, should be seeking the truth and not just the victory.

Disparaging Commentary About the Defendant, or the Defense Counsel or Case

Prosecutors are obliged to use criminal trials as quests to find the truth and achieve justice; thus, a prosecutor's disparaging comments about the defendant, defense counsel, or defense case and arguments can be deemed prosecutorial misconduct. From the prosecutor's perspective, trials should be exercises in applying the law to the facts. Unnecessarily emotional and *ad hominem* attacks that nullify the jurors by turning them away from their role as factfinders are neither law nor facts, and so are improper.

Other Jury Nullification and Appeals to the Jury's Emotion, Passion, or Prejudice

In a related sense, since the prosecutor should use the jury only to find the facts and apply the law to those facts, emotion, passion, and prejudice should play no role in a juror's deliberations, particularly when suggested or welcomed by the prosecutor. That is not to say trials are unemotional or that prosecutors must present the facts in dispassionate ways. Rather, it means that if emotion, passion, or prejudice sway the jury away from pure determination of the facts or reasoned application of law to those facts, the prosecutor is departing from the obligation to seek the truth as an administrator of justice. Similarly, arguing in the trial-in-chief that the jury must convict to protect the community from this dangerous defendant is an improper call to emotion that diverts a jury from its true role in the criminal justice system.

Vouching for Testimony of State's Witnesses or Offering the Prosecutor's Own Opinion

It is improper and can be deemed misconduct for a prosecutor to personally vouch for a witness or inject the prosecutor's own personal opinion into a criminal case, particularly before a jury. Jurors may give inordinate weight to the prosecutor's opinions about witnesses and evidence, since jurors may reasonably believe that prosecutors know far more about the case than what they are permitted to present in court. Thus, a prosecutor vouching for (or against) a trial witness or injecting the prosecutor's own opinion into a trial is tantamount to the prosecutor putting a thumb on the scales of justice. That is prosecutorial misconduct.

Knowing or Reckless Introduction of False Evidence or Misrepresenting Evidence

Prosecutors are the last line of defense to protect justice from misconduct by governmental and other actors prior to and during trial. For example, if an expert witness for the State intends to testify to scientific matters unsupported by the science or the evidence, the prosecutor can and must prevent that witness from taking the stand. Or if a State DNA expert presents the DNA evidence in a way that overstates its import or that otherwise misleads the jury, the prosecutor must prevent that from reaching the jury. Indeed, the prosecutor has an obligation to correct the record if such improper evidence is admitted before the jury. Along the same path, once evidence is providently admitted, the prosecutor may not misrepresent its meaning or value. Instead, the prosecutor must zealously guard the record to prevent misleading, improper, and inadmissible evidence from tainting the process and adversely affecting the quantum of due process the defendant receives.

Certain other intentional acts by prosecutors may also suffice as prosecutorial misconduct, including vengeful, vindictive, or retaliatory prosecution (Lieb, 2014); extra-judicial statements compromising defense interests (ABA Standards 3–1.10(c); Gershman, 2016); destroying evidence; hiding evidence (a variant of *Brady v. Maryland* (1963)); misleading the defense about the availability of a key state witness; failing to correct a known misstatement; failing to disclose to the judge controlling authority adverse to the prosecutor's case; allowing the continuation of a case that no longer has a substantial probability of success beyond a reasonable doubt at trial (ABA Standards 3–4.3(b)); allowing forensic testing that consumes all available evidence without prior notice to the defense; prosecuting a case where the prosecutor has a conflict of interest; improper leverage and overcharging to coerce a negotiated guilty plea (Gold, Hessick, & Hessick, 2017); and knowingly offering evidence the trial judge had suppressed, among others (Ridolfi & Possley, 2010), can all constitute prosecutorial misconduct.

Remedies and Consequences for Prosecutorial Misconduct

Although there are generally no remedies or consequences for mere prosecutorial error, there can be substantial remedies and consequences for prosecutorial misconduct. Indeed, without such remedy or consequence, prosecutorial misconduct can be committed with impunity, thus sullying the trial process and procedural justice. Leading remedies and consequences for prosecutorial misconduct are discussed below.

Mistrial With or Without Prejudice

If a criminal case has, in the judgment of the trial judge, been irredeemably despoiled by prosecutorial misconduct, the judge may order a mistrial, terminating that trial. If the case was being tried by a jury, double jeopardy attached when the jury was sworn, so absent a specific court order to the contrary, a mistrial would bar retrial of the defendant for charges arising out of the same incident. However, if the prosecutorial misconduct was not unduly extensive, damaging, or intentional, the judge may order the mistrial to be "without prejudice," thereby allowing the prosecutor to re-charge the defendant for that incident. Otherwise, the mistrial will be deemed "with prejudice" and therefore without possibility of being recharged. Of course, a mistrial with prejudice harms the victim far more than the prosecutor, and some mistrials are granted for defense misconduct, so most mistrials are granted without prejudice.

Dismissal of One or More Counts

When the prosecutorial misconduct relates to a single pending charge or subset of pending charges, the judge may dismiss one or more charges as a consequence for prosecutorial misconduct. If such dismissals do not reach all pending counts, the trial merely continues with the jury restrained from considering the dismissed charges.

New Trial

If the trial results in conviction, but the trial judge believes the conviction was based in substantial part on the impact of prosecutorial misconduct, the judge in most jurisdictions can order a new trial in response to a post-conviction relief petition. Similarly, if on appellate review the appeals court finds substantial prosecutorial misconduct that tarnished the conviction(s), the appeals court can order a remand back to the trial court for a new trial.

Suppression of Evidence

Particularly where the prosecutorial misconduct occurred pretrial, the court can remedy that misconduct by ordering that the affected evidence be suppressed – that is kept out of the trial and away from the jury. If the suppressed evidence effectively precludes the prosecutor from mounting a winnable case, the prosecutor can file a pretrial (interlocutory) appeal to challenge that suppression before an appellate court. That pretrial appeal option is critically important, because if the trial proceeds without it and the defendant is acquitted, the prosecutor cannot appeal post-conviction as that would, obviously, violate the defendant's right to be free from double jeopardy – being twice put in jeopardy of life or liberty for a single criminal incident.

Prepare and Distribute a Brady *Violation Disclosure Letter*

At least one commentator (Kreag, 2019) recommends that when a prosecutor has failed to disclose *Brady* material to the defense, a "*Brady* Violation Disclosure Letter" be prepared then disseminated to all the key stakeholders in the original trial tainted by the *Brady* violation. In that way, at least some of the sting and adverse impact of the prosecutor's *Brady* violation can be blunted and remedied in the light of day.

Actions Against the Prosecutor's Law License

In some circumstances of prosecutorial misconduct, an aggrieved party or even the judge can recommend an action against the prosecutor's license to practice law. Perhaps unfortunately, this option has very rarely resulted in any substantive license consequences for the prosecutor committing the misconduct (MacLean & Wilks, 2012, 2014). State attorney licensing entities have exhibited extraordinary willingness to avoid serious license consequences for prosecutors and judges and opposing attorneys are often loath to report prosecutor misconduct for fear of prosecutorial retaliation in future cases. More unfortunately, such after-the-fact actions against a prosecutor's license (fines, public or private admonition, censure, caution, reprimand, suspension, up to disbarment) do not offer any real remedy for the defendants harmed by the prosecutor's misconduct. Furthermore, such license consequences may do little to lead errant prosecutors toward refraining from misconduct in the future, since many courts refrain from identifying the prosecutor in their prosecutor admonition, caution, and censure orders.

Prosecutorial Immunity and its Impact on Vindicating Prosecutorial Misconduct and Error

Title 42 of the United States Code section 1983 purports to provide an avenue for civil damages for persons whose constitutional rights have been violated by persons acting under color of state law. Nonetheless, the United States Supreme Court has repeatedly granted, and upheld against challenges, virtually absolute immunity for civil claims under section 1983 against prosecutors' personal assets for actions in furtherance of the prosecutor's statutory duties, "no matter how severe," at least in the absence of affirmative bad faith by the prosecutor (*Imbler v. Pachtman*, 1976). The theory goes that "prosecutors performing their official duties are quasi-judicial officials, not non-judicial functionaries and should be able to vigorously proceed with their tasks unhampered by the fear of unlimited civil litigation" (*Venckus v. Iowa City*, 2019). In the *Imbler* case, the defendant Imbler, who had been acquitted in a criminal trial, alleged in a subsequent civil case under 42 U.S.C. § 1983 that the prosecutor and police officers had conspired to deprive him of a fair trial by knowingly offering perjured testimony at trial and failing to disclose exculpatory *Brady* material. Despite that factual record, the Supreme Court granted the prosecutor absolute immunity, because the alleged actions had arisen within the prosecutor's exercise of statutory duties. The one loophole clearly remaining after *Imbler* is to sue prosecutors for behavior deemed outside of the prosecutor's statutory duties, such as when the prosecutor makes improper extrajudicial statements or when the prosecutor violates a subject's constitutional rights when helping law enforcement in investigative design and execution, which are considered to be beyond the prosecutor's prosecutorial obligations and beyond the judicial phase of the criminal justice process.

The United States Supreme Court has also repeatedly granted virtually unlimited immunity for civil claims against prosecuting offices, at least in the absence of a clear pattern of similar misconduct from those offices, especially as evidenced by a municipal policy (*Connick v. Thompson*, 2011). In *Connick*, the Court held that when a prosecutor failed to disclose *Brady* material in a criminal case, the defendant could not successfully sue that prosecutor's office seeking money damages for failure to properly train that prosecutor absent evidence the office knew of a pattern of similar *Brady* violations by the office's prosecutors; in other words, civil actions against a prosecutor's office may only proceed when the office caused or contributed to the misconduct.

Many reformers have argued that absolute prosecutorial immunity inures to the detriment of defendants, suspects, justice, and due process, and serves as a shield behind which unscrupulous prosecutors can protect themselves from consequences for clear misconduct (Niles, 2017). These reforms are not likely to take hold unless and until the United States Supreme Court retreats from its unwavering support for prosecutorial immunity.

Systemic Response Options for Prosecutorial Misconduct and Error

In the disaggregated and distributed United States criminal justice system, it is very difficult to apply a systemic response to any flaw, including prosecutorial misconduct. There are simply too many jurisdictions with too many independent decision-makers to make it easy to cast a single wide net (Zack, 2020). Nonetheless, each jurisdiction could consider the following local options to address prosecutorial misconduct.

License Consequences with Teeth

As mentioned above, consequences involving a prosecutor's license to practice law are rarely applied and even more rarely applied in ways that yield strong and tough sanctions on errant prosecutors. Those license consequences, depending on the jurisdiction, are determined and applied most often by the state bar association, the state attorney licensing board, the state supreme court, or a combination of those. Therefore, legislating a solution here would be pyrrhic. Instead, local interests could apply pressure or lobbying efforts on the local bar association, licensing board, or supreme court to ask them to impose license consequences with teeth when prosecutors violate constitutional, statutory, and ethical requirements and codes (Adachi & Calloway, 2019). Enhancing the level of license consequence for unethical prosecutors should match the severity of the prosecutor's misconduct and be sufficient to underscore society's displeasure with the current state of affairs and *laissez faire* approach to prosecutorial misconduct. In other words, consequences affecting prosecutors' licenses to practice law should be severe enough and should happen often and predictably enough to send a message to that prosecutor and all others and thereby substantively deter future bad prosecutor conduct.

Adopt a Proactive Approach to Prosecutor Discipline

At least one commentator (Holuta, 2020) has recommended that disciplinary committees move beyond ex post and reactive disciplinary actions and move toward proactively imposing preventative measures to guide prosecutors' offices toward reduced misconduct. That would allow regulators to inspect prosecution offices' internal and external charging and disposition policies with an eye toward improving their viability and power to direct ethical prosecutor conduct.

Publicize Prosecutors' Names

An important first step is to reduce the frequency with which the state bar associations, state licensing boards, and state supreme courts issue their rulings in private or publicly but without disclosing the disciplined prosecutors' identities. Prosecution, more than most attorney work, is work on behalf of the public; thus, most license consequences for prosecutorial misconduct should identify the prosecutor and be disseminated publicly.

Money Sanctions v. Prosecuting Offices and Prosecutors and Relaxation of Immunity Protections

Those who are charged with crimes and hailed into criminal court suffer losses as a result – sometimes including lost freedom, lost money resources, lost relationships, lost time, lost employment, and losses affecting reputation. Absolute immunity exists, in part, to allow prosecutors the flexibility and freedom to manage a criminal case as they deem appropriate. Immunity is also allegedly necessary to make it easier to attract and retain attorneys to serve in prosecutorial roles. However, immunity may not be necessary to ensure flexibility or prevent wholesale exodus from prosecution practice. Instead, immunity's most salient effect may be to prevent undeniably harmed defendant-plaintiffs from recovering money damages for their losses when those losses flowed from governmental – prosecutorial – misconduct.

Required Training and Policies

In appropriate cases, consequences for prosecutorial misconduct could include required training or retraining and could include an obligation for the prosecutor's office to promulgate appropriate policies to guide prosecutors away from misconduct in future cases. That re-training and those policy revisions should, of course, fit the violation such that each would be likely to reduce recurrence of the misconduct.

Dismissal with Prejudice

In prosecutorial misconduct cases where the prosecutor's behavior was egregious and compromised justice, due process, or the system of criminal justice, decision-makers should, at least, consider dismissing the criminal case with prejudice where the victim (if any) still has other available and feasible remedies (beyond the prosecution case alone) and dismissal with prejudice best serves the public interest.

Create and Empower a Statewide Prosecutorial Oversight Board

Caldwell (2014, 2017) recommended creation of statewide prosecutorial oversight boards to centrally assess prosecutorial misconduct and determine tiered consequences based on the severity of the misconduct and whether the errant prosecutor has a history of misconduct. Caldwell's vision restricted those boards to consideration only of prosecutorial misconduct found and affirmed first by an appellate court, but other options could be arranged such as statewide boards that act on complaints from aggrieved claimants even if they did not appeal. These statewide boards would take the pressure off supreme courts and attorney licensing boards and would begin to create a common database of appropriate ranges of attorney license consequences based on the type and breadth of the prosecutorial misconduct. On a related note, New York State briefly maintained the first and only Prosecutorial Misconduct Commission in the nation between 2019 and 2020. Creation and operation of the Commission was later deemed unconstitutional in 2020 (Center on Media, Crime, and Justice at John Jay College, 2020; Roy, 2020) only to be revived by new legislation signed into law in June 2021 (Mahoney, 2021) creating a slightly modified Prosecutorial Misconduct Commission that proponents hope will be less arguably violative of separation of powers and other principles enshrined in the New York State Constitution.

Create a Public Registry of Errant Prosecutors

Some have recommended that public disclosure of prosecutors committing serious misconduct is only part of the solution and recommend creation of nationwide prosecutor misconduct registries (Center for Prosecutor Integrity, n.d.) so the public and those harmed by prosecutors' actions or inactions can easily identify past misconduct, which often requires fifty or more internet searches, jurisdiction by jurisdiction. The registry could catalogue all errant prosecutors or just those exhibiting patterns of misbehavior or just those displaying serious prosecutorial misconduct.

Treat Prosecutorial Misconduct as Obstruction of Justice and Proceed Against the Office

At least one commentator (Thompson, 2017) has argued that errant prosecutors are likely not just "bad apples," that is, rogue operators in an otherwise ethical prosecution office. Rather, "[p]rosecutorial misconduct flows from an environment that tolerates it, oversees it, and encourages it" (p. 623); thus, its remedy requires treating it as obstruction of justice and acting not just against the individual prosecutor but against the prosecution office that condoned or permitted the misconduct.

Other consequences and remedies for prosecutorial misconduct could also be devised. Generate and assess those other options as you consider the exercises below.

Exercises

These exercises are offered as a platform for the reader to think critically and creatively about prosecutorial misconduct issues and to devise creative and insightful action plans to help address prosecutorial misconduct in ways that will reduce the frequency of such misconduct in the future, provide aggrieved plaintiffs adequate remedies for prosecutorial misconduct, and still allow prosecutors the flexibility they need to prosecute criminal cases on behalf of the public.

Exercise One

Assume you have been selected by the Chief Justice of your state supreme court to serve as a public member on a select committee to offer recommendations on (1) how the supreme court should best respond to prosecutorial misconduct; (2) what array of consequences are appropriate for prosecutorial misconduct; (3) what degree of prosecutorial and prosecuting office immunity is appropriate for prosecutorial misconduct and in what circumstances; and (4) what systems, boards, or commissions should administer prosecutorial misconduct responses, and using what procedures. Present and defend your recommendations and rule out other approaches as appropriate.

Exercise Two

Imagine you are the trial court judge to whom a criminal sexual conduct case that involves a twelve-year-old victim has been assigned. During the jury trial, the prosecutor (A) led the state's forensic witness to claim the DNA evidence proved far more than it did, (B) failed to disclose that the lead investigator is the minor victim's third cousin, (C) failed to disclose that the alleged victim initially reported that someone other than the defendant was the actual perpetrator of the sexual assault, and (D) indicated to the jury in closing argument that you did not hear any denial from the defendant so the prosecution's evidence is uncontroverted. The defendant sought an immediate recess after the prosecutor's closing argument and has moved for you to (1) grant a mistrial with prejudice given the severity of the prosecutorial misconduct and the multiple incidents of misconduct, (2) grant, in the alternative, a mistrial without prejudice but striking the two most serious counts as a consequence for the prosecutor's misconduct, (3) grant, in the alternative, a mistrial without prejudice and without dismissing any counts, and (4) levy sanctions against the prosecutor as a consequence for the misconduct. What would you order and why? Be specific and detailed.

Exercise Three

You are the elected lead prosecuting attorney in your county. The statutes in your state require every elected prosecuting attorney to adopt and disseminate a set of guidelines and procedures that are intended to reduce or eliminate prosecutorial misconduct in (A) charging cases, (B) resolving cases, and (C) trying cases before juries. Identify at least a dozen provisions you would include in your set of prosecutorial guidelines and procedures related to those three prosecution duties, and explain and defend each one.

Exercise Four

After an illustrious career as a criminal defense attorney, you have been appointed and confirmed to serve as an Associate Justice on the United States Supreme Court. The Chief Justice has assigned you to draft the Supreme Court's majority opinion in a case challenging absolute immunity for prosecutors "no matter how severe" the misconduct. The majority of the Supreme Court has decided to reduce or limit the degree of immunity or the circumstances to which immunity applies for prosecutor misconduct within the prosecutor's official duties. Please discuss the main arguments you would offer in defense of the Supreme Court majority decision to reduce or limit absolute prosecutorial immunity.

Exercise Five

After much introspection, you have decided that aspirational standards for prosecutors are, too often, ignored. Therefore, you have decided to propose a nationwide, required set of standards that applies to all prosecutors in all jurisdictions. Practically speaking, is that possible? If you deem it impossible, explain your reasoning in detail. On the other hand, if you deem it possible, describe in detail the mechanism by which you would strive to put that nationwide set of standards into place and enforce it (for example, would you intend to create and enforce it by federal statute, a model code adopted state-by-state, a set of attorney license requirements prepared for each state to review and adopt, or some other mechanism).

Note

1 Chuck MacLean was the principal author of this chapter.

References

Adachi, J., & Calloway, P. (2019, May 21). One simple way to hold bad prosecutors accountable: State bar associations have the power to discipline prosecutors, but they studiously ignore bad behavior. *The Appeal*. Available at https://theappeal.org/prosecutorial-misconduct-jeff-adachi-commentary/.

American Bar Association (2017). *Criminal justice standards for the prosecution function*, fourth edition ("ABA Standards, 2017"). Available at https://www.americanbar.org/groups/criminal_justice/standards/ProsecutionFunctionFourthEdition/.

American Bar Association (1983 and as subsequently amended). *Model rules of professional conduct*, Rule 3.8. Available at https://www.americanbar.org/groups/professional_responsibility/publications/model_rules_of_professional_conduct/rule_3_8_special_responsibilities_of_a_prosecutor/comment_on_rule_3_8/.

Batson v. Kentucky, 476 U.S. 78 (1986).

Brady v. Maryland, 373 U.S. 83 (1963).

Brown, D. K. (2020). Does it matter who objects? Rethinking the burden to prevent errors in criminal process. *Texas Law Review*, 98, 615–677.

Caldwell, H. M. (2014). The prosecutor prince: Misconduct, accountability, and a modest proposal. *Catholic University Law Review*, 63(1), 51–101.

Caldwell, H. M. (2017). Everybody talks about prosecutorial conduct but nobody does anything about it: A 25-year survey of prosecutorial misconnect and a viable solution. *University of Illinois Law Review, 2017*(4), 1455–1486. Available at https://www.illinoislawreview.org/wp-content/uploads/2017/08/Caldwell.pdf.

Center on Media, Crime, and Justice at John Jay College (2020, January 29). NY judge strikes down prosecutor misconduct panel. Available at https://thecrimereport.org/2020/01/29/ny-judge-strikes-down-prosecutor-misconduct-panel/.

Center for Prosecutor Integrity (n.d.). Registry of prosecutorial misconduct. Available at http://www.prosecutorintegrity.org/registry/.

Connick v. Thompson, 563 U.S. 51 (2011).

Doyle v. Ohio, 426 U.S. 610 (1976).

Federal Rules of Criminal Procedure, Rule 24. Available at https://www.uscourts.gov/sites/default/files/rules-of-criminal-procedure.pdf.

Gershman, B. (2016). The prosecutor's duty of silence. *Albany Law Review*, 79(3), 1183–1219.

Gold, R. M., Hessick, C. B., & Hessick, F. A. (2017). Civilizing criminal settlements. *Boston University Law Review*, 97, 1607–1660. Available at https://scholarship.law.unc.edu/cgi/viewcontent.cgi?article=1420&context=faculty_publications.

Gross, S. R., Possley, M. J., Roll, K. J., & Stephens, K. H. (2020). Government misconduct and convicting the innocent: The role of prosecutors, police and other law enforcement. National Registry of Exonerations. Available at https://repository.law.umich.edu/cgi/viewcontent.cgi?article=1165&context=other.

Harker, T. C. (2018). Faithful execution: The persistent myth of widespread prosecutorial misconduct. *Tennessee Law Review*, 85(4), 847–895.

Hatch, A., & Gerstein, T. (2020, Winter). Re-envisioning the roles of prosecutors and attorneys general to make the justice system work for everyone. *Stanford Social Innovation Review*. Available at https://ssir.org/articles/entry/re_envisioning_the_roles_of_prosecutors_and_attorneys_general_to_make_the_justice_system_work_for_everyone.

Holuta, C. B. (2020). Proactive regulation of prosecutors' offices: Strengthening disciplinary committees' oversight of prosecutors' offices across the United States with ABA Model Rule 5.1. *Fordham Law Review*, 89, 695–729.

Imbler v. Pachtman, 424 U.S. 409 (1976).

Innocence Project (2018, September 6). 6 reasons we need prosecutorial accountability. Available at https://innocenceproject.org/6-reasons-we-need-prosecutorial-accountability/.

Innocence Project (n.d.). Andre Hatchett: Time served-25 years. Available at https://innocenceproject.org/cases/andre-hatchett/.

Jackson, R. H. (1940, June). The federal prosecutor. *Journal of the American Judicature Society*, 24, 18–20.

J.E.B. v. Alabama ex rel. T.B., 511 U.S. 127 (1994).

Kepple, R. (2018, January–February). Setting the record straight on prosecutorial misconduct – Five years later. Texas District & County Attorneys Association. Available at https://www.tdcaa.com/journal/setting-the-record-straight-on-prosecutorial-misconduct-five-years-later/.

Kreag, J. (2019). Disclosing prosecutorial misconduct. *Vanderbilt Law Review*, 72(1), 297–352.

Lieb, D. (2014). Vindicating vindictiveness: Prosecutorial discretion and plea bargaining, past and future. *Yale Law Journal*, 123, 1014–1069.

MacLean, C. E., Berles, J. J., & Lamparello, A. (2015). Stop blaming the prosecutors: The real causes of wrongful convictions and rightful exonerations, and what should be done to fix them. *Hofstra Law Review*, 44(1), 151–200.

MacLean, C. E., & Wilks, S. (2012). Keeping arrows in the quiver: Mapping the contours of prosecutorial discretion. *Washburn Law Journal*, 52, 59–96.

MacLean, C. E., & Wilks, S. (2014). A tale of two countries: Comparing the regulation of prosecutorial discretion and misconduct in Canada and the United States. *Supreme Court Law Review 2d*, 65, 107–144.

Mahoney, J. (2021, June 21). Prosecutors, Cuomo split on oversight commission. *The Daily Star*. Available at https://www.thedailystar.com/news/local_news/prosecutors-cuomo-split-on-oversight-commission/article_b019bac7-1fd1-5341-ada2-801fa1939507.html.

National Association of Criminal Defense Lawyers (2019, April 25). Examples of prosecutorial misconduct. Available at https://www.nacdl.org/Content/ExamplesofProsecutorialMisconduct.

National District Attorneys Association (2009). *National prosecution standards*, third edition. Available at https://ndaa.org/wp-content/uploads/NDAA-NPS-3rd-Ed.-w-Revised-Commentary.pdf.

Niles, M. C. (2017). A new balance of evils: Prosecutorial misconduct, Iqbal, and the end of absolute immunity. *Stanford Journal of Civil Rights and Civil Liberties*, 13, 137–187.

Ramirez, A. (2016, Fall). Plain error review is just plain confusing: How the confused state of plain error review led the Seventh Circuit to get it wrong. *Seventh Circuit Review*, 12 (1), article 2, 1–32. Available at https://scholarship.kentlaw.iit.edu/cgi/viewcontent.cgi?article=1191&context=seventhcircuitreview.

Ridolfi, K. M., & Possley, M. (2010, October). *Preventable error: A report of prosecutorial misconduct in California 1997–2009*. Northern California Innocence Project Publications, Book 2. Available at https://www.nacdl.org/getattachment/613c709f-b20c-4390-a8cd-856c2ee53cb6/preventableerror.pdf.

Roy, Y. (2020, January 29). Judge: Prosecutorial Misconduct Commission unconstitutional. *Newsday*. Available at https://www.newsday.com/news/region-state/cuomo-district-attorneys-misconduct-1.41207316.

Thompson, A. C. (2017). Retooling and coordinating the approach to prosecutorial misconduct. *Rutgers University Law Review*, 69, 623–690.

United States Code, title 42, § 1983.

United States Constitution, Amendment V (U.S. Const. amend. V).

Venckus v. Iowa City, 930 N.W.2d 792 (Iowa 2019).

Wojcik, M. E. (2019). Extending *Batson* to peremptory challenges of jurors based on sexual orientation and gender identity. *Northern Illinois University Law Review*, 40(1), 1–43.

Womack, B. (2019, Spring). Prosecutorial accountability: The epidemic of prosecutorial misconduct in America. *Public Interest Law Reporter*, 24(2), 161–167. Available at https://lawecommons.luc.edu/cgi/viewcontent.cgi?article=1572&context=pilr.

Zack, E. (2020, April 23). Why holding prosecutors accountable is so difficult. *Innocence Project*. Available at https://innocenceproject.org/why-holding-prosecutors-accountable-is-so-difficult/#:~:text=Prosecutorial%20misconduct%20occurs%20when%20a,senior%20litigation%20counsel%20Nina%20Morrison.

PART III

Sentencing and Corrections

This part of the book examines issues in the United States' correctional institutions, including sentencing law and policy (chapter 7), the death penalty (chapter 8), mass incarceration and private prisons (chapter 9), and the treatment of mentally ill offenders in the criminal justice system (chapter 10). In so doing, these chapters require you to critically analyze the practical and conceptual complexities in these areas and propose innovative and workable solutions that will effectuate greater fairness and equality in the criminal justice system.

DOI: 10.4324/9781003163411-9

7

SENTENCING[1]

This chapter presents the question of whether sentencing should be discretionary, such that judges have the power to individualize sentences based on the facts of a particular case, or standardized, which would require judges to impose substantially similar sentences on defendants convicted of the same or similar crimes. For many years, sentencing in the United States was discretionary, which allowed judges to impose on defendants any sentence within a broad statutory range. Unfortunately, this practice led to widely disparate sentences, and these disparities were often based on factors such as the defendant's race, gender, and socioeconomic status. Thus, sentencing in the discretionary regime was unprincipled and unfair.

To remedy these intolerable disparities, Congress, and most state legislatures, implemented sentencing guidelines that pre-determined the sentences for specific crimes and substantially restricted judges' ability to deviate from those guidelines in specific cases. The goal was to effectuate uniformity in sentencing; however, this approach created similar injustices that were equal to, if not worse, than sentencing disparities in the pre-Guidelines era. First, the standardized sentences to which judges were bound to impose in all but the most extraordinary cases were merely the mathematical averages of the unprincipled sentences imposed in pre-Guidelines cases, rendering the guidelines' sentences equally purposeless and arbitrary. Second, the guidelines unduly and unnecessarily restricted judges from imposing individualized sentences where the defendant's personal history regarding, for example, mental illness, prior abuse, or intellectual disability justified a sentence outside the pre-determined range. Third, the guidelines failed to address a fundamental issue that has plagued sentencing jurisprudence: sentences for many offenses are simply too long, and prolonged incarceration has such a harmful effect on many inmates that successful reintegration into society upon release is often difficult, if not impossible, thus leading many to re-offend.

DOI: 10.4324/9781003163411-10

Ultimately, legislators and policymakers must have a substantive and comprehensive discussion designed to develop a principled sentencing system that furthers the purposes of criminal punishment and facilitates inmates' social and economic stability upon release. This includes, but is not limited to, examining whether the length of sentences for certain crimes is too long, considering whether to offer more robust mental health and educational services, and commit to offering comprehensive support to inmates upon release to maximize offenders' likelihood of achieving economic and social stability upon release. Part of this effort should include prohibiting, in some instances, employers from discriminating against applicants based on prior criminal history, as doing so presents obstacles to successful re-integration into society and increases the likelihood of re-offending.

To be clear, this chapter does not condemn imprisonment as a criminal punishment. Indeed, for some defendants, such as those convicted of murder and rape, imprisonment for life may be appropriate in some circumstances. However, for some crimes, sentences are too long, are purposeless, fail to help inmates struggling with mental health and other issues, and are ineffective at minimizing recidivism rates. For these reasons, a new approach to sentencing law and policy is legally and morally necessary.

Chapter Highlights

- For many decades, intolerable disparities and inequities characterized sentencing law and policy, as factors such as race, ethnicity, and socioeconomic level impacted the length of sentences that defendants received.
- In response to this problem, standardized sentencing guidelines were adopted at the federal level and in most states to reduce judges' discretion and ensure uniformity in sentencing.
- The standardization of sentences was far too restrictive and failed to give judges sufficient discretion to individualize sentences based on factors unique to a defendant and that impacted a defendant's culpability.
- The focus on whether to adopt a standardized or an individualized model ignored the fact that sentences, regardless of the model, were often far too long.
- Additionally, many sentences were unprincipled, involved incarceration exclusively, and did not serve any of the purposes of criminal punishment.
- As such, sentencing practices often harm, rather than rehabilitate, offenders convicted of non-violent crimes and contribute to unacceptably high rates of recidivism.
- Federal and state sentencing guidelines should be reformed to shorten the length of sentences for many crimes while retaining severe sentences for violent crimes.
- Judges should be afforded more discretion to individualize sentences and to impose "blended" sentences that include penalties other than incarceration, provided that judges explain how a particular sentence furthers one or more of the purposes of criminal punishment.

Introduction

Jimmy Baker is twenty-two years old and lives with his three siblings, Bobby, Christina, and Nicole, who are six, eight, and fourteen, respectively.

Sadly, two years ago, Jimmy' father, Robert, who was sixty-two years old and a pilot at Heavenly Airways, died tragically in a plane crash that stunned the nation. The flight, which departed from Los Angeles International Airport and was to land at Newark, New Jersey's Liberty International Airport, was Robert's final flight before retiring from Heavenly Airways. Unfortunately, while on final approach to Newark Airport, a strong wind shear, coupled with a rudder malfunction, caused the plane to suddenly invert and plunge into the ground, killing Robert and all 127 passengers. Robert's wife Victoria, along with Jimmy, Bobby, Christina, and Nicole, were devastated and miss Richard tremendously. To make matters worse, one month after Robert's death, Victoria was diagnosed with advanced-stage pancreatic cancer and died six weeks later.

In the weeks and months after Robert and Victoria's deaths, Jimmy, who had just graduated from a highly regarded university, assumed responsibility for taking care of his siblings. Jimmy worked three jobs, seven days a week, and was often exhausted as he attempted to support his siblings financially and emotionally. However, Jimmy simply did not earn enough money and feared for his own and his siblings' welfare.

Then, while lying in his bed one night unable to sleep, Jimmy had an idea. He would rob Heavenly Bank and steal enough money to ensure that Bobby, Christina, and Nicole would be able to live comfortably for the foreseeable future. Jimmy had never violated the law before, but he knew that this was a matter of desperation and preservation. He couldn't allow his family to sink into poverty and struggle to survive, particularly after the trauma that they had endured.

One week later, Jimmy, dressed in all black and wearing a hockey mask, entered Heavenly Bank with an AR-15 rifle and demanded that the clerk immediately open the bank's vault and provide him with $200,000 in cash. Although shocked and traumatized, the clerk summoned the bank's manager, who proceeded to open the vault and get the money. While this occurred, Jimmy heard the sound of police sirens in the distance and began to panic. Then, a customer in the bank tackled Jimmy and attempted to take the gun and subdue Jimmy while law enforcement officers were on their way to the scene. Unfortunately, during this struggle, the gun went off and struck an elderly woman who was standing nearby. She died instantly.

Jimmy continued to struggle with the customer for a few moments before law enforcement officers suddenly burst through the front door with guns drawn and instructed everyone to lay down with their hands behind their heads. At this point, Jimmy pulled the trigger, hoping to shoot the customer, who had placed his hands around Jimmy's neck and begun to choke him while screaming, "Die!" Jimmy pulled the trigger and struck the customer in the chest, killing him instantly. Also, when Jimmy pulled the trigger, one of the law enforcement officers fired at Jimmy, striking him in the back. Jimmy was rushed to the hospital, and, after an emergency surgery, doctors informed Jimmy that he would be paralyzed from the waist down.

Jimmy expressed remorse for the incident, stating to investigators that he was just trying to provide for his family after the death of his parents.

The prosecutor charged Jimmy with one count of attempted armed robbery, one count of first-degree murder for shooting the customer, and one count of second-degree murder for the death of the elderly woman. If convicted on all charges, Jimmy could face life imprisonment without the possibility of parole.

After a two-week jury trial, Jimmy was convicted.

***

What sentence would you impose on Jimmy? What purposes does your sentence serve? Explain your reasoning given the relevant facts and address all relevant counter-arguments. Also, you need not be familiar with any particular murder statute or legal standard. Instead, your opinion should be based solely on the facts and criteria that you believe are relevant.

Discussion

Sentencing in the United States Before the Federal (and State) Sentencing Guidelines

Before 1987, sentencing in the United States was unprincipled and largely purposeless. Judges had nearly unfettered discretion to sentence a defendant to any term of imprisonment within a wide statutory range for a particular crime (Lamparello, 2004, pp. 648–659). For example if a statute authorized a term of twenty-five years to life imprisonment for first-degree murder, a judge had the power to impose terms of imprisonment anywhere in this range without explaining the purposes underlying imposition of a particular sentence.

Not surprisingly, sentencing in the pre-Guidelines era often led to unjustifiable disparities in the sentencing of similarly situated criminal defendants.

> To put it bluntly, federal sentencing in the pre-Guidelines era can be appropriately characterized as "lawless" because the judiciary was not required to enunciate any principles or objective factors by which lower courts in subsequent cases could channel and apply their discretionary authority. In fact, "sentencing decision-makers operated within a system that not only allowed but implicitly encouraged rendering decisions without explicit 'explanation or purported justification.'" Trial judges were not required to "explain the reasons for their sentencing decisions on the record." Moreover, since appellate review of the propriety of such sentences was, save for constitutional issues, precluded, no substantive sentencing law existed. In this way, the discretionary sentencing regime vested in judges and parole and probation agencies the greatest degree of uncontrolled power over the liberty of human beings that one can find in the legal system.
>
> *(Lamparello, 2004, pp. 648–649)*

Indeed, the evidence was

> conclusive that judges of widely varying attitudes on sentencing, administering statutes that confer huge measures of discretion, mete out widely divergent sentences where the differences are explainable only by the variations among the judges, not by material differences in the defendants or their crimes.
>
> *(Frankel, 1973, p. 21)*

Because these variations were sometimes predicated on factors such as race and socioeconomic status, sentencing in the United States was lawless, arbitrary, and purposeless.

Sentencing in the Guidelines Era – From Disparity to Uniformity

In 1984, the United Congress decided to act. Former Senator Edward Kennedy lamented that Congress has not "built any standards or safeguards into the sentencing process," and argued that unjust disparities in sentencing were created "by conferring unlimited discretion on the sentencing judge" without any explanation of the "purposes ... criteria or Guidelines to be considered by the sentencing judge" (Berman, 1999 (quoting S. 2699, 94th Cong. (1975)).

To remedy this problem, Congress focused on eliminating disparity and achieving uniformity in sentencing for similarly situated offenders. As part of the Sentencing Reform Act of 1984, Congress created the United States Sentencing Commission, which was responsible for drafting sentencing guidelines that judges would be required to apply in all but the most extraordinary cases.

The Federal Sentencing Guidelines were complex and rigid, requiring judges to identify an applicable – and quite narrow – sentencing range for a particular crime though a multi-step process that considered both offender and offense characteristics. Indeed, this process involved "an intricate, nine-step process in which a sentencing court assesses the seriousness of a defendant's current offense and past crimes to establish an 'offense level' and a 'criminal history score' which are then used to determine the defendant's applicable sentencing range from within a 258-box grid known as the Guidelines Sentencing Table, or 'heartland'" (Berman, 2002, p. 443). Put simply, the "heartland" represented the specific sentencing range for a particular crime that a judge was *required* to impose in nearly all cases.

To be sure, the Guidelines only permitted judges to depart from the predetermined sentencing ranges – and thus impose an individualized sentence – in limited circumstances. Specifically, a judge could only depart from the Guidelines heartland if they found "an aggravating or mitigating circumstance of a kind, or to a degree, not adequately taken into consideration by the Sentencing Commission in formulating the Guidelines that should result in a sentence different from that described" (18 U.S.C. § 3553(b) (2000)). The problem, of course, is that in its exhaustive evaluation of pre-Guidelines sentencing practice, the Sentencing Commission considered nearly every possible offense and offender characteristic that judges had relied upon when sentencing defendants. Indeed, the Guidelines sentencing manual is "now over four hundred pages in length and contains over 100 multi-section Guidelines, indicating that the Commission 'adequately considered' all but the most esoteric sentencing factors" (Lamparello, 2004, pp. 657–658). In fact, the Sentencing Commission stated that "the guidelines, offense by offense, seek to take account of those factors that the Commission's data indicate made a significant difference in pre-Guidelines sentencing practice" (United States Guidelines Manual, ch.1, pt. A, introductory cmt., 2002). As the Commission stated:

> The Commission intend[ed] the sentencing courts to treat each guideline as carving out a "heartland," a set of typical cases embodying the conduct that each guideline describes. When a court finds an atypical case, one to which a guideline linguistically applies but where conduct significantly differs from the norm, the court may consider whether a departure is warranted.
>
> *(USG Manual, 2002)*

Thus, the Commission's message was clear: it expected that departures would be rare, and that judges would apply the Guidelines in the vast majority of cases. As the Commission stated, "Despite the courts' legal freedom to depart from the Guidelines, they will not do so very often," as departures should be "highly infrequent" (USG Manual, 2002).

The Guidelines unquestionably revolutionized federal sentencing law. The question, however, is whether the Guidelines significantly improved federal sentencing law. The answer, from both scholars and judges, is no. To begin with, the Guidelines sentencing ranges failed to import purpose and principle into federal sentencing jurisprudence. Instead, they represented nothing more than a codification of the purposeless sentences that were imposed in pre-Guidelines jurisprudence. The Sentencing Commission's approach can be summarized as follows:

> In determining the appropriate sentencing ranges for each offense, the Commission estimated the average sentences served within each category under the pre-Guidelines sentencing system .... While the Commission has not considered itself bound by pre-Guidelines sentencing practice, it has not attempted to develop an entirely new system of sentencing .... Guidelines sentences, in many instances, will approximate pre-Guidelines practice and adherence to the Guidelines will help to eliminate wide disparity.
>
> *(USG Manual, 2002)*

In other words, although the Guidelines' drafters largely eliminated sentencing disparities, they did create a purpose-driven sentencing regime. The result was that sentences imposed in the Guidelines era were just as unfair and unjust as the sentences imposed in the pre-Guidelines era:

> [C]ould one persuasively argue that the Guidelines are calculated to do justice? The Guidelines' well known birth process makes such a claim implausible … the Commission did not deduce sentencing Guidelines from principles of justice, or logical principles of any sort. The Sentencing Reform Act took judges out of the sentencing philosophy business so that a single, centralized authority—the Commission—could sort through the competing arguments and come to a single conclusion on sentencing philosophy for a given case. But the Commission never undertook this analysis. Instead, it based its sentences on mathematical averages of past practice of federal sentencing judges, with minor and equally irrational adjustments.
>
> *(Robinson, 1997, pp. 1241–1242)*

The result, sadly, is that the Guidelines failed to explain in any depth *why* specific sentences were adopted for particular offenses:

> The effect of this foundation of the Guidelines is that no one, Commissioner or judge, can give an explanation for any Guidelines sentence other than to say that the sentence is what has been done in the past, or worse, that the sentence is a mathematical average of what has been done in the past … such mathematical averaging often ensures irrational sentences. Judges may have disagreed, for example, whether it is best to give drug users who sell to support their habit a purely rehabilitative, non-prison sentence to a drug treatment program, or whether it is better to give a long prison term to provide a dramatic deterrent. Both approaches have a logic and can be rationally defended. The same cannot be said for a mathematical average of the two, which may be too short for the dramatic deterrent and yet not provide the drug rehabilitation.
>
> *(Robinson, 1997, pp. 1241–1242)*

In other words, the Guidelines' drafters failed, both in developing the sentencing ranges and severely restricting judges' discretion, to explain whether, and to what extent, the sentencing ranges further one or more of the purposes of criminal punishment:

> Attempted applications of policies of deterrence, incapacitation, rehabilitation, and desert have more often been the stuff of dissenter's laments, or district court opinions overturned on appeal, than the basis of majority rulings on appeal. When district courts have premised departures on the conclusion that there is an unusually small likelihood that the defendant will re-offend, the courts of appeals have brushed such reasoning aside. When district judges have found that defendants show good prospects for rehabilitation, or have already, prior to sentencing, made unusual strides in treatment programs, the circuit courts have almost always invalidated the resulting departures. The appellate opinions … seldom make any nod to the statutory authorization to evaluate

> sentences in light of the underlying goals of punishment .... Presumably, in the jurisprudential world of federal guideline appeals, such cornerstone policies have already been "adequately considered" by Congress and the Commission.
>
> *(Reitz, 1997, pp. 1468–1470)*

The problem was that the Guidelines were focused solely on achieving uniformity in sentencing and eliminating disparities at all costs. However, uniformity for the sake of uniformity only produces the same problems as a system of unguided discretion: it lacks principle and purpose in theory and in fact.

Furthermore, the Guidelines left judges with far too little discretion to impose individualized sentences where the facts warranted. Instead, as stated above, the Guidelines required judges to impose a within-Guidelines sentence in all but the most extraordinary cases, prompting many judges to criticize the Guidelines' framework:

> Rightly or wrongly, many trial judges view the Guidelines as too rigid ... [J]udges confront cases in a highly individualized, highly contextualized micro framework. They are most sensitive to the impact of the sentence on the particular defendants and their family, because these are the people with whom they deal. Many judges believe that offender characteristics that should have a bearing on sentences were wrongfully de-emphasized by Congress and are not adequately accounted for by the Guidelines .... Further, many judges think that the overall sentence lengths that result from the Guidelines are simply too long ....
>
> *(Schulhofer & Nagel, 1997, pp. 1299, 1301)*

Moreover, judges widely criticized the Guidelines, stating that they were "mechanistic and unprincipled," and posed "a serious credibility problem with many sentencing judges" (Robinson, 1997, p. 1240). In fact, the Guidelines were described as an attempt "to transform the venerable ritual of sentencing into a puppet theater," a "dark, sinister, and cynical crime management program," and "the greatest travesty of justice in our legal system in this century" (Stith & Cabranes, 1998, p. 84). Such statements are very troubling considering that the Guidelines were supposed to *reform* and *improve* sentencing practice.

The reason that they failed to do so is because the Guidelines' drafters swung the pendulum too far in the opposite direction. They imported purposeless sentences into the Guidelines' heartland and then gave judges minimal discretion to depart from those ranges. The result was a sentencing regime no better than that which it replaced. Still, the most significant problems with the Guidelines were yet to be discovered. As the United States Supreme Court held in *United States v. Booker*, the Guidelines were unconstitutional.

Sentencing in the Advisory Guidelines Era

In *United States v. Booker* (2005), the United States Supreme Court held that the Guidelines were unconstitutional. Amazingly, one of the authors of the majority opinion – Justice Steven Breyer – was also a member of the United States Sentencing Commission and helped to draft the Guidelines. The Court held that the Guidelines violated the Sixth Amendment to the United States Constitution because they enabled judges to make factual determinations relating to an offense and increase a defendant's sentence above the applicable range based on such determinations (*Booker*, 2005). The Court held that, under the Sixth Amendment, only juries could make findings of fact that result in a sentence above the applicable range (*Booker*, 2005).

Accordingly, the Court held that the Guidelines were no longer mandatory. Thus, judges were no longer required to apply the Guidelines' ranges when sentencing defendants. Rather, appellate courts would simply review sentences to ensure that they were "reasonable," although the criteria for determining reasonableness were largely subjective. In theory, therefore, the *Booker* decision returned sentencing laws to the pre-Guidelines era, as judges now had discretion to impose sentences within the broad statutory ranges for particular crimes.

As a practical matter, however, judges did not exercise this renewed discretion in a principled and purposeful manner. Rather, in the majority of cases, judges simply applied the Guidelines now-advisory sentencing ranges, in substantial part because sentences within the advisory ranges were considered presumptively reasonable, and because it was easier for judges to impose sentences that had already accounted for most offense and offender characteristics. The courts' decisions to continue applying the Guidelines advisory ranges was ironic: for years, judges had complained that the Guidelines gave judges insufficient discretion to impose individualized sentences. Yet, when given the opportunity to exercise increased discretion, most judges rejected that opportunity and instead decided to continue to impose sentences within the advisory Guidelines' ranges. The result was that, after *Booker*, sentencing was in the proverbial no man's land.

Not surprisingly, therefore, sentencing jurisprudence remains plagued by the same problems that arose in the pre-Guidelines era: sentences are unprincipled and purposeless. The fundamental problem is not with uniformity or disparity in sentencing *per se*. It is with the failure to explain the reasons underlying uniform or disparate sentences for particular crimes, thus rendering sentencing jurisprudence unhinged from the purpose of criminal punishment that it is expected to vindicate.

Exercises

Exercise One

Tiffany Peterson is twenty-one years old and a student at an elite university. She is a pre-med student and hopes to attend a prestigious medical school upon graduation. However, recently Tiffany has experienced severe fatigue and for two weeks has missed most of her classes and been unable to concentrate on her schoolwork. Tiffany scheduled an appointment with a physician at the university's health center. The physician conducted an examination and ordered a blood test, which revealed no abnormalities. The physician recommended that Tiffany rest for a week and see a counselor to address what he perceived was Tiffany's high level of stress.

However, final examinations were only a week away and Tiffany was determined to maintain her high grade point average. Thus, she decided to push herself to work diligently regardless of the fatigue she experienced. One evening, Tiffany's best friend Melissa Thompson noticed how tired Tiffany appeared and decided to act.

"Tiffany, here are some pills that will give you so much more energy and focus," Melissa said.

> "What are they?" Tiffany said. "I'm not taking anything dangerous or illegal."
> "It's just Adderall," Melissa said. "Everyone takes it."

Tiffany decided to try one pill and, within a few minutes, felt more energetic and focused. Melissa gave Tiffany twenty pills to help her succeed on the final examinations.

The next morning, however, Tiffany was found dead in her dorm room. An autopsy revealed that Tiffany had a rare heart disorder, and that the Adderall caused Tiffany to suffer a fatal arrythmia.

***

Should Melissa be charged with a crime and, if so, what sentence should she receive if convicted? Explain how your sentence furthers one or more of the purposes of criminal punishment and address all relevant counterarguments.

Exercise Two

Steven Carson is seventeen years old and a senior at Hope High School. For years, Steven has struggled with major depression and has experienced periods where he contemplated suicide. Fortunately, Steven has a very caring doctor and has been prescribed two anti-depressant medications that have enabled him to achieve mental and emotional stability. However, Steven still endures intermittent periods of suicidal depression, and his parents have been worried that one day Steven might impulsively commit suicide.

Recently, Steven has been struggling through a major depressive episode and, sadly, contemplating suicide. His best friend, Shannon Foster, who has known of his mental illness for years, tried to help him, but Steven sank further into a dangerous depression. A few days later, Steven and Shannon had the following exchange via text message:

STEVEN: I am really thinking about doing it this time.
SHANNON: You should. You have suffered for too long. End it. Go to heaven.
STEVEN: Are you serious?
SHANNON: Yes. It's time. You shouldn't suffer anymore. You won't get better. Get it over with. Now.
STEVEN: But I'm scared

SHANNON: Just do it. Stop being a wimp. It is for the best.
STEVEN: You think so?
SHANNON: Yes.

About an hour later, Steven hung himself in his bedroom and was discovered by his parents, who recovered Steven's cell phone and read the text messages Shannon had sent immediately before Steven's death. A few days later, the district attorney charged Shannon with murder in connection with Steven's death.

***

Should Shannon be charged with murder? If so, and if she is convicted, what sentence should she receive? Explain how your sentence furthers one or more of the purposes of criminal punishment and address all relevant counterarguments.

Exercise Three

Bethany Jones and Wendy Grant are sixteen and seventeen years old, respectively. They attend Eternity High School. They have been best friends for years. Unfortunately, Bethany and Wendy never made other friends at Eternity High School, and are frequently bullied and ridiculed by other students. As such, Bethany and Wendy have often felt alienated and alone.

One day when Bethany and Wendy were hiking in Eternity State Park, they met a girl named Christina Boyd, who was hiking with her boyfriend, and who had recently graduated from Eternity High School. They immediately connected with Christina and began discussing their experiences at Eternity High School.

> "Everyone picked on me," Christina stated, "but then I found true friends that will last a lifetime."
>
> "What do you mean?" Bethany asked.
>
> "His name is Colton," Christina replied. "He owns a ranch where he welcomes and inspires everyone. You and your friend should come to the ranch with us and become members of our family!"

Desperate to be accepted and meet new friends, Bethany and Wendy go to the ranch and are introduced to Colton, who welcomes them with open arms.

> "Everyone is loved here," Colton tells Bethany and Wendy, smiling. "We live in a beautiful world where all of your dreams will come true."

Over the next several weeks, Bethany and Wendy spend most of their time at the ranch and met many new friends, including Daniel and Sabrina, who have been living at the ranch for two years. They both graduated from Eternity High School and were bullied in the same manner as Bethany and Wendy.

> "This is a family," Colton said while they were all having dinner one evening, "and one of the things we do is help others to become better people. Especially those who have harmed us."

Colton asked Bethany and Wendy to make a list of the people at Eternity High School who had harmed them. They immediately named Brenda Smith and Kerry Bergen, who were extremely popular at Eternity High School and had repeatedly bullied and ridiculed Bethany and Wendy.

> "You must sacrifice them to the higher power," Colton said, "and you must do this to show that you are a part of this family."

Bethany and Wendy were shocked at this suggestion, which they interpreted as a command to kill Brenda and Kerry. Then, Daniel and Sabrina intervened.

> "You aren't going to harm anyone," Daniel said, as Sabina nodded approvingly. "You are delivering them to a better place where they can learn how to love."
>
> "And you are showing that you know how to love," Colton said.

Bethany and Wendy were so inspired that they agreed to "sacrifice" Brenda and Kerry. A few days later, Colton commanded Bethany, Wendy, Daniel, and Sabrina to go to Brenda and Kerry's homes and "sacrifice them for the greater good." However, Colton instructed them that only Brenda and Wendy were permitted to "sacrifice" Brenda and Kerry, and that Daniel and Sabrina would accompany them to "ensure that the sacrifice is completed."

That evening, Bethany and Wendy broke into Brenda and Kerry's homes and stabbed them to death. During the murders, Daniel and Sabrina subdued Brenda and Kerry's parents, who woke up during the attacks. However, they were not harmed.

The next day, Eternity High School's students were traumatized when they heard the news that Brenda and Kerry had been murdered, and that Bethany and Wendy had been arrested for their murders.

The district attorney charged Bethany, Wendy, Daniel, Sabrina, and Colton with first-degree murder.

***

If convicted, what sentences should Bethany, Wendy, Daniel, Sabrina, and Colton receive? Would they differ for one or more of the defendants? Explain how your sentence furthers one or more of the purposes of criminal punishment and address all relevant counterarguments.

Exercise Four

Jeremy and Joanne Bullock have been married for twelve years and have two daughters named Amy and Kimberly, who are four and seven, respectively. Jeremy and Joanne have had a wonderful marriage and are planning on having another child together.

Sadly, however, Joanne was recently diagnosed with a particularly aggressive form of cancer and given between six and twelve months to live. Jeremy was devastated by this news and when he informed Amy and Kimberly, they were likewise devastated.

Unfortunately, as the months progressed, Joanne's condition deteriorated substantially and, despite being on pain medication, she suffered terribly. One evening, Joanne looked at Jeremy and said, "Please help me die. I can't suffer anymore. Let me go." Jeremy began crying and held Joanne's hand. As much as he loved her, Jeremy didn't want Joanne to suffer anymore. The next morning, Jeremy gave Joanne a lethal dose of her pain medication and held her as she passed away peacefully. Amy and Kimberly were traumatized when they learned of their mother's death.

The district attorney charged Jeremy with murder. Although sympathetic to Jeremy, the district attorney stated that, unless acting in self-defense, no one has the right to murder another individual.

***

If convicted, what sentence would you impose on Jeremy? Explain how your sentence furthers one or more of the purposes of criminal punishment and address all relevant counterarguments.

Exercise Five

For the Walsh family, July 4th is a special holiday. In addition to celebrating the Independence Day, July 4th is the wedding anniversary of William and Karen Walsh, who have been married for twenty years and have two children: Brandon, aged eighteen, and Mark, aged fifteen. Brandon and Mark love July 4th because their parents host a large party with friends and extended family members. The boys get to enjoy delicious food and set off many fireworks in their large backyard under William and Karen's close supervision.

This year, on July 1, Brandon and Mark went to Bob's Fireworks Warehouse to purchase fireworks for the upcoming party. Brandon had saved over $500 from his part-time job working at Bill's Burger Joint, where he was a server. Brandon and Mark searched through the store and, after about an hour, they decided to purchase the following fireworks:

- *Bob's bottle rockets.* These are ignited and fly dangerously fast for approximately fifty to seventy-five feet. Brandon purchased ten.
- *Bob's might mortars.* These fireworks are placed in a small tube with a fuse attached to the bottom. The user lights the fuse and quickly runs away before the it ignites and lights up the sky.
- *Bob's atomic bomb.* This is one of the most dangerous fireworks. Shaped and designed to look like an actual bomb, it requires the user to light a fuse at the bottom of the "bomb" and throw it in an open area where people are at least 100 feet away.

Brandon and Mark were extremely excited about this year's fireworks, which they believed would be the best they had ever used at the party. However, when they arrived home, William and Karen told Brandon and Mark that the fireworks were far too dangerous to be used at the party. Although the boys were not forced to return the fireworks, William and Karen told them that could only be used after the party and under their supervision.

The July 4th party was fun and festive, as over forty guests enjoyed beautiful weather, great music, and William's outstanding barbecued ribs.

During the party, Brandon and Mark were bored and upset that they could not use any of the fireworks, Then, Brandon had an idea. "Let's just light one of the atomic bombs," Brandon said. "We can just throw it in to the backyard when nobody is around."

> "I don't know," Mark said. "Mom and dad will be so mad if anything goes wrong."
>
> "It won't," Brandon replied. "Trust me. I know what I am doing."

Mark agreed and, while the guests were inside their house enjoying William's barbecued ribs, the boys went outside with one of *Bob's atomic bombs*. Brandon followed the instructions carefully, lighting the fuse and then throwing it toward an open area in the backyard when no one was within 100 feet.

Unfortunately, Brandon threw the *Bob's atomic bomb* too far. It landed in their neighbor's backyard, where the neighbors and approximately fifteen of their friends were enjoying an outdoor barbecue.

When the bomb went off, it made a thundering sound and released an enormous amount of smoke into the air. When the smoke cleared, Brandon and Mark raced to the neighbor's backyard, hoping that no one was injured. Sadly, that was not true. The bomb's force killed two of the guests instantly with blunt force trauma, and caused three others to suffer major injuries. One of the injured guests was immediately taken to the hospital where, despite doctors' best efforts, his right leg had to be amputated.

Brandon and Mark were arrested. They were charged with two counts of murder and three counts of assault with a deadly weapon.

***

If convicted, what sentence would you impose on Brandon and Mark? Explain how your sentence furthers one or more of the purposes of criminal punishment and address all relevant counterarguments.

Solutions

As the discussion in this chapter illustrates, sentencing law and policy in the United States should be reformed at the federal and state level. First, for many crimes, sentences are too long. Second, many sentences are purposeless and unprincipled. Third, insufficient consideration is given to imposing alternative sentences.

Sentences For Many Crimes Are Too Long – And For a Few Offenses, Too Short

In the United Sates, sentencing for various crimes is far too long (Miller & Harawa, 2019). As a threshold matter, consider the realities of a prison environment. Inmates spend most of their days locked in a small prison cell with minimal social interaction or recreational activity. They receive, at best, modest opportunities for educational advancement. The medical care is substandard. Psychiatric services and psychological counseling is inadequate. The food lacks meaningful nutritional value, and prisoners often gain weight and develop health issues due to the prolonged exposure to an unhealthy diet. Inmates are also subject to physical and sexual abuse. In many prisons, the living conditions are deplorable. Contact with loved ones is severely limited. In short, prison is a horrible and, in some areas, inhumane environment. Imagine spending one week in this environment. It would be horrible. Now imagine spending years in this environment. The effects on a person's mental and physical health might be irreversible upon release (US-HHS, 2001).

Importantly, the United States Department of Justice, Bureau of Statistics' report on the average time spent in prison for the most common criminal offenses demonstrates that sentences for some crimes are far too long (Kaeble, 2018). For example, individuals convicted of drug possession spend an average of one year and three months in prison before they are released. So, the college student who is arrested for possessing cocaine – a drug frequently used on college campuses – will spend, on average, over a year in prison? That makes no sense. The college student harmed no one. The conduct of which he was convicted, although criminal, is not uncommon among college students. Yet, this student's life will now be ruined. Shouldn't there be an alternative sentence available?

Additionally, individuals convicted of burglary spend an average of two years and two months incarcerated before they are released. Of course, burglary is a serious criminal offense and should result in a period of incarceration. Still, sending someone to jail for over two years seems absurd considering the debilitating effects of prison. For example, assume that an individual unlawfully enters a family's home while they are on vacation and steals valuable jewelry. The suspect is later apprehended and pleads guilty. Should this offender spend over two years incarcerated? Why? Given the conditions of prison, why wouldn't a one-year sentence suffice?

To be clear, these sentences are only averages, and the individual circumstances of an offense often vary substantially among offenders, thus justifying a lesser or more severe sentence. The fact remains that the average sentences for many offenses are too high. Furthermore, apart from these averages, for most crimes, states provide judges with significant discretion to impose sentences within a wide statutory range. As a result, in thousands of cases, judges have imposed truly outrageous sentences. For example, one forty-six-year-old offender was sentenced to twenty-five years' imprisonment for selling $1,800 worth of pain medication (Fuchs, 2013). Another offender received a twenty-year sentence for attempting a single sale of crack cocaine (Fuchs, 2013). The list goes on and on, and the examples are illustrative of how sentencing law desperately requires reform.

To be sure, there is no evidence that severe sentences deter crime more than a lesser sentence (Adwar, 2014). Indeed, the United States Department of Justice commissioned a report regarding the deterrence value of severe sentences. One commentator summarized the results as follows:

> [T]he report argues that the certainty and imminence of punishment are more likely to deter crime than length. In a Hawaii program, for example, offenders on probation who faced the certain, but brief, punishment of one to two days of confinement for failing drug tests had far fewer positive tests than offenders who didn't face that punishment. Overall, the report recommends that federal and state officials alter criminal justice policies to reduce nationwide incarceration rates "[g]iven the small crime prevention effects of long prison sentences and the possibly high financial, social, and human costs of incarceration."
>
> *(Adwar, 2014)*

Substantial evidence exists that, by the age of forty, most individuals "age out" of crime and thus no longer present a risk to public safety (Goldstein, 2015). So what is the justification for sentencing a forty-six-year-old offender to twenty-five years in prison for selling $1,800 worth of painkillers? None. And to the extent that such sentences result from mandatory minimum sentence laws, which they often do, such laws should be abolished because they are ineffective (Families Against Mandatory Minimums, n.d.). Instead of mandatory minimum sentences, there should be mandatory minimum caps on sentences for various crimes, and in reforming sentencing law, legislators must confront these and other issues to ensure that sentences are fair and serve a legitimate purpose other than over-punishing for crimes that warrant less, or alternative, sentences. Also, for some certain crimes, the law should allow inmates to seek sentencing reductions if they can demonstrate that they are no longer a danger to society and have shown behavioral improvement while incarcerated.

Moreover, the length of sentences must be considered in light of the collateral consequences of imprisonment on the offender and the offender's family. As stated above, the prison environment involves being locked in a small cell every day for most of the day, and the short and long-term psychological effects are undeniable (US-HHS, 2001). Furthermore, if the offender has a spouse and children while incarcerated, the effects on them are substantial. Indeed, an offender's family often struggles to survive financially and provide necessary support to their children. To make matters worse, upon release, offenders face many obstacles to successfully reintegrate into society. Many employers, for example, will deny employment to individuals with a criminal record, and many universities will deny admission to those same individuals. Put simply, the cost of incarceration is immeasurable and, in some instances, irreparable and that should matter when fashioning an appropriate sentence.

To be clear, the point is not that all sentences are too long or that imprisonment should be disfavored. In fact, for some offenses, lengthy prison terms are appropriate and, currently, far too low. For example, the average sentence that an offender serves in state prison for rape and related sexual crimes is a little over six years (Kaeble, 2018). Additionally, the average time that individuals convicted of murder, including manslaughter, spend in prison is fifteen years. Think about that: a person can be sentenced to twenty-five years' imprisonment for selling $1,800 of a pain medication yet only serve six for violating another person in arguably the most egregious way possible and only fifteen for taking another person's life. It should be the other way around.

In short, the United States' sentencing laws are hopelessly flawed. On one hand, the federal sentencing guidelines and mandatory minimum sentencing laws unduly restrict judges from exercising discretion to individualize sentences where, for example, the offender's history reduces or aggravates culpability. On the other hand, giving too much discretion can result in the imposition of entirely unjust sentences. Where is the proper balance?

It should begin with a belief that sentences should be shorter and, as discussed below, include penalties that do not involve incarceration.

The rest is for you to decide – if you can.

Sentences Are Largely Purposeless

In the United States, the fundamental purposes of criminal punishment are retribution, deterrence, and rehabilitation. Thus, sentences of imprisonment should further at least one of these purposes. In many cases, however, they do not.

Consider the death penalty. What purpose does the death penalty serve? Perhaps one might argue that is serves a retributive purpose. But what is the criteria to determine if a punishment is appropriately retributive? At the very least, the punishment would have to be considered proportionate to the crime. That determination, however, is difficult, if not impossible, to make because of the challenge in quantifying the many factors that impact a defendant's culpability. After all, it's not as simple as "an eye for an eye." If a defendant intentionally murders another person, but is diagnosed with schizophrenia, a sentence of death cannot possibly be deemed proportional. Further, the problems with proportionality extend beyond the individual level. Assume that ten defendants each intentionally murder another person, but only three of them get the death penalty, while the others receive life imprisonment. Does this mean that the death sentences are appropriately retributive, and the life sentences are not? It means that the determination of who receives the death penalty is arbitrary. Statistics overwhelmingly show that the likelihood of receiving the death penalty depends not on principled proportionality determinations, but on factors such as where a defendant lives, the race of the defendant and victim, and the defendant's socioeconomic status. To make matters worse, studies have repeatedly shown that the death penalty does not deter crime (Amnesty International, 2009). In fact, in states without the death penalty, the murder rate is *lower* (Bonner & Fessenden, 2021). Thus what purpose does the death penalty serve? None.

Unfortunately, that is the case with the vast majority of sentencing laws in the United States. First, judges are rarely, if ever, required to explain on the record why they are imposing a particular sentence or identify the purposes served by that sentence (i.e., retribution, deterrence, rehabilitation). Moreover, what should a judge do when an alternative sentence would further different purposes? For example, a term of imprisonment may, in some instances, serve retributive or deterrence purposes, but a sentence of commitment to a mental health facility might also further rehabilitative purposes. Which purpose should take priority? And how can a judge quantify the impact of various offense and offender characteristics to make this determination? The answer is not that they can't; the answer is that they don't. Sentences are imposed without a true understanding of what societal purposes they serve. For example, why should a defendant receive a twenty-year prison term for attempting a single sale of cocaine? What criteria or standards would justify different or similar sentences for fifty defendants convicted of that crime? For example, imagine five defendants convicted of the same crime, who are from the same background, and who have each struggled with the same mental illness in their past. Otherwise, no facts differentiate them regarding their respective culpability. It is almost certain that the judges would impose different sentences because of their subjective values. Specifically, one judge might view the presence of a mental illness as a mitigating factor, while another may view it as an "excuse" that is not worthy of consideration. This is precisely where sentencing law fails. It lacks a principled foundation. This does not mean that judges should be required to impose the same sentences. It means that they should be required to explain in detail why they are imposing a particular sentence.

Most importantly, what is the reasoning behind specific prison terms for specific crimes? Why, for example, do offenders convicted of drug-related offenses in Minnesota receive a mean sentence of eight years imprisonment while individuals convicted of drug-related offenses in Oklahoma receive a sentence of three years (Security.org, 2019)?

Admittedly, individuals convicted of the same crime, whether in or across states, may deserve different sentences. Factors such as the offender's prior criminal record and history of mental illness, along with the nature and circumstances of the crime, may certainly warrant different sentences. The issue is not with disparity *per se*. The problem is that judges rarely give principled and purpose-driven sentencing opinions to explain *why* disparate sentences are justified, or to explain *why* a term of imprisonment of twenty years is warranted over ten years. Of course, the courts do rely on recommendations set forth in sentencing reports by probation officers, and on sentencing guidelines, but rarely do judges explain in any depth precisely what purpose or purposes a sentence serves. For example, if a defendant is convicted for a second time of physically assaulting his wife, should a judge sentence the defendant to one year in prison? Or should the defendant be sentenced to 1,000 hours of community service in a battered women's shelter while being placed on house arrest but permitted to continue his current occupation and thus continue supporting his family? The failure to explain why we sentence – and identify what purposes those sentences serve – has rendered criminal sentencing a largely arbitrary endeavor.

Insufficient Consideration is Given to Imposing Alternative Sentences

For some crimes, prison is not an optimal or even desired sentence, particularly if other sentences would serve important purposes, such as protecting public safety or reducing the likelihood that a defendant will re-offend upon release. However, insufficient consideration is given to alternative sentencing schemes because prison is the default sentence in many cases. Still, for some crimes, prison makes no sense or, at the very least, is not the best option.

For example, in a report titled *How Many Americans are Unnecessarily Incarcerated*, the authors found that 39% of offenders are incarcerated even though they pose little, if any, threat to public safety (Brooke-Eisen & Chettiar, 2016). The authors explained as follows:

> How did we get to this number [39% imprisoned without a sufficient rationale]? First, many people who are in prison shouldn't have been sent there in the first place. For example, we found that 25% of prisoners (364,000 people), almost all non-violent, lower-level offenders, would be better served by alternatives to incarceration such as treatment, community service, or probation. Second, another 14% (212,000 prisoners) have already served long sentences for more serious crimes and can be safely set free.
>
> *(Brooke-Eisen & Chettiar, 2016, brackets added)*

The study's results suggest that, for some crimes, prison is simply ineffective and unwarranted. Moreover, given the collateral consequences that prison exacts on an offender upon release (e.g., difficulty obtaining employment, the stigma of being incarcerated), the decision to sentence an offender to prison should, in some circumstances, be rejected.

For example, consider a young male who is addicted to Fentanyl, a powerful prescription pain medication. One evening, he attempts to purchase $300 worth of Fentanyl from an individual who poses as a drug dealer but is actually an undercover police officer. The male is arrested and charged with the attempt to purchase a controlled substance. Should he be sentenced to prison? If so, why? What purpose would that serve? Obviously, he suffers from a drug addiction. Why not sentence him to in-patient treatment at a recovery facility? Doing so would maximize the likelihood that he would overcome the addiction and become a productive member of society. Placing him in prison would almost ensure that he does not receive the necessary treatment and is released in the same state as when he arrived: addicted to drugs. Thus, the likelihood that he will break the law again is substantially higher. How does that serve any of the purposes of criminal punishment and, most importantly, how does that protect safety? It doesn't. That is the problem. Sentencing in the United States is largely purposeless and ineffective.

Ultimately, for some crimes, alternatives to imprisonment should be considered. In so doing, states will reduce the prison population. In states that have already implemented alternative punishments, crimes has also been reduced. Put simply, you can reduce the prison population – and crime – simultaneously (Brooke-Eisen & Chettiar, 2016).

***

You are appointed to the United States Sentencing Reform Commission and responsible for reforming sentencing law in the United States. Specifically, you are asked to:

- Propose new sentencing ranges for the most common criminal offenses. In so doing, you must explain why, how, and to what extent these ranges further one or more of the purposes of criminal punishment, are consistent with fairness and justice, and accurately account for the aggravating or mitigating factors that may impact an offender's culpability.
- Identify alternative punishments, such as commitment in a mental health facility, that you consider appropriate for particular crimes. In so doing, be sure to consider alternative punishments to incarceration and explain why these punishments better reflect an offender's culpability and are likely to achieve one or more of the purposes of criminal punishment.

You are asked to use the Table below to summarize your recommendations for the following crimes. The goal should be to give judges sufficient discretion to individualize sentences where the facts so warrant, but to guide that discretion in a manner that eliminates unjustifiable disparities and produces a principled and purposed sentencing regime. How will you strike the right balance?

Crime	*Length of sentence range*	*Justification (retribution, deterrence, incapacitation)*	*Factors that would mitigate and justify a lesser sentence*	*Factors that would aggravate and justify a more severe sentence*	*Services available to the offender while incarcerated*	*Services available to released inmates to facilitate re-entry into society*
First-degree murder						
Second-degree murder						
Voluntary manslaughter						
Involuntary manslaughter						
Assault						
Rape						
Kidnapping						
Robbery						
Burglary						
Fraud						

Note

1 Adam Lamparello was the principal author of this chapter.

References

Adwar, C, (2014, May 28). Here's evidence that insanely long prison terms are a bad way to deter crime. *Business Insider*. Available at https://www.businessinsider.com/report-says-long-sentences-dont-deter-crime-2014-5.

Amnesty International (2009, June 18). *A clear scientific consensus that the death penalty does not deter*. Available at https://www.prisonpolicy.org/scans/famm/Primer.pdf.

Berman, D. A. (1999). A common law for this age of federal sentencing: The opportunity and need for judicial lawmaking: It remains critically important for federal judges to embrace their opportunities to actively cultivate a common law of sentencing. *Stanford Law & Policy Review*, 11, 93–111.

Berman, D. A. (2002). From lawlessness to too much law? Exploring the risk of disparity from differences in defense counsel under guidelines sentencing. *Iowa Law Review*, 87, 443–463.

Bonner, R. & Fessenden, F. (2021, June 7). States with no death penalty share lower homicide rates. *New York Times*. Available at https://deathpenaltyinfo.org/stories/states-with-no-death-penalty-share-lower-homicide-rates.

Brooke-Eisen, L. & Chettiar, I. (2016, December 9). 39% of Prisoners Should Not Be in Prison. *Time Magazine*. Available at https://time.com/4596081/incarceration-report/.

Families Against Mandatory Minimums (n.d.). Mandatory sentencing was once America's law-and-order panacea. Here's why it's not working. Available at https://www.prisonpolicy.org/scans/famm/Primer.pdf.

Frankel, M. E. (1973). *Criminal sentences: Law without order*. New York NY: Hill & Wang Publishing.

Fuchs, E. (2013, April 23). Ten people who received outrageous sentences for drug convictions. *Business Insider*. Available at https://www.businessinsider.com/10-most-outrageous-mandatory-minimum-2013-4.

Goldstein, D. (2015, March 20). Too old to commit crime? Why people age out of crime, and what it could mean for how long we put them away. *The Marshall Project*. Available at https://www.themarshallproject.org/2015/03/20/too-old-to-commit-crime.

Kaeble, D. (2018, November). Time served in state prison, 2016. *United States Department of Justice, Bureau of Statistics*. Available at https://bjs.ojp.gov/content/pub/pdf/tssp16.pdf.

Lamparello, A. (2004). Introducing the "heartland departure." *Harvard Journal of Law & Public Policy*, 27 (2), 643–689. Preprint available at https://papers.ssrn.com/sol3/papers.cfm?abstract_id=2363087.

Miller, B. & Harawa, D. S. (2019, September 3). Why America needs to break its addiction to long prison sentences: Shorter sentences will end prison crowding and even reduce crime. *Politico*. Available at https://www.politico.com/magazine/story/2019/09/03/why-america-needs-to-break-its-addiction-to-long-prison-sentences-227999/.

Reitz, K. R. (1997). Sentencing guideline systems and sentence appeals: A comparison of federal and state experiences. *Northwestern University Law Review*, 91, 1441–1506.

Robinson, P. H. (1997). The federal sentencing guidelines: Ten years later: An introduction and comments. *Northwestern University Law Review*, 91, 1231–1246.

Schulhofer, S. J. & Nagel, I. H. (1997). Plea negotiations under the federal sentencing guidelines: Guidelines circumvention in the post-*Mistretta* period. *Northwestern University Law Review*, 91, 1284–1316.

Security.org (2019, March 14). Crimes and convictions: Examining United States Sentencing Commission federal sentencing statistics. Available at https://www.security.org/resources/crime-sentencing-by-state/.

Stith, K. & Cabranes, J. A. (1998). *Fear of judging: Sentencing guidelines in federal courts*. Chicago IL: University of Chicago Press.

United States Code, title 18, section 3553(b) (18 U.S.C. § 3553(b)) (2020).

United States Department of Health and Human Services ("US-HHS") (2001, December). The psychological impact of incarceration: Implications for post-prison adjustment. Available at https://aspe.hhs.gov/reports/psychological-impact-incarceration-implications-post-prison-adjustment-0.

United States Guidelines Manual ("USG Manual") (2002), ch.1, pt. A, introductory cmt.

United States v. Booker, 543 U.S. 220 (2005).

USG Manual. See United States Guidelines Manual.

US-HHS. See United States Department of Health and Human Services.

8

CAPITAL PUNISHMENT[1]

In the United States, capital punishment is reserved for a narrow category of defendants considered the "worst of the worst," namely, those whose crimes are so heinous that they are deemed deserving of the death penalty. For example, Timothy McVeigh, who bombed a federal building in Oklahoma City, Oklahoma and killed over 160 people, was executed. Likewise, Ted Bundy, who murdered over thirty women, was executed. John Wayne Gacy, who murdered at least thirty-three young boys, was also executed. These individuals can surely be considered the "worst of the worst."

The problem with the death penalty is that often it has not been reserved for the "worst of the worst." Rather, the death penalty has been imposed inconsistently, arbitrarily, and unfairly. In many instances, the likelihood of receiving the death penalty depends not on whether a defendant constitutes "the worst of the worst," but on arbitrary factors such as the state in which the defendant resides, the race of the victim, and the defendant's socioeconomic status. To make matters worse, many defendants who could not possibly be considered "the worst of the worst" have been executed, such as those with severe mental illnesses, brain damage, and intellectual disabilities. As a result, the death penalty is now imposed arbitrarily and unfairly – and there exists no evidence that the death penalty deters crime. But that does not mean that the death penalty should be abolished. Individuals such as Timothy McVeigh, Ted Bundy, and John Wayne Gacy should have been executed, if for no other reason than to express society's moral condemnation at such heinous acts of violence. However, for the death penalty to remain viable, and to ensure that it is imposed consistently and fairly, courts or legislators must establish objective standards to identify precisely what narrow category of defendants constitutes the "worst of the worst." In doing so, the criminal justice system can ensure that the death penalty is reserved for the "worst of the worst" while excluding those, such as severely mentally ill and cognitively impaired defendants, for whom

DOI: 10.4324/9781003163411-11

imposition of the death penalty would be fundamentally unjust and barbaric. Additionally, this approach would ensure that arbitrary things, such as race or socioeconomic status, would not be factors in determining whether the death penalty should be imposed.

Chapter Highlights

- In the United States, the death penalty is reserved for offenders considered the "worst of the worst," who comprise the narrow category of offenders for which capital punishment is warranted.
- Although constitutionally permissible and theoretically justifiable, the death penalty has often been arbitrarily and inconsistently imposed upon individuals who cannot be considered the "worst of the worst."
- For example, individuals with severe mental illnesses, intellectual and cognitive disabilities, and brain damage have been executed, and substantial evidence exists supporting the proposition that innocent individuals have been executed. Additionally, the death penalty has been disproportionately imposed on the basis of race and gender.
- Notwithstanding, there remains a category of offenders whose crimes are so heinous, and the harm caused so nefarious, that they fall into the narrow category of offenders for whom the death penalty is justified, particularly to express society's moral condemnation of such acts.
- The courts, however, have never identified or quantified the factors that place a defendant within this narrow category, thus causing the death penalty to be imposed in an arbitrary and often unjust manner.
- To solve this problem, the death penalty should not remain in its current form, but it should not be abolished. Rather, courts should create objective criteria upon which to determine death-eligibility, and abandon the subjective "aggravating versus mitigating factors" approach that prevails in jurisdictions throughout the United States. Doing so will lead to consistency and fairness in imposing the death penalty, and reserve death for those who are truly the "worst of the worst."
- Retaining the death penalty should not be for deterrence or even retributive purposes, but to express society's collective moral outrage at conduct so heinous that death may be deemed by many as the only acceptable remedy.

Introduction

John and Shannon have been married for ten years. They have an eight-year-old son named Anthony. In the last few years, John has developed an alcohol and drug problem, and frequently comes home late at night and physically abuses Shannon. In fact, on one occasion, Shannon suffered a broken nose and concussion after John, in an alcohol and drug-infused rage, struck her in the face several times. To make matters worse, in the last few months, John has repeatedly raped Shannon and threatened to kill her if she ever informed law enforcement.

One evening, John arrived home from work visibly intoxicated and, upon entering, punched Anthony in the face and told Shannon that he would "deal with her" after taking a shower. After getting out of the shower, Shannon seduced John in their bedroom and, in so doing, tied him to their bed. Once John was tied to the bed, Shannon retrieved a knife from the kitchen and stabbed John over 100 times. Anthony heard John's horrifying screams and ran to the bedroom, where he witnessed Shannon stabbing John violently. After ensuring that John was dead, Shannon attempted to cover up the murder by cleaning the bedroom and burying John in the backyard. Traumatized by what he witnessed, Anthony called the police and told them what Shannon had done. Ultimately, Shannon confessed to the crime.

Should Shannon receive the death penalty? Explain your reasoning and address all relevant counterarguments.

Discussion

In the United States, the death penalty is arguably constitutional. The text of the Fourteenth Amendment to the United States Constitution provides in relevant part that "No state … shall … deprive any person of life, liberty, or property without due process of law" (U.S. Const. amend. XIV). The text unquestionably demonstrates that the Amendment's drafters contemplated and, in fact, countenanced imposition of the death penalty for certain crimes and offenders.

Importantly, the United States Supreme Court has held that the death penalty can – and should – only be imposed on defendants who are considered the "worst of the worst," namely, criminal defendants who comprise a narrow category of offenders and whose crimes are so heinous that the penalty of death is justified (Sarat, 2020). Unfortunately, however, neither the courts nor legislatures have attempted to define precisely who constitutes the "worst of the worst," thus leading to injustices of the most unconstitutional kind.

There are some defendants who can certainly be classified as the "worst of the worst." For example, John Wayne Gacy was an American serial killer who tortured and killed thirty-three young men (Jenkins, 2021). Ted Bundy was an American serial killer who confessed to thirty homicides, most of which consisted of young women (Bonn, 2019). Timothy McVeigh orchestrated the 1995 bombing of a federal building in Oklahoma City that killed 168 people (Janos, 2021). These men received the death penalty and were executed.

Did Gacy, Bundy, and McVeigh deserve the death penalty? Arguably, *yes*.

However, many defendants who could not possibly be considered the "worst of the worst" have been executed. For example, Cecil Clayton, who was convicted of murder but had an IQ of 68, was also executed (DPIC-a, nd.). Likewise, Alfred Bourgeois, who allegedly had an IQ of 75, was executed (Bishop, 2020). In fact, 26% of those executed in the United States had a history of mental illness or were treated with psychiatric medication (Frieden, 2018). Additionally, individuals with brain damage and prior histories of severe childhood abuse and poverty have been executed (Human Rights Watch, 2001).

Did these individuals constitute the "worst of the worst" and thus deserve the death penalty? *No.*

Nonetheless, they were executed because legislatures and courts have never endeavored to create an objective and non-discretionary standard by which to identify what offenses and offenders constitute the "worst of the worst." Due to this failure, the death penalty has been imposed on offenders – including those with low IQs, cognitive impairments, and mental illnesses – who should never have been executed because they could not possibly be considered "the worst of the worst" (Amnesty International, 2017). Put simply, the United States Supreme Court's admonition that the death penalty must be reserved for a narrow category of offenders considered the "worst of the worst" has proven illusory. That, in a nutshell, is the point – and the problem.

The answer, however, is not to categorically abolish the death penalty. After all, many would maintain that the justice system – and society – should retain the right to execute individuals like John Wayne Gacy and Ted Bundy. By the same token, the justice system should relinquish the right to execute those, like Robert Clayton, whose culpability renders a sentence of death arbitrary and unfair.

Thus, rather than viewing the death penalty in black-and-white terms, namely, continuation versus abolition, courts, scholars, and legislatures should embrace a more nuanced approach. In so doing, they should develop a *non-discretionary* list of factors that standardizes the process by which courts in every state identify the "worst of the worst." This paradigm will ensure that the death penalty is truly reserved for the narrow category of offenders constituting the "worst of the worst," and thus imposed fairly consistently, and rarely.

A Troubled History – Failing to Define the "Worst of the Worst" and Arbitrarily Imposing the Death Penalty

Capital punishment has a long and troubled history in the United States. The reason is that, from its inception and continuing until the late twentieth century, the death penalty was arbitrarily, inconsistently, and unfairly applied to those who arguably were not among the "worst of the worst." Indeed, in no state did there exist standards or criteria upon which to determine which defendants constituted the "worst of the worst" and thus were among the narrow category of offenders for whom the death penalty was justified. In fact, the determination regarding death eligibility rested exclusively with prosecutors, whose decisions were guided by little more than their subjective and sometimes discriminatory judgment. To make matters worse, substantial evidence emerged that factors such as the defendant's race and socioeconomic status, along with the race of the victim, influenced the prosecutor's decision about whether to seek the death penalty in a given case. For example, black and poor defendants (of all races), some of whom were intellectually disabled or suffered from mental illness, were more likely to face the death penalty for crimes that were arguably less severe than those of their white counterparts. The most tragic aspect of this standardless system is that the death penalty was imposed on defendants who were innocent.

In the 1970s, the United States Supreme Court recognized that the arbitrariness and unfairness that infused the determination of death eligibility violated the Eighth Amendment to the United States Constitution, which prohibits the imposition of cruel and unusual punishments (*Furman v. Georgia*, 1972). To be sure, although the death penalty, based on the language of the Fourteenth Amendment, is not unconstitutional in *theory*, its arbitrary and unfair imposition rendered it unconstitutional *in fact*. Specifically, in *Furman v. Georgia* (1972), the Court invalidated all death penalty statutes in the United States, holding that states could not impose the death penalty unless and until they implemented policies to eliminate its arbitrary and discriminatory impact.

The states responded by passing statutory schemes that purportedly addressed these concerns. For example, the state of Georgia enacted legislation requiring that a jury or judge weigh specific *aggravating* and *mitigating* factors when making the decision whether to impose the death penalty (*Gregg v. Georgia*, 1976). This approach would, therefore, require jurors or a judge to consider aggravating factors such as the number of victims and whether the defendant tortured a victim, and mitigating factors such a defendant's mental health history, socioeconomic status, and prior history of sexual abuse. The purpose was to identify those defendants who truly constituted the worst of the worst. In *Gregg v. Georgia* (1976), decided four years after *Furman*, the Court upheld Georgia's statutory scheme. The Court held that, as a constitutional matter, the death penalty did not *always* violate the Eighth Amendment (*Gregg v. Georgia*, 1976). Furthermore, the Court held that the death penalty could be imposed in states like Georgia that provided objective criteria to guide and limit the death eligibility decision, that required the jury to consider the defendant's character and prior record, and that provided for meaningful appellate review (*Gregg v. Georgia*, 1976). Thus, the Court permitted executions to resume in all states that complied with these requirements. Shortly thereafter, the states enacted statutes similar to Georgia's that mandated a consideration of aggravating and mitigating factors.

Critically, however, the decision to impose the death penalty remained *discretionary* and *standardless*. Indeed, although state statutes provided for the consideration of aggravating and mitigating factors, there were no standards to guide a jury concerning *how* to quantify or weigh each aggravating or mitigating factor. Many statutes included an exhaustive list of precisely which factors could be considered aggravating or mitigating, thus arguably precluding the consideration of factors that could be relevant to the death eligibility determination. For example, consider the following colloquy between hypothetical jurors:

JUROR NO. 4: The attorney for the defendant said he suffered from depression his whole life, but my son gets depressed sometimes and doesn't kill anyone.

JUROR NO. 1: Also, who cares if the defendant was poor. My best friend grew up in a poor home. She worked hard and obeyed the law. It's no excuse.

JUROR NO. 6: And the defense attorney kept saying how the defendant was sexually abused as a child. Well, I was too but I never thought of killing anyone.

JUROR NO. 10: Right, and since the defendant murdered another person, it's only right for him to die. I'm tired of defendants blaming their crimes on stuff like mental illness or abuse.

Ultimately, the jury votes unanimously to impose the death penalty. The jury's decision would be upheld in every jurisdiction in the United States, despite the fact that the jurors are not experts in determining the impact of mental illness, prior abuse, or socioeconomic status on criminality, and regardless of the fact that the jurors' biases and uninformed assumptions unquestionably influenced their decisions about whether a person should live or die. In essence, the balancing test involving aggravating and mitigating circumstances is more of a superficial cover for the very arbitrariness that *Furman* condemned yet comprises the death eligibility determination that the Court now countenances.

The hypothetical deliberation above underscores the infirmities in the aggravating versus mitigating circumstances approach, and the necessity of a standardized and non-discretionary approach. Justice William Douglas warned in *Furman v. Georgia* (1972), "discretion is pregnant with discrimination" and thus a recipe for subjectivity and arbitrariness.

***

Not surprisingly, after *Gregg,* nothing has changed. Due to the lack of objective criteria, the death penalty continues to be imposed in an arbitrary, discriminatory, and unfair manner. In *Glossip v. Gross* (2015), Justice Stephen Breyer highlighted the infirmities that continued to plague the death penalty's administration, and that rendered its constitutionality dubious (*Glossip v. Gross*, 2015 (Breyer, J., dissenting)).

First, there is substantial evidence that innocent defendants have been executed in the post-*Gregg* era. As Justice Breyer explained:

> [T]he evidence that the death penalty has been wrongly *imposed* (whether or not it was carried out), is striking. As of 2002, this Court used the word "disturbing" to describe the number of instances in which individuals had been sentenced to death but later exonerated. At that time, there was evidence of approximately 60 exonerations in capital cases ... Since 2002, the number of exonerations in capital cases has risen to 115 ... Last year, in 2014, six death row inmates were exonerated based on actual innocence. All had been imprisoned for more than 30 years (and one for almost 40 years) at the time of their exonerations.
>
> *(Glossip v. Gross, 2015 (Breyer, J., dissenting))*

Put simply, "despite the difficulty of investigating the circumstances surrounding an execution for a crime that took place long ago, researchers have found convincing evidence that, in the past three decades, innocent people have been executed" (*Glossip v. Gross*, 2015 (Breyer, J., dissenting)). In fact, as Justice Breyer noted, "researchers estimate that about 4% of those sentenced to death are actually innocent" (*Glossip v. Gross*, 2015 (Breyer, J., dissenting)).

Second, the arbitrariness that characterized the death penalty before *Furman* remained after *Gregg* and the advent of the aggravating versus mitigating factors balancing test. As Justice Breyer stated:

> A recent study ... examined all death penalty sentences imposed between 1973 and 2007 in Connecticut, a State that abolished the death penalty in 2012. The study reviewed treatment of all homicide defendants. It found 205 instances in which Connecticut law made the defendant eligible for a death sentence. Courts imposed a death sentence in 12 of these 205 cases, of which 9 were sustained on appeal. The study then measured the "egregiousness" of the murderer's conduct in those 9 cases, developing a system of metrics designed to do so. It then compared the egregiousness of the conduct of the 9 defendants sentenced to death with the egregiousness of the conduct of defendants in the remaining 196 cases (those in which the defendant, though found guilty of a death-eligible offense, was ultimately not sentenced to death). Application of the studies' metrics made clear that only 1 of those 9 defendants was indeed the "worst of the worst" (or was, at least, within the 15% considered most "egregious"). The remaining eight were not. Their behavior was no worse than the behavior of at least 33 and as many as *170* other defendants (out of a total pool of 205) who had not been sentenced to death.
>
> *(Glossip v. Gross, 2015 (Breyer, J., dissenting))*

Simply put, after *Gregg*, the decision to impose the death penalty remained standardless and, as such, a recipe for arbitrariness. Moreover, such arbitrariness manifested in several ways that are anathema to fairness and justice. For example, as Justice Breyer explained, factors other than the seriousness of the offense, such as race, gender, and geography have materially impacted who receives the death penalty.

Regarding race, "individuals accused of murdering white victims, as opposed to black or other minority victims, are more likely to receive the death penalty" (*Glossip v. Gross*, 2015 (Breyer, J., dissenting)). Table 8.1 demonstrates that the death penalty is imposed most frequently when the victim is white.

Moreover, the death penalty disparately impacts African-Americans, who, despite being only 13% of the population, comprise 34.1% of those executed (DPIC-b, n.d.).

TABLE 8.1 Race of Victims in Death Penalty Cases Since 1976

Race	*Percentage*
White	75.7%
Black	15.2%
Hispanic	6.9%
Other	2.2%

(DPIC-b, n.d.)

Furthermore, many studies "have found that the gender of the defendant or the gender of the victim makes a not-otherwise-warranted difference" (*Glossip v. Gross*, 2015 (Breyer, J., dissenting)). Additionally, the likelihood of receiving the death penalty depends in substantial part on the state and county within which a defendant lives. As Justice Breyer emphasized, "[b]etween 2004 and 2009, for example, just 29 counties (fewer than 1% of counties in the country) accounted for approximately half of all death sentences imposed nationwide" (*Glossip v. Gross*, 2015 (Breyer, J., dissenting)). The explanation for the county-by-county disparity was attributable to the fact that local prosecutors retained almost exclusive authority to determine which defendants were eligible for the death penalty, and that in these counties the public defenders often lacked the resources to effectively represent a defendant (*Glossip v. Gross*, 2015 (Breyer, J., dissenting)). In fact, Table 8.2 demonstrates that, in the United States, many states provide far too few resources to public defenders, thus compromising their ability to effectively represent indigent clients.

Also, the racial composition of particular counties influences the rate at which the death sentence is imposed (*Glossip v. Gross*, 2015 (Breyer, J., dissenting)). Finally, political pressures on judges, particularly in conservative states where some judges are elected and not appointed, increases the likelihood that a defendant will be sentenced to death. In the state of Alabama, for example, studies have shown that elected state judges, faced with electoral pressures, are far less likely to reverse a jury's flawed recommendation of death (*Glossip v. Gross*, 2015 (Breyer, J., dissenting)).

Justice Breyer's dissent – and the facts on which he relies – illustrates that the decision to impose the death penalty often depends on factors that have nothing to do with the severity of the offense or the culpability of the defendant. Rather, factors such as the defendant's race, the race of the victim, and the state within which a defendant lives often determine the likelihood of imposing a death sentence. As Justice Breyer stated:

TABLE 8.2 Per capita spending for public defenders by state

State	*Amount (approximately)*
Alaska	$42
Massachusetts	$27
Oregon	$24
New York	$22
Montana	$18
Indiana	$6
Arkansas	$5
Utah	$4
Missouri	$4
Mississippi	$3

Lee, Levintova, & Brownwell, 2013

> [W]hether one looks at research indicating that irrelevant or improper factors—such as race, gender, local geography, and resources—*do* significantly determine who receives the death penalty, or whether one looks at research indicating that proper factors—such as "egregiousness"—do *not* determine who receives the death penalty, the legal conclusion must be the same: The research strongly suggests that the death penalty is imposed arbitrarily.
>
> *(Glossip v. Gross, 2015 (Breyer, J., dissenting))*

Put simply, although "the constitutionality of capital punishment rests on its limited application to the worst of the worst," the relevant evidence "suggests that it is not so limited" (*Glossip v. Gross*, 2015 (Breyer, J., dissenting)). Accordingly, the Court's attempt after *Gregg* to confine the death penalty to those considered the "worst of the worst" was an abject failure, as the infirmities that attended the death penalty's imposition before *Furman* and *Gregg* remain. That is the problem with the death penalty today – and historically.

Justice Breyer's dissent also demonstrates that the aggravating and mitigating circumstances approach is not sufficient because it can lead to the very arbitrariness and inconsistencies that the Constitution – and basic principles of fairness – strive to avoid. Indeed, when jurors apply this balancing test, there exists a possibility that bias, racism, and other improper factors may influence their calculus.

As such, the many flaws in the death penalty's administration beg the question: should the death penalty be abolished?

The answer to many is *no*.

Why Abolition Is Not Necessarily Advisable

Abolishing the death penalty is not advisable because there are some offenders whose conduct warrants this punishment. Individuals like John Wayne Gacy, Ted Bundy, and Timothy McVeigh, for example, committed crimes so heinous that the death penalty is seen by many as the appropriate sanction to reflect society's collective moral outrage at and condemnation of such crimes. At the same time, there are many offenders who have been executed, such as Robert Clayton and Albert Bourgeois, that did *not* deserve the death penalty, including some who were innocent.

The critical task, therefore, is to define – using objective and non-discretionary factors – precisely what offenders constitute the "worst of the worst," thus excluding all defendants who do not belong in this category due to factors such as mental illness and cognitive impairments, and who are executed due to arbitrary factors such as race, gender, and geographic location. If that task proves unworkable, then the death penalty *should* be abolished.

Consequently, legislatures must create truly objective and non-discretionary criteria that identify with precision the offense and offender characteristics that define a defendant as the "worst of the worst." Most importantly, this criteria cannot be too broad because it will lead to the same subjectivity and arbitrariness that the aggravating and mitigating circumstances paradigm engenders. Rather, the criteria should be sufficiently specific such that there can be no dispute regarding whether they are satisfied in a particular case. For example, factors such as whether a defendant murdered multiple victims, had two more violent felonies, tortured the victim, or murdered a child under the age of twelve, admits of no subjectivity. However, factors such as whether a defendant demonstrated "depraved indifference to human life," or "showed insufficient remorse for the crimes resulting in conviction" invites precisely the arbitrariness that is anathema to fairness and justice.

Defining the "worst of the worst" is extraordinarily difficult because it requires policymakers to identify – and quantify – the factors that qualify or disqualify a defendant from death eligibility. The gravity and permanency of death demands that lawmakers undertake this task to ensure that the death penalty is imposed rarely, consistently, and fairly.

Before endeavoring to develop the criteria by which to identify the "worst of the worst," the abolition argument must be addressed. Many will argue that the inequities and injustices that accompany imposition of the death penalty support its abolition. Furthermore, abolitionists will argue that the death penalty serves none of the purposes of criminal punishment – retribution, deterrence, and rehabilitation. Of course, for obvious reasons, rehabilitation cannot possibly serve as a justification for the death penalty.

Regarding retribution, abolitionists are correct that, in its current form, the death penalty is not truly retributive. The death penalty is applied so inconsistently and arbitrarily – as Justice Breyer's dissent underscores – that whatever retributive principle it vindicates is limited. Furthermore, retribution depends on *proportionality*, that is, a reasoned deliberation concerning whether a punishment is proportionate to a particular crime. This determination is inherently subjective and will vary within and across jurisdictions. In short, what is retributive for one person (or court) will be considered unjust for another person or court. Moreover, except in limited circumstances, identifying a proportional punishment is a futile endeavor. For example, if an abused wife intentionally murders her abusive husband, is the death penalty proportionate simply because she intentionally took another's life? If a sixteen-year old boy who suffers from bi-polar disorder murders several classmates in a school shooting, should he be executed? The answer depends invariably on the subjective moral values of a particular individual, not upon objective and largely agreed-upon moral considerations. For these reasons, proponents cannot argue that the death penalty is truly retributive.

In short, who should die and who should be spared?

The answer most will embrace is that only the "worst of the worst" should die, but the challenge is to identify precisely what defendants fall into this rare category. Developing consistent and fair standards that account for the complexities and nuances in all cases is the only way for the death penalty to remain constitutionally and morally justifiable. Of course, that too relies in part on subjective considerations, but there are certainly factors that, if agreed upon by the majority of policymakers, will eliminate the arbitrariness that characterizes the death penalty and provide the fairness and consistency that its imposition requires. For example, and as discussed in more detail below, most reasonable people would agree that, if a defendant with no history of mental illness or cognitive impairment intentionally murders fifty people and has no remorse whatsoever, the defendant would constitute the "worst of the worst" and thus be death eligible. However, if a defendant with schizophrenia and an IQ of 72 murders two people, many would disagree on whether the death penalty is appropriate. And that is the point. Where reasonable people can disagree, the death penalty should not be imposed. Developing standardized and non-discretionary criteria that garners the support of a majority of policymakers is essential to ensure that we narrow the class of death eligible offenders to those who are truly the "worst of the worst." Otherwise, the death penalty cannot be considered retributive.

Those who claim that such an undertaking is impractical need only refer to the Sentencing Reform Act of 1984 and, concomitantly, the Federal Sentencing Guidelines, which standardized sentencing practice for every federal crime, with the goal of effectuating uniformity and consistency in sentencing. If Congress and the Federal Sentencing Commission can standardize sentencing for every federal crime, they can certainly do so for the death penalty.

Concerning deterrence, empirical evidence suggests strongly that the death penalty does not deter others from committing crimes that may warrant its imposition. In fact, as Table 8.3 demonstrates, the murder rate in *non-death penalty* states is lower than in death penalty states.

Moreover, the inconsistency with which the death penalty is applied, coupled with the fact that it often takes decades to execute an individual who was sentenced to death, suggests that those who commit murder do so without considering the likelihood that they will receive the death penalty.

Given these facts, what possible justification exists to retain the death penalty yet limit its application to only the "worst of the worst?" In certain circumstances, the death penalty reflects *society's collective moral outrage at certain crimes and criminals for acts so heinous that a sentence of death is appropriate to vindicate society's values regarding the sanctity and dignity of human life.* This justification applies to individuals like John Wayne Gacy, who tortured and killed at least *thirty-three* young men. It applies to Ted Bundy, who brutally murdered at least *thirty* women. It applies to Timothy McVeigh, who caused the deaths of *168* people – including children – when he bombed a federal building in Oklahoma City, Oklahoma.

For these reasons, abolition is not advisable *unless* there is no practical way by which to identify the narrow class of offenders who constitute the "worst of the worst" and thus are eligible for the death penalty.

TABLE 8.3 Murder Rates in Death Penalty States Versus Non-Death Penalty States

Year	*1997*	*1998*	*1999*	*2000*	*2001*	*2002*	*2003*
Death Penalty States	7.09	6.54	5.86	5.74	5.83	5.82	5.92
Non-Death Penalty States	4.99	4.63	4.59	4.24	4.23	4.27	4.12

DPIC-c, n.d.

After all, society's collective moral outrage is not vindicated by executing a defendant who, regardless of the offense's severity, is intellectually disabled, cognitively impaired, or schizophrenic. The problem with the death penalty is that it doesn't reliably make these distinctions and, in so doing, executes defendants who cannot be considered the "worst of the worst."

For these reasons, the current approach to identifying death-eligible offenders is also not advisable.

The solution is for Congress to develop a comprehensive, objective, and non-discretionary model that identifies the "worst of the worst," and thus removes the death penalty decision from the subjective predilections of juries and judges. Otherwise, the infirmities identified by Justice Breyer in *Glossip* will remain in perpetuity and indeed justify abolition.

Before turning to the challenge of developing objective and non-discretionary criteria to identify the "worst of the worst," consider the following hypothetical cases and whether you would impose the death penalty on the respective defendants.

Exercises

Below are five hypotheticals involving murder. Identify which, if any, of the defendants constitute the "worst of the worst" and thus fall into the narrow category of defendants who should receive the death penalty. In so doing, consider what factors influenced your decision.

Exercise One

Dylan lives in *Hope, Virginia,* is nineteen years old, and is struggling to cope with the traumatic events that he endured for years as a child. Specifically, for several years, beginning when he was eight years old, Dylan's father Neil physically and sexually abused him, and told Dylan that if he ever told anyone, he would be thrown out of the house. Dylan's mother Maria suspected that Neil was abusing Dylan, but did nothing to protect Neil. Ultimately, the abuse stopped when Neil entered high school. Last year, Neil died after a prolonged struggled with lung cancer.

As a result of the abuse, Dylan suffers from major depression, anxiety, and post-traumatic stress disorder. After Neil's death, Dylan sought counseling and has been seeing a psychologist on a weekly basis. Dylan's progress has been slow, however, as he harbors extraordinary resentment toward Neil and Maria, who is fifty-four years old and lives alone in the home where Dylan was raised.

One evening, while watching the evening news, Neil sees a breaking news story about a thirty year-old male, Steven Ray, who lives in *Hope* and was recently charged with four counts of aggravated sexual assault. Ironically, Steven was one of Neil's best friends, and Dylan had visited Steven's home with Neil and Maria several times during his childhood. Prosecutors allege that Steven repeatedly molested his seven-year-old daughter Melissa. Additionally, prosecutors claim that Steven physically abused Melissa on numerous occasions, which resulted in Melissa being recently hospitalized for a concussion and severe bruising. Notwithstanding, Steven was released on $150,000 bond pending trial.

When Dylan saw the story, it triggered the memories of his childhood and the trauma he suffered. Dylan decided that it was time to exact revenge on the people who preyed on children and committed such heinous acts. Later that evening, Dylan drove to Steven's home armed with a shotgun. He walked up to the front door and rang the bell. When Steven opened the door, Dylan shot him twice in the chest, killing Steven instantly.

Dylan calmly walked back to his car, drove to his childhood home, and knocked on the front door. When Maria answered, Dylan shot her once in the head, also killing her instantly.

Dylan was arrested an hour later and charged with two counts of first-degree murder.

***

Should Dylan receive the death penalty? Explain the basis for your decision, and address all relevant counterarguments.

Exercise Two

Amy is thirty-one years old, married, and the mother of six children. Since childhood, Amy has suffered from severe anxiety and schizophrenia. For the past ten years, Amy has seen a psychiatrist and taken medication for her condition. However, in recent months, Amy's condition has worsened. Her husband Tim, who struggles to support his family financially, is opposed to psychiatric medication and requires Amy to home school their six children. Additionally, Tim has become verbally and, at times, physically abusive.

These circumstances have caused Amy to become very depressed. In recent weeks, she has suffered many panic attacks on a daily basis and, at the urging of her husband, has stopped taking her medication. Shortly thereafter, Amy began to experience hallucinations.

One morning, after Tim had left for work, Amy's condition deteriorated substantially, and she began to believe that God was giving her divine messages. One of those messages told Amy to kill her children and "send them to heaven." Shortly thereafter, Amy strangled her six children while they were sleeping in their beds, believing that it was God's wish. Amy was arrested and charged with six counts of first-degree murder.

***

Should Amy receive the death penalty? Explain the basis for your decision, and address all relevant counterarguments.

Exercise Three

Mike and Sharon are the proud parents of three children – Amanda, who is twelve years old, Brandon, who is eight years old, and Maria, who is two years old.

Recently, while walking home from school, Amanda was kidnapped by two men. While in their custody, Amanda was tortured and repeatedly raped. The two men drove Amanda to a remote area, threw her out of the vehicle, and told her that they would kill her if she ever told anyone about this horrific incident. Amanda suffered serious injuries requiring hospitalization for several weeks. Unfortunately for the two men, a local resident witnessed Amanda's abduction and identified the two men who kidnapped, tortured, and raped Amanda. The men were arrested, charged with kidnapping, aggravated rape, and aggravated assault, and released on $500,000 bail.

Devastated over the trauma that Amanda endured, Mike and Sharon decided to get revenge. One evening, they traveled to the residence where the two men were staying. They broke into the residence and, upon finding the two men sleeping upstairs, beat them both to death with an axe. Before leaving, Mike and Sharon set fire to the residence. They didn't know, however, that three children, aged one, four, and seven, who were the children of one of the two men, were also in the residence. The three children died from smoke inhalation and severe burns.

★★★

Should Mike and Sharon receive the death penalty? Explain the basis for your decision, and address all relevant counterarguments.

Exercise Four

Jason is a pilot with Heavenly Airways, a popular commercial airline that offers services from most cities in the United States to Hawaii. Recently, however, Jason was diagnosed with schizophrenia, a debilitating mental illness that caused Jason to suffer paranoia and hallucinations. Jason did not inform Heavenly Airways about his diagnosis, because he feared losing his job.

On a recent flight from New York to Aruba, Jason suffered hallucinations. Specifically, Jason believed that God was telling him to crash the plane. Thus, when his co-pilot left the cockpit to use the restroom, Jason immediately placed the plane in a nosedive. Ultimately, the plane crashed into the Pacific Ocean, killing 157 out of the 181 passengers. Miraculously, Jason survived, although he suffered severe injuries and is paralyzed from the waist down.

Jason was charged with 157 counts of first-degree murder.

★★★

Should Jason receive the death penalty? Explain the basis for your decision, and address all relevant counterarguments.

Exercise Five

Christopher is a nurse at Mercy Hospital and responsible for caring for patients who are suffering from inoperable cancers. On many days, Christopher experiences tremendous sadness when seeing his patients suffering. Therefore, one day Christopher decided to take action to end the suffering of some of his sickest patients.

Specifically, Christopher injected certain extremely ill patients with a lethal dose of morphine, which caused them to die peacefully. In doing so, Christopher believed that he was relieving these patients of continued suffering and "uniting them with God and their loved ones who have passed."

Christopher continued this behavior for several years, during which time over forty patients died from morphine overdose. Eventually, based on the patients' autopsy results, and the fact that Christopher was the patients' primary care nurse and responsible for administering morphine, investigators suspected that Christopher may be responsible for their deaths. Upon questioning, Christopher admitted to "ending their suffering" so that they would not "endure any more pain."

Christopher is charged with forty counts of first-degree murder.

***

Should Christopher receive the death penalty? Explain the basis for your decision, and address all relevant counterarguments.

Solutions

Implement a moratorium immediately to address the social and racial inequities that the death penalty's administration causes

Currently, as Justice Breyer discussed in *Glossip v. Gross,* the death penalty is administered in an unfair and unjust manner. The decision to seek and impose the death penalty often depends on arbitrary factors such as the defendant's race and socioeconomic status, the victim's race, and the state in which the defendant resided. The result is that the death penalty is not imposed consistently and fairly. For that reason, a moratorium should be imposed on the death penalty until standards are developed to address these inequities.

Develop detailed and workable criteria to identify the "worst of the worst"

To ensure that the death penalty is applied consistently and fairly, federal and state legislators should develop detailed and workable criteria by which to identify the narrow class of offenders whose crimes are so heinous that the death penalty is warranted. In so doing, legislators must recognize that it is not even remotely sufficient to create broadly worded criteria to guide the determination of which defendants constitute the "worst of the worst." The result of such an approach would be to give judges and juries far too much discretion to interpret and define the relevant criteria in a manner that reflects their subjective policy preferences and pre-existing biases. In essence, a broad standard is no standard at all. It is a recipe for arbitrariness and injustice of the most unconstitutional kind. If the death penalty is to pass constitutional muster, the criteria for identifying the "worst of the worst" must be specific. The criteria must meaningfully differentiate the "worst of the worst" from other offenders, particularly concerning moral culpability. And the criteria must eliminate the possibility that impermissible factors such as race, ethnicity, sex, religion, and socioeconomic status, will influence the death eligibility determination.

***

You were recently appointed to the United States Capital Sentencing Commission to develop the criteria upon which to identify the "worst of the worst" offenders and thus ensure that the death penalty is consistently and fairly applied. In so doing, you must consider, among other things, the severity of the crime, the personal history and characteristics of the defendant (e.g., mental illness, personality disorders, intellectual disability), and the extent to which imposition of the death penalty furthers a legitimate purpose of punishment. Most importantly, you must *quantify* or, at the very least, *specify* the weight that should be afforded to each offender characteristic when determining death eligibility.

Below are tables to assist you in determining which defendants constitute the "worst of the worst." Use these tables and any other information to create a comprehensive solution that ensures fairness and due process in the administration of the death penalty. The tables provide a few examples of offense and offender characteristics that should be considered, but you are responsible for inputting additional offense and offender characteristics that you deem relevant to identifying the "worst of the worst."

Offense	*Death-eligible (Yes/no)*
First-degree murder (one victim)	
Rape	

Offense characteristics	*Death Eligible (Yes/No)*	*Death Ineligible (Yes/No)*
Torture of the victim		
Age of the victim		
Race of the victim		

Offender characteristics (in addition to the crime of conviction)	*Death Eligible (Yes/No)*	*Death Ineligible (Yes/No)*
Prior violent felony		
IQ under 80		
Mental illness – schizophrenia		
Mental illness – depression, bipolar disorder, post-traumatic stress disorder, anxiety		
Prior physical or sexual abuse		

Note

1 Adam Lamparello was the principal author of this chapter.

References

Amnesty International (2017, May 18). *Death penalty and mental illness*. Available at https://www.amnestyusa.org/issues/death-penalty/death-penalty-facts/death-penalty-and-mental-illness/.

Bishop, W. (2020, December 12). Justices permit execution of Alfred Bourgeois to proceed. *Legal Torts*. Available at https://thelegaltorts.com/justices-permit-execution-of-alfred-bourgeois-to-proceed/.

Bonn, S. A. (2019, December 30). Examining serial killer Ted Bundy. *Psychology Today*. Available at https://www.psychologytoday.com/us/blog/wicked-deeds/201912/examining-serial-killer-ted-bundy.

Death Penalty Information Center ("DPIC-a") (n.d.). Mentally ill prisoners who were executed. Available at https://deathpenaltyinfo.org/policy-issues/mental-illness/mentally-ill-prisoners-who-were-executed.

Death Penalty Information Center ("DPIC-b") (n.d.). Executions by race and race of victim. Available at https://deathpenaltyinfo.org/executions/executions-overview/executions-by-race-and-race-of-victim.

Death Penalty Information Center ("DPIC-c") (n.d.). Murder rate of death penalty states compared to non-death penalty states. Available at https://deathpenaltyinfo.org/facts-and-research/murder-rates/murder-rate-of-death-penalty-states-compared-to-non-death-penalty-states.

DPIC. See Death Penalty Information Center.

Frieden, J. (2018, October 28). Some prisoners executed despite mental illness diagnosis. *MedPage Today*. Available at https://www.medpagetoday.com/meetingcoverage/aapl/75973.

Furman v. Georgia, 408 U.S. 238 (1972).

Glossip v. Gross, 135 S. Ct. 2726 (2015).

Gregg v. Georgia, 428 U.S. 153 (1976).

Human Rights Watch (2001, March 5). *Beyond reason: The death penalty and offenders with mental retardation*. Available at https://www.hrw.org/report/2001/03/05/beyond-reason/death-penalty-and-offenders-mental-retardation.

Janos, A. (2021, June 9). Timothy McVeigh's death: The final days of the Oklahoma City bomber. *Arts & Entertainment (A&E) TV*. https://www.aetv.com/real-crime/timothy-mcveigh-death.

Jenkins, J. P. (2021, May 6). John Wayne Gacy. *Brittanica.com*. Available at https://www.britannica.com/biography/John-Wayne-Gacy.

Lee, J., Levintova, H., & Brownwell, B. (2013, July 1). Charts: Why you're in deep trouble if you can't afford a lawyer. *Mother Jones*. Available at https://www.motherjones.com/politics/2013/05/public-defenders-gideon-supreme-court-charts/.

Sarat, A. (2020, June 9). The illusory quest to only execute the "worst of the worst." *Verdict: Legal Analysis and Commentary from Justia*. Available at https://verdict.justia.com/2020/06/09/the-illusory-quest-to-execute-only-the-worst-of-the-worst.

9

MASS INCARCERATION AND PRISON PRIVATIZATION[1]

The term "mass incarceration" is misleading and ideologically driven. The fact is that incarceration – for lengthy periods or life in some instances – is the appropriate penalty for crimes such as murder, rape, and other violent crimes. In fact, over 70% of incarcerated persons have been convicted of violent crimes and should be incarcerated. Nonetheless, serious problems plague the United States' carceral policy. First, individuals are often treated inhumanely while incarcerated. For example, in the United States, incarceration is intended primarily to punish and incapacitate – not to rehabilitate and re-socialize. As a result, incarcerated persons often spend years in an isolated prison environment, faced with inhumane conditions, deprived of social interaction, and without opportunities to receive meaningful educational and social support services. To make matters worse, many incarcerated persons, particularly those who are elderly and mentally ill, are at high risk for physical and sexual assault by other inmates. The result is that many incarcerated persons are released from prison in a physically and psychologically compromised state, with their prospects for successfully reintegrating into society minimal and their likelihood of reoffending quite high. Second, for many defendants, incarceration is neither a principled nor a just response to the crime for which they were convicted. For example, defendants convicted of minor drug offenses would benefit from rehabilitation-based sentences that are designed to address their underlying addictions and thus maximize their likelihood of achieving economic and social stability upon release. Third, sentences for some crimes, such as drug possession, theft, burglary, and other property crimes, are simply too long. Fourth, federal and state prisons do not provide sufficient re-entry programs to facilitate offenders' transition into society, the result of which is a high rate of recidivism.

The problem with private prisons is that they perpetuate the same problems that characterize government-run prisons: they often subject inmates to inhumane conditions, present minimal opportunities for rehabilitation and re-socialization,

DOI: 10.4324/9781003163411-12

and place inmates at high risk for abuse by other prisoners. The result is the same: inmates are released with little, if any support, in the re-entry process and frequently fail to achieve economic and social stability upon release. As such, the recidivism rate remains high and public safety is threatened.

For these reasons, the United States should rethink four issues: who should be incarcerated, how long we should incarcerate, what we should prioritize during incarceration (e.g., whether incarceration should be rehabilitative rather than retributive), and how we can successfully support incarcerated persons upon release to minimize their likelihood of reoffending. To do so, the United States should consider the rehabilitation-based approaches other countries pursue because these approaches reduce crime and recidivism rates, and thus protect public safety more effectively. The result would be a more comprehensive and efficacious carceral policy that punishes where appropriate, that rehabilitates when justified, and that prioritizes protection of the public.

Chapter Highlights

- The term "mass incarceration" is somewhat misleading; although the United States leads the world in the number of citizens incarcerated per capita, a substantial portion of prisoners are incarcerated for violent crimes, and *should be* in prison.
- Private prisons create a marketplace for crime that incentivizes private prison officials to advocate for, and courts to impose, lengthy prison terms to keep such prisons operating at full capacity.
- Private prisons continue to emphasize retribution and incapacitation over rehabilitation and resocialization, despite evidence that this approach is ineffective and leads to higher recidivism rates.
- The conditions in some private prisons are deplorable, subject inmates to an inhumane and unsafe environment, and fail to provide rehabilitative services that increase the likelihood of successful reintegration into society upon release.
- Legislators should not focus solely on *whether* to incarcerate individuals for certain crimes; rather, they should focus on *how* the criminal justice system incarcerates, consider alternative models of incarceration, and reduce the length of incarceration because many sentences are too long.

Introduction

Brian Sheldon and his wife, Amy, have spent the last year struggling to help their twenty-seven-year-old daughter Meredith, who is a graduate of a prestigious university in California, and who had dreamed of attending law school and becoming a criminal defense lawyer. On the evening after Meredith's graduation ceremony, she attended, along with her parents, a graduation party that was hosted by her sorority at a well-known restaurant in the downtown Los Angeles area. At the party, Meredith consumed several glasses of wine and two shots of tequila while celebrating with her friends and family.

The party ended at approximately 1:00 a.m., and Meredith agreed that she would drive to the hotel where her parents were staying and say goodbye to them before they returned home to New Jersey. Sadly, on the way to the hotel, Meredith accidentally drove through a stop sign at an intersection and struck a vehicle that was passing through the intersection. Meredith's car struck the driver's side door at approximately thirty-eight miles per hour. After the collision, Meredith immediately called for emergency assistance and law enforcement officers, along with paramedics, arrived within minutes. Tragically, the driver of the car that Meredith hit, a seventy-five-year-old woman who was driving home from her sister's birthday party, was severely injured and died at a hospital in Los Angeles four days later.

Law enforcement officers immediately smelled alcohol on Meredith's breath and administered a breathalyzer test, which revealed a blood alcohol level of .09, which was above the legal limit of .08. Meredith was arrested for driving while intoxicated and, after the passenger died, Meredith was charged with criminally negligent homicide.

Meredith and her parents were devastated. Her parents hired a well-known criminal defense attorney who negotiated a plea bargain whereby Meredith would plead guilty to involuntary manslaughter in exchange for a sentence of one year in prison. At the sentencing hearing, however, the judge rejected the plea bargain. Distraught and remorseful, Meredith told her attorney that wanted to plead guilty and to "get this over with" and "hope that the judge understands that I never intended to hurt anyone." Although Meredith's attorney objected and argued that he could negotiate a new deal with the prosecutor, Meredith insisted.

Thus, two weeks later Meredith plead guilty and expressed her sincere remorse to the victim's family and to the judge. However, the judge was not moved by Meredith's statement. Citing an increase in alcohol-related driving death over the past two years, the judge sentenced Meredith to five years' imprisonment, which was the maximum sentence allowed under state law.

Meredith spent the next five years in prison, where she was sexually assaulted twice by a prison guard, attacked by one of the inmates, and allowed only one hour of recreation time each day. During this time, Meredith suffered from severe depression, anxiety, and post-traumatic stress disorder. After her release, Meredith's parents retained a psychiatrist to treat Meredith and supported her in every way possible.

However, Meredith soon realized that her life was ruined. She applied to ten law schools, hoping that she would receive a second chance to live the life she had always dreamed. Every law school rejected Meredith. Sher also applied for numerous jobs in her community, hoping that one employer would give her a second chance. Every employer rejected her application.

Alone and hopeless, Meredith committed suicide by hanging herself in the backyard of her parents' home. Amy discovered Meredith in the backyard when she was returning home from work. Upon seeing Meredith's body, Amy ran inside, grabbed a knife, and slit her wrists.

Brian arrived home an hour later to discover his wife and daughter dead. At that moment, Brian wanted to die.

Over the next two years, after receiving intensive therapy, Brian was able to begin moving on with his life, although her remained in a fragile mental state. One evening, however, Brian had an idea: the best way to honor Meredith and Amy was to advocate for change in the criminal justice system. Brian decided to run for Congress, and his personal story captured the sympathy and admiration of voters.

Brian was elected in a landslide.

A week after the election, Brian hired you to be his policy advisor on criminal justice reform. Brian told you that the one thing he wanted to do as a congressman was to ensure that no one would ever experience the suffering that he endured when Meredith and Amy died. He directs you to propose reforms to the criminal justice system, particularly concerning how we sentence criminal offenders, how we treat offenders while incarcerated, and how we can help offenders successfully reintegrate into society upon release.

What reforms would you propose? Why? In developing this proposal, be sure to address all relevant counterarguments.

Discussion

The term "mass incarceration" is misleading because the majority of incarcerated persons have been convicted of violent crimes and other offenses that threaten public safety.

Admittedly, as the statistics below demonstrate, the United States leads the world in the number of citizens incarcerated per capita.

However, the idea that the United States is incarcerating individuals needlessly and unjustifiably is somewhat misleading. As Table 9.2 reveals, a substantial portion of offenders are incarcerated in state prisons for violent and property crimes.

TABLE 9.1 Rates of Incarceration per 100,000

Country	*Rate per 100,000*
United States	639
El Salvador	566
Turkmenistan	552
Thailand	549
Palau	522
Rwanda	511
Cuba	510
Maldives	499
Bahamas	442
Grenada	429

World Population Review, n.d.

TABLE 9.2 Number of Incarcerated Persons in State Prisons for Specific Crimes (Prison Policy Initiative, n.d.)

Crime	*Number of Incarcerated Persons*
Murder	183,000
Manslaughter	17,000
Rape/Sexual Assault	165,000
Robbery	169,000
Assault	136,000
Other Violent Crimes	42,000
Burglary	122,000
Theft	44,000
Car Theft	10,000
Other Property Crimes	25,000
Fraud	26,000
Drug Possession	45,000
Other drug offenses	145,000
Driving Under the Influence	25,000
Other Public Order Offenses	74,000
Weapons Offenses	55,000
Other Offenses	8,000

Prison Policy Initiative, n.d.

Indeed, of the approximately 1,291,000 individuals housed in state prisons, 73% – nearly three-fourths – of inmates housed in state prisons are serving sentences for violent and property-related crimes. Furthermore, the vast majority of drug offenders who are imprisoned for drug-related offenses have been convicted of manufacturing or distributing drugs, not mere possession (U.S. Department of Justice, Bureau of Justice Statistics, *Drug Offenders in Federal Prison: Estimates of Characteristics Based on Linked Data* (Oct. 2015), available at: Drug Offenders in Federal Prison: Estimates of Characteristics Based on Linked Data (ojp.gov)).

There can be little doubt that for these individuals, incarceration is, in most instances, necessary to protect public safety and express society's condemnation of deplorable conduct that often causes irreparable harm. Thus, although reforms to sentencing and carceral policies are necessary, the term "mass incarceration" is somewhat misleading because in a significant portion of cases, incarceration is justified.

Notwithstanding, in some instances, both the decisions to incarcerate and the length of incarceration are both unjust and draconian. They lead to terrible outcomes for prisoners and often fail to serve any societal goal, such as protecting public safety or reducing recidivism rates. Private prisons are responsible for continually supporting an incarceration-based approach to criminal punishment, even where alternative sanctions would more effectively rehabilitate an offender and decrease recidivism rates, thus protecting public safety.

Private Prisons Create a Marketplace for Crime and Emphasize Incarceration as the Primary Mode of Criminal Punishment

Private prison corporations, such as the Corrections Corporations of America, have existed for decades and promote incarceration as the primary method by which to punish criminal offenders. That should not be a surprise. Private prisons are corporations, and their motive is to maximize profits, which only occurs when private prisons are near full capacity.

> Private prison company directors, managers, and their lobbyists currently work doggedly to increase profits by: (1) influencing carceral policy so that greater numbers of Americans face incarceration; (2) exploiting those imprisoned through private prison labor contracts; (3) lobbying government officials tirelessly to privatize entire state and federal prison systems; (4) reducing the quality of food and degree of safety for prisoners to cut costs at privately run facilities; (5) drafting legislation and lobbying for passage of draconian sentencing policies including mandatory minimums, three-strikes, and illegal immigration legislation; (6) bribing judges and government officials to fill private prison facilities with children on dubious charges; (7) requiring governments that contract for their services to maintain capacity in the private prisons at ninety percent or risk breach of contract and higher per diem fees; and (8) building new prison facilities despite no government contract or ready prisoners to fill them.
>
> *(Cummings & Lamparello, 2016, p. 414)*

Put simply, "the perverse and immoral incentives underlying the private prison industry translate into a demand for more prisons and prisoners" (Cummings & Lamparello, 2016, p. 415).

Indeed, a private prison corporation's ability to profit from its contracts with state and federal government officials depends on maximizing the number of prisoners in its facility.

> Although private prison corporations claim to save money for local governments by attempting to win prison contracts, the fundamental basis upon which private prison companies receive income is through contracts with municipal, state, and federal governments that promise payment of taxpayer funds to the private prison companies in exchange for warehousing the government's criminals in either privately-owned facilities or government-owned facilities. This transfer of taxpayer funds to corporate coffers is based on a per diem rate where governments contractually owe private prisons a certain fee per bed or per prisoner Thus, the greater the number of prisoners, the greater the payout from taxpayers to corporate coffers.
>
> *(Cummings & Lamparello, 2016, pp. 415–416)*

In fact, in most contracts with private prisons, states are required to ensure that private prisons remain at nearly full capacity, with ninety percent of prison beds occupied (Cummings & Lamparello, 2016, p. 429). As such, "the state is obligated to keep prisons almost full at all times or pay for the beds anyway, so the incentive is to incarcerate more people and for longer in order to fill the quota" (Cummings & Lamparello, 2016, p. 429).

Predictably, to maximize profits, "[n]early all for-profit corporations engage in activities to influence policymaking in their favor by paying lobbyists, providing campaign contributions, and supporting election campaigns of those legislators" who are "tough on crime" and supportive of incarceration as the primary sanction for criminal offenders (Cummings & Lamparello, 2016, pp. 416–417). To be sure, "the private prison regime and its lobby have literally fanned the flames of the War on Drugs, convincing Congress to repeatedly adopt more draconian sentencing policies for even the most minor of drug offenses" (Cummings & Lamparello, 2016, p. 417).

Ultimately, "profit maximization incentives underlying private prisons have proven too perverse and injurious to the basic civil rights of inmates," and further a carceral policy that has proved ineffective in reducing or deterring crime (Cummings & Lamparello, 2016, pp. 417–418).

Private Prisons Often Subject Prisoners to Deplorable and Dangerous Conditions

To maximize profits, private prison officials reduce costs as much as possible, which has the effect of creating deplorable and dangerous prison environments. Private prisons operate in a market economy where maximizing profits is vital to sustainability and thus a driving factor in corporate decision-making (Cummings & Lamparello, 2016, p. 420). This approach undeniably compromises the rights and safety of inmates that are housed in private prisons.

> The cost-cutting focus of private corporations translates to reduced staffing levels, reduced investment in training of prison guards, increased ratios of inmates to correctional officers, and lower wages for private correctional officers. Low pay, poor training, and high turnover may contribute to higher levels of violence in the private sector prisons. This may in turn encourage private prison employees to violate prisoners' rights – rights that would be better safeguarded if government employees in government-run facilities guarded the prisoners. This is the predicament of the privately housed federal prisoner.
>
> *(Cummings & Lamparello, 2016, p. 421)*

Indeed, the cost-cutting measures and profit maximation motives underlying private prisons have subjected prisoners to intolerable abuse and harm. For example, one study of a private prison operated by the Correction Corporation of America in Youngstown, Ohio revealed the following:

> CCA [Corrections Corporation of America] managers employed brutal policies [,] … engaged in excessive use of force against prisoners, failed to maintain control over weapons, and failed to implement numerous security procedures. As a result, there were two homicides, numerous stabbings, extreme levels of violence, and six escapes within the first 14 months.
>
> *(Cummings & Lamparello, 2016, pp. 425–426)*

In fact, the rates of violence in private prisons are higher than in government-run prisons.

> When comparing for-profit prisons with public, a nationwide study found that assaults on guards by inmates were [forty-nine percent] more frequent in private prisons than in government-run prisons. The same study revealed that assaults on fellow inmates were [sixty-five percent]more frequent in for-profit/private prisons. Another study concluded that, "Privately operated prisons appear to have systemic problems in maintaining secure facilities" concluding that for-profit/private prisons have significantly more escapes, homicides, assaults, and drug abuse compared to government-run prisons.
>
> *(Cummings & Lamparello, 2016, pp. 426–427)*

Similarly, "a study in Mississippi found that 'privately run prisons in the state had assault rates three to five times higher than the public facilities'" (Cummings & Lamparello, 2016, p. 426; Thompson, 2014).

Furthermore, some inmates in private prisons are subject to deplorable and dangerous conditions. Indeed, the American Civil Liberties Union conducted a study of one private prison and concluded as follows:

> At Reeves County Detention Center in late 2008 and early 2009, after a prisoner died from inadequate medical care, prisoners organized uprisings that got so out of control they ended with prisoners setting fire to the facility. Then, in the summer of 2013, prisoners started a petition to protest crowded conditions, bad food, and lack of medical care. When prison staff learned of the petition, they reportedly sought out the protest organizers, tear-gassed their dormitories, shot at them with rubber bullets, and then locked in isolation cells both the organizers and bystanders who objected to being tear-gassed.
>
> *(Cummings & Lamparello, 2016, p. 428; American Civil Liberties Union, n.d.)*

Also, a class action lawsuit against a privately run youth correctional facility asserted that "children there are forced to live in barbaric and unconstitutional conditions and are subjected to excessive uses of force by prison staff" (Cummings & Lamparello, 2016, p. 428).

The evidence regarding private prisons portrays a troubling and unjust picture: inmates are often incarcerated under deplorable conditions and with minimal rehabilitative or educational services, and at risk for abuse by correctional officials or other inmates. What purpose does this serve? None.

Legislators Should Support an Approach to Incarceration that Is Conducive to Rehabilitation and that Is Likely to Reduce Recidivism

Prison and lengthy terms of incarceration are sometimes appropriate for particular crimes. In the United States, however, the problem runs far deeper, and casts doubt on the wisdom of a criminal justice system that incarcerates for nearly all criminal offenses yet achieves little progress in reforming offenders or reducing recidivism. As the Vera Institute of Justice reported:

> The U.S. prison population has increased 700 percent in the last 40 years, and state corrections expenditures reached $53.5 billion in 2012. Despite this massive investment in incarceration, the national recidivism rate remains at a stubborn 40 percent—meaning that four in 10 incarcerated people will return to prison within three years of release.
>
> *(Vera Institute of Justice, 2013)*

As such, the need for substantive and principled reforms is obvious. Among these reforms, legislators should consider alternatives to incarceration, address the length of sentencing that often appears far too draconian, and focus on crime prevention efforts through community-based programs.

At the very least, legislators should reform prisons to focus on rehabilitation and successful reintegration into society upon release. Examining the practices of other countries can provide a perspective that can inform reformation efforts in the United States. For example, Germany and the Netherlands are "organized around central tenets of resocialization and rehabilitation," with a focus on "normalization" that strives to make "life in prison as similar as possible to life in the community" (Vera Institute of Justice, 2013). Thus, prisoners are not kept behind bars in crowded prisons and substandard living environments. Rather, prisons are apartment-style buildings (York, 2019). Germany's approach to incarceration differs substantially from the United States. As one commentator explains:

> The American prison system is looked upon by many countries as punitive punishment. The German prison system is rehabilitative-centered. Human dignity is very important to Germans. In Germany, correctional officers and prison management are required to help the inmates better themselves. Specific rules state the prison sentence is the punishment and the inmates will not have bad housing or bad treatment.
>
> *(York, 2019)*

Perhaps most importantly, Germany's approach results in substantially lower incarceration rates (Vera Institute of Justice, 2013).

When considering relevant reforms, legislators should consider the efficacy of Germany's and other countries' carceral policies. After all, the goal of criminal punishment should not simply be to punish. For many offenders, criminal penalties should incorporate rehabilitative and educational aspects because the majority of offenders will be released from prison. The goal, therefore, should be to maximize the likelihood that offenders will achieve financial and social stability upon release and thus have no incentive to commit additional offenses. This approach will likely reduce recidivism, protect public safety, and create a more principled criminal justice system.

Exercises

Read the following five exercises and consider the sentence you would impose on the defendants in each exercise. In so doing, explain whether, and to what extent, your sentence, including the length of the sentence and services available to the offender while confined, furthers one or more of the purposes of criminal punishment, and serves important societal goals. Additionally, consider whether a sentence other than incarceration may be appropriate. In so doing, be creative. Think outside the box.

Exercise One

Jimmy Harrison was raised in New Jersey and has struggled with significant adversity in his life. When Jimmy was nine years old, his father died from cancer, forcing his mother to raise Jimmy while working three jobs to support them and afford the rent in their small apartment. Despite this adversity, Jimmy performed extremely well in school, and in high school Jimmy obtained a perfect grade point average and graduated first in his class while also working a part-time job as a server at a local restaurant.

Jimmy was accepted to Princeton University, which is one of the most prestigious universities in the world. The only problem was that Jimmy could not afford to attend Princeton. Although Jimmy applied for educational loans from the federal government, they were not sufficient to cover the high cost of tuition. Jimmy was incredibly disappointed that he would not be able to attend Princeton, particularly because he had overcome so much adversity and worked so hard to gain acceptance to the prestigious university and to pursue his dream of becoming a doctor.

However, one of Jimmy's friends, Jason Wilkins, had an idea. Jason's family was poor, and he had lived most of his life in a low-income neighborhood. Yet, Jason had secretly saved nearly $50,000 because he began selling illegal drugs, including cocaine and heroin, a few years earlier. Jason told Jimmy that he could "help him get started" and promised Jason that he would "make a ton of money and be able to easily pay for college." At first, Jason hesitated, believing that it was wrong to sell drugs and that the risk of getting caught was too high, but when Jason thought of the possibility that he would be unable to attend Princeton, he decided that selling drugs was worth it if it meant being able to pursue his education.

During the summer before Jimmy was to begin his freshman year at Princeton, he sold a large amount of drugs and, coupled with his loans, he was able to pay the tuition for the first semester. Thus, Jimmy began his studies at Princeton, although he knew that, to continue at Princeton, he would have to keep selling drugs to afford the tuition. Jimmy's continued doing so for the next year and was able to remain at Princeton, where he received extremely high grades and was well-respected by the students and professors. However, just before the end of his second year at Princeton, Jimmy was arrested by an undercover officer to whom he attempted to sell a large amount of cocaine.

Jimmy was devastated. His mother was shocked and angry.

Jimmy was charged with the possession of and intent to distribute cocaine. If convicted, Jimmy faced a substantial term of imprisonment. Upon his conviction, Princeton would almost certainly expel Jimmy and his dream of becoming a doctor would be unattainable.

What sentence would you impose on Jimmy? Explain how your sentence furthers one or more of the purposes of criminal punishment, and identify the factors, aggravating and mitigating, that influenced your chosen sentence. Also, consider whether an alternative sentence would be appropriate.

Exercise Two

Scott Blakely recently moved to Recovery, Massachusetts to begin a new life. For the past fifteen years, Scot had lived in his hometown of Pleasant, Pennsylvania working as a gym teacher at Pleasant High School. Scott disliked his job and lamented the fact that he never pursued his dreams in life, one of which was to become a clinical psychologist, as Scott was passionate about helping people and making a difference in the world. Unfortunately, Scott was never a good student and failed out of college after the first year. Thus, Scott lacked the credentials to be admitted into a graduate program in psychology.

Notwithstanding, when Scott moved to Recovery, Massachusetts, he was determined to live out his dream. Using nearly all of the money he had saved over the past fifteen years, Scott rented a modest office space in downtown Recovery and represented to the community that he was an experienced clinical psychologist.

Within a week, Scott saw his first patient, and, over the next few months, Scott gained an excellent reputation as a caring and effective psychologist. As such, many of Recovery's residents sought Scott's services and, after six months, Scott had over thirty clients. His clients, who shared extremely personal information about their lives during their counseling sessions, uniformly commended Scott for his authenticity and unique approach to treatment, which involved forcing every patient to develop their own treatment plan through intensive introspection and increased self-awareness. Scott's clients viewed his approach as empowering and instilling a sense of personal responsibility and accountability to their lives. Indeed, many clients claimed that Scott had helped them to overcome the adversity they were facing and lead happier lives. In so doing, Scott had finally achieved his dream of making a meaningful difference in the lives of other people.

Scott's career, however, was about to end abruptly.

Another psychologist in town, Arthur Middleton, was suspicious of Scott's rapid rise to success in Recovery, and bothered by the fact that he had lost many clients who decided to seek Scott's services. Arthur decided to research Scott online to confirm that he was a properly educated and credentialed psychologist. Upon doing so, Arthur discovered Scott's picture and biography on Pleasant High School's website, which administrators at the high school had inadvertently failed to remove. The biography stated that Scott graduated from Pleasant High School and attended Pleasant Community College for one year before deciding to pursue a career as a gym teacher.

Stunned and concerned for the welfare of Recovery's residents, Arthur reported Scott to the Recovery Police. After a brief investigation, Scott was arrested and charged with fraudulently impersonating a mental health services professional. Scott pled guilty shortly thereafter.

***

What sentence would you impose on Scott? Explain how your sentence furthers one or more of the purposes of criminal punishment, and identify the factors, aggravating and mitigating, that influenced your chosen sentence. Also, consider whether an alternative sentence would be appropriate.

Exercise Three

Victoria is an extremely talented college student at a top-ranked university. She majors in English and Music, and is already a nationally known concert pianist and a published poet. Victoria has obtained a perfect 4.0 grade-point average and plans to enroll in law school when she graduates. She is also in a relationship with her high school sweetheart Brian, who attends the same university. They plan to get married when they graduate next year.

Unfortunately, Victoria also suffers from schizophrenia, with which she was diagnosed when she was a child. Victoria has taken a prescription medication for years that has successfully mitigated the effects of her condition, although the medication has often led to somewhat severe side effects, such as insomnia and tardive dyskinesia, which affects the nervous system and causes involuntary movements, such as facial grimacing.

Striving to eliminate these embarrassing and debilitating side effects, Victoria decided to stop taking her medication, believing that she had successfully overcome schizophrenia and could live normally without her medication.

Approximately six weeks after stopping her medication, Victoria began to experience hallucinations and symptoms consistent with paranoia. As her condition deteriorated, Victoria began to hear voices telling her that Brian had met another woman and intended to kill Victoria to "get her out of the picture." In a state of panic, and believing that she was in mortal danger, Victoria purchased a gun and shot Brian while he was sleeping, killing him instantly.

Victoria was arrested, charged with first-degree murder, and convicted. After the trial a few of the jurors explained that Victoria's mental illness had no effect on their deliberations.

What sentence would you impose on Victoria? Explain how your sentence furthers one or more of the purposes of criminal punishment, and identify the factors, aggravating and mitigating, that influenced your chosen sentence. Also, consider whether an alternative sentence would be appropriate.

Exercise Four

Bobby Delaney lives in Twilight, South Carolina and owns a three-bedroom house on approximately two acres of land. For the past ten years, Bobby has taught English and Social Studies at Twilight High School, and he is also the head coach of Twilight High School's football team.

However, on the weekends, Bobby devotes his time to activity that would shock both students and administrators at Twilight High School: he operates a dogfighting ring. This activity violates the law in Twilight, South Carolina, which imposes criminal penalties for dogfighting and expressly prohibits any activity that involves the "maiming, mutilation, or torture of animals." The statute also authorizes increased penalties if an animal's death results from such conduct.

Every Saturday night, Bobby holds dogfights on his property, which often attract between fifty and seventy-five people. At these events, two dogs fight each other, with the winner declared only after one of the dogs dies. Bobby has been operating the dogfighting ring for nearly two years, during which time over 200 dogs have died. Additionally, Bobby has personally tortured and killed twenty dogs that were unable to perform due to malnourishment.

At Bobby's last dogfighting event, immediately before two of Bobby's dogs began to fight, a spectator threw an empty bottle of beer at one of the dogs, striking it in the side of the head. The dog became enraged and attacked the spectator, inflicting a deep wound that severed the spectator's carotid artery. The spectator died within minutes. Law enforcement officers arrived shortly thereafter and, upon discovering the dogfighting event, arrested Bobby. A few weeks later, Bobby pled guilty to operating an illegal dogfighting ring and admitted that over 200 dogs had died during the past two years, and that he personally had killed twenty dogs that were unable to fight.

★★★

What sentence would you impose on Bobby? Explain how your sentence furthers one or more of the purposes of criminal punishment, and identify the factors, aggravating and mitigating, that influenced your chosen sentence. Also, consider whether an alternative sentence would be appropriate.

Exercise Five

Kristen Johnson is twenty-eight years old and teaches English and Social Studies at Aspire High School, which is considered one of the best high schools in the

Northeast. Many students are admitted to prestigious universities every year, and the teachers are exceptionally well-qualified. Kristen was thrilled when, after graduating college and obtaining her teaching certification, she received an offer to teach at Aspire High School.

The job offer was particularly gratifying because Kristen had overcome extraordinary adversity in her life. Sadly, Kristen was raised in a low-income family where her parents struggled to provide for Kirsten and her two siblings. In addition, Kristen was sexually abused by her uncle for several years, and she has struggled for years to cope with the trauma that this abuse caused. To make matters, worse, at the time Kristen received the job offer from Aspire High School, she was in the midst of a divorce after discovering that her husband had been having an affair with one of Kristen's friends.

Despite these difficulties, Kristen persevered and, for the last two years, she has been regarded as one of the best teachers at Aspire High School. The students report that she is a dynamic and inspiring teacher, and is always available to help any student in whatever way they need. In fact, last year, Kristen won Aspire High School's Teacher of the Year Award.

Several months ago, however, everything changed. One of Kristen's students, Dylan Walsh, who was a senior at Aspire High School, asked to meet with Kirsten privately. During their first meeting, Dylan revealed that he was struggling with severe depression because his girlfriend had recently ended their relationship, and because his grandmother, with whom Dylan had an extremely close relationship, had died two weeks ago from cancer. Being no stranger to adversity, Kristen understood Dylan's pain and tried to support him in every possible way. She met with Dylan weekly and, during one of their meetings, shared her personal struggles with Dylan and explained how she learned to cope with and overcome adversity. In so doing, a sincere trust and true friendship began to develop between Kristen and Dylan.

As their meetings continued, Kristen and Dylan began to grow closer. A couple of weeks later, Kristen invited Dylan to her home for dinner. During the dinner, they discussed Dylan's future, including the colleges he hoped to attend and the career he intended to pursue. In the midst of their conversation, Dylan told Kristen how much she meant to him and how much he would miss her when he graduated. Dylan hugged Kristen and, in a moment when they were both overcome with emotion, they kissed. Shortly thereafter, they had sexual intercourse.

Over the next few months, Kristen and Dylan continued their relationship and fell in love. One evening, however, a teacher from Aspire High School saw Dylan leaving Kristen's house. To make matters worse, the teacher saw Kristen kiss Dylan as he was leaving.

The next day, the teacher informed Aspire High School's principal of what she had seen, and the principal contacted local law enforcement officials, who questioned Dylan about the nature of their relationship. Dylan admitted that he had been having a sexual relationship with Kristen for the past several months, and that it was entirely consensual.

Kristen was charged with statutory rape and sexually assaulting a minor. She pled guilty to both crimes.

***

What sentence would you impose on Kristen? Explain how your sentence furthers one or more of the purposes of criminal punishment, and identify the factors, aggravating and mitigating, that influenced your chosen sentence. Also, consider whether an alternative sentence would be appropriate.

Solutions

Private prisons represent a troubling continuation of a carceral policy in the United States that has failed to assist offenders in successfully reintegrating into society upon release and, concomitantly, contributed to high recidivism rates and a failure to protect public safety. Responsible criminal justice reform should focus on: (1) reducing the number of individuals who are forced to remain in prison for months, sometimes years awaiting trial; (2) discouraging prosecutors from overcharging and instead encouraging them to file charges that are consistent with the defendant's culpability; (3) reforming prison environments to ensure that inmates are treated with dignity and provided with rehabilitative and educational programs that maximize their likelihood of successfully re-integrating into society upon release; and (4) designing community-level programs and relationships that will prevent crime.

The Number of People Incarcerated While Awaiting Trial Should Be Responsibly Reduced (But Not Eliminated)

Undoubtedly, there are some individuals who should be incarcerated pending trial, such as those who are accused of violent crimes and who present a flight risk if released. These people should not be given bail under any circumstances. Courts should also be reluctant to grant bail to individuals with several prior criminal offenses. After all, there are far too many examples of dangerous individuals who were released on bail only to commit another violent crime.

However, far too many individuals who are accused of relatively minor crimes – and who present little, if any, risk to the public – are held for months, and sometimes years awaiting trial. They are incarcerated pending trial because they are poor and cannot afford bail. This practice should end immediately. Allowing individuals to languish and, in some cases, decompensate in prison while awaiting trial in the notoriously slow criminal justice system is unacceptable. In the United States, individuals are innocent until proven guilty and they should be released on bail unless they pose a flight risk or threat to public safety.

Prosecutors Should Be Prohibited from Overcharging, as Charges Should Reflect Accurately the Culpability of an Individual's Conduct

In many cases, prosecutors will "overcharge, which means that they will add additional charges against a defendant, some of which are more severe than the culpability that the defendant's conduct reflect" (Williams, 2018). In so doing, the prosecutor is attempting to effectuate a plea bargain in which the defendant agrees to plead guilty to a lesser charge to avoid going to trial and risking a conviction on the higher charge. Essentially, because the prosecutor has unfettered discretion to decide the charges to file against the defendant, the defendant is placed in an unequal bargaining position and often forced to plead guilty for fear of losing at trial and being subject to a much higher sentence than would be imposed pursuant to a plea bargain.

In many cases, however, the prosecution and defense fail to agree on a plea bargain, yet the prosecution nonetheless "overcharges" and frequently obtains a guilty verdict based on conduct that, although technically satisfying the elements of the charged crime, does not accurately reflect the defendant's culpability. As a result, many defendants are subject to prison terms that are far longer than warranted by their conduct and culpability. For example, assume that a woman had to be hospitalized for ten days with a broken jaw and three broken ribs. When the woman leaves the hospital, she decides that she cannot take any more abuse. When her husband returns home from work a couple of days after she is released from the hospital, she shoots and kills her husband.

The prosecutor could certainly charge the woman with first degree murder, which if convicted would subject her to a possible sentence of life imprisonment. Or the prosecutor could charge her with involuntary manslaughter, which upon conviction could result in a sentence of ten years' imprisonment. The prosecutor's decision, therefore, will have a determinative impact on the length of imprisonment that she will face. Because of the immense power that the prosecutor yields in this context, the exercise of that power should not be unchecked. Rather, courts should assume a more active role in ensuring that the charges reasonably reflect the defendant's culpability.

Legislators Should Support a Law Requiring Private and Public Prisons to Create Humane and Rehabilitative Prison Environments

Legislators at the state and federal level should revisit and reform the conditions under which prisoners in the United States are incarcerated. Even a single visit to a prison in the United States reveals the deplorable and borderline inhumane conditions to which inmates, including those awaiting trial, are subject. Consider, for example, the Metropolitan Correctional Center New York City. This prison, which houses inmates who are awaiting trial on federal charges, is unquestionably inhumane (Theoharis, 2019). As one commentator explains:

> The real scandal is that the horrors of MCC [Metropolitan Correctional Center] have existed for decades, hidden in plain sight. The journalist Aviva Stahl published a searing exposé last year in *Gothamist* on conditions at MCC that documented the filth, rodents, overflowing sewage, deeply substandard medical care, wrenching isolation, and often indifferent—and at times, cruel—staff. From reports from lawyers and people imprisoned there, to the legal

> motions they have filed attempting to mitigate the inhumane conditions, to the hundreds of administrative remedies prisoners have filled out to request remediation (the first step prisoners must take to document problems with their conditions), to the research of scholars and human-rights organizations, the abusive and corrupt conditions at MCC are well documented.
>
> *(Theoharis, 2019)*

In fact, one inmate at the Metropolitan Correctional Center secretly recorded a video of the conditions inside the prison, and described the deplorable conditions inside the facility.

> The inmate says that 26 inmates sleep on bunk beds in a dark, crowded space. Mice, rats and water bugs live in a rusty heater that doesn't work. A trail of rodent droppings shows the critters are trying to raid inmates' lockers. Mold grows in the bathroom ceiling. The inmates share one shower, a toilet and a urinal. Water never stops running from the shower or sink. A toilet plunger has no stick, meaning inmates have to put extra elbow grease into clearing a clog.
>
> *(Theoharis, 2019)*

Put simply, the United States is operating "a high-rise dungeon in Manhattan's financial district" (Theoharis, 2019). These conditions are intolerable in a society that is purportedly committed to preserving fairness and human dignity. And the worst aspect is that the inmates subject to these deplorable conditions are awaiting trial; they have not been convicted of any crime.

Additionally, one component of reforming prison conditions should involve prohibiting solitary confinement except where unquestionably necessary to protect an inmate from harm or from harming others. Solitary confinement should not be punitive because, as the table below demonstrates, the effects of such confinement are severe and, in some instances, irreparable.

Simply put, solitary confinement is inhumane and barbaric. It should be abolished or, at the very least, restricted only to the "worst of the worst" inmates. Additionally, inmates should never be subject to solitary confinement for a prolonged period of time and the conditions of solitary confinement should be more humane. For

TABLE 9.3 Increased Risk of Death After Release for Inmates Who Were Placed in Solitary Confinement

Cause of Death	*Percentage of Increased Risk Due to Solitary Confinement*
Suicide	55%
Homicide	29%
Opioid Overdose	26%
Any Death	17%

Fenster, 2020

example, inmates should not be locked in a small cell for twenty-three or twenty-four hours and permitted only one hour of exercise (Solitary Watch, 2015). Indeed, it is not difficult to imagine that subjecting individuals to these conditions would result in a deterioration of their physical and mental health. In short, solitary confinement is cruel and unbecoming of a country dedicated to respecting the basic dignity of every human being.

Finally, sentences for many crimes are too long and keep inmates incarcerated even though they remain no threat to public safety, and the crime for which they were convicted, such as theft or selling drugs, did not justify a lengthy sentence. For example, in Mississippi, a defendant who had two prior convictions for non-violent drug crime was sentenced – under Mississippi's habitual offender law – to sixty years imprisonment for selling $40 worth of cocaine (Myers, 2012). That is simply ridiculous.

Ultimately, in addressing prison reform, legislators can learn from other countries. Consider Germany's approach to incarceration and the fact that German citizens commit crimes at a rate far lower than in the United States. To begin with, prisoners in Germany are housed in humane, apartment-style buildings and the focus during incarceration is on rehabilitation and resocialization, the effects of which substantially reduce the likelihood of re-offending upon release and maximize the likelihood of successful reintegration into society. Conversely, in the United States, the focus of incarceration is primarily punitive, and the conditions of confinement often deplorable. Many prisons offer only a bare minimum of rehabilitative, mental health and educational services, while subjecting inmates to prolonged periods of isolation and limited opportunities for recreation. The result is that many inmates decompensate while incarcerated and find it nearly impossible to achieve financial and social stability upon release. It should come as no surprise, therefore, that the recidivism rate is high in the United States.

Public Officials Should Focus on Preventing Crime through Community-Level Programs

In the United States, there is an insufficient focus on preventing crime by addressing its root causes and creating innovative, community-level programs that support families and young people. For example, in poor communities, the government should create opportunity centers that offer a variety of services to the community, such as after school programs, tutoring, mentoring, counseling, and part and full-time employment. Additionally, law enforcement agencies should focus on building relationships with the community that foster trust with citizens. Perhaps most importantly, citizens should work together to improve their communities, such as through neighborhood watches and clean ups, which will foster pride in the community and deter criminal conduct. These solutions are only a sample of the innovative ways in which crime prevention can be addressed and lives can be changed – and saved.

★★★

You are a United States Senator and appointed to the Prison Reform Task Force, where you are required to draft a proposal that addresses the following issues:

- The possibility of creating a new type of "residential community" prison environment that focuses on rehabilitation and resocialization for some offenders. In addressing these issues, you are required to identify the types of crimes and offenders for which traditional incarceration would be appropriate. Also, you must be specific about what types of rehabilitative, social, and educational services you would offer to inmates.
- Develop a detailed and workable community-based program that will reduce crime and build positive relationships between law enforcement officers and community members.

Write the proposal and, in so doing, consider all relevant counterarguments.

Note

1 Adam Lamparello was the principal author of this chapter.

References

American Civil Liberties Union (n.d.). Warehoused and forgotten: Immigrants trapped in our shadow private prison system. Available at https://www.aclu.org/other/warehoused-and-forgotten-immigrants-trapped-our-shadow-private-prison-system.

cummings, a. d. p. & Lamparello, A. (2016). Private prisons and the new marketplace for crime. *Wake Forest Journal of Law and Policy*, 6, 407–440.

Fenster, A. (2020, October 13). New data: Solitary confinement increases risk of premature death after release. *Prison Policy Initiative*. Available at https://www.prisonpolicy.org/blog/2020/10/13/solitary_mortality_risk/#:~:text=A%20recently%20published%20study%20of,canaries%20in%20the%20coal%20mine.

Myers, R. (2012, August 13). Extreme sentencing. *American Civil Liberties Union*. Available at https://www.aclu.org/blog/smart-justice/mass-incarceration/extreme-sentencing.

Prison Policy Initiative (n.d.). How many people are locked up in the United States? Available at https://www.prisonpolicy.org/graphs/pie2020.html.

Solitary Watch (2015). What is solitary confinement? Available at https://solitarywatch.org/wp-content/uploads/2017/09/Solitary-Confinement-FAQ-2015.pdf.

Theoharis, J. (2019, August 16). I tried to tell the world about Epstein's jail. No one wanted to listen. *The Atlantic*. Available at https://www.theatlantic.com/ideas/archive/2019/08/real-scandal-mcc/596257/.

Thompson, C. (2014, December 18). Everything you ever wanted to know about private prisons. *The Marshall Project*. Available at https://www.themarshallproject.org/2014/12/18/everything-you-ever-wanted-to-know-about-private-prisons.

U.S. Department of Justice, Bureau of Justice Statistics, *Drug Offenders in Federal Prison: Estimates of Characteristics Based on Linked Data* (Oct. 2015). Available at Drug Offenders in Federal Prison: Estimates of Characteristics Based on Linked Data (ojp.gov).

Vera Institute of Justice (2013, October). Sentencing and prison practices in Germany and the Netherlands: Implications for the United States. Available at https://www.vera.org/publica

tions/sentencing-and-prison-practices-in-germany-and-the-netherlands-implications-for-the-united-states.

Williams, C. L. (2018, December 5). Overcharging in a criminal case. *JustCriminalLaw.com*. Available at https://www.justcriminallaw.com/criminal-charges-questions/2018/12/05/overcharging-criminal-case/.

World Population Review (n.d.). Incarceration rates by country 2021. Available at https://worldpopulationreview.com/country-rankings/incarceration-rates-by-country.

York, G. (2019, January 8). What can U.S. corrections learn from the German prison system? *Corrections1*. Available at https://www.corrections1.com/correctional-healthcare/articles/what-can-us-corrections-learn-from-the-german-prison-system-Hgvc02nL77KqAjhG/.

10

MENTALLY ILL OFFENDERS[1]

This chapter is dedicated to Marc Lamparello (January 28, 1982 to April 17, 2020)

Marc Lamparello, who suffered from schizophrenia, died a little over a month after he was released from Riker's Island Correctional Facility in New York. While incarcerated for nearly a year awaiting trial on attempted arson charges, Marc decompensated substantially. When released pursuant to a plea agreement that required Marc to receive intensive mental health care, he was denied that care for over a month. When the hospital responsible for his treatment finally agreed upon a plan to treat Marc, it was too late; he had committed suicide by jumping off the Verrazano Bridge in New York.

In the United States, the quality of mental health care is abysmal and morally indefensible. At the community level, millions of individuals lack access to any mental health services, often due to socioeconomic status. Upon arrest, mentally ill individuals often languish in federal and state prisons for months, if not years, because the criminal justice system is alarmingly slow in processing cases. While awaiting trial, mentally ill individuals live in isolation and lack access to competent psychological and psychiatric care, thus it comes as no surprise that, like Marc, these individuals decompensate while incarcerated, despite being presumed innocent of the crime(s) for which they are charged. During trial, the only way that mentally ill defendants can demonstrate that their illness, not their moral depravity, was responsible for their criminal conduct is through the insanity defense. However, this defense is no defense at all. In most jurisdictions, the insanity defense requires defendants to show not only that they were mentally ill, but that their illness prohibited them from knowing the difference between right and wrong. Such a standard is nearly impossible to satisfy and, as such, the insanity defense is used on only 1% of criminal cases. In these cases, defendants lose 75% of the time. Thus, most mentally ill defendants are found guilty and incarcerated for substantial periods of time, where they receive substandard

DOI: 10.4324/9781003163411-13

mental health care and, under such conditions of isolation with minimal social contact, deteriorate significantly.

Upon release, mentally ill individuals have little, if any, chance of achieving economic and social stability, thus resorting to crime or, like Marc, committing suicide. This state of affairs is a tragedy and a stain on a criminal justice system that is supposedly dedicated to fairness and equal protection of the law.

The solution is three-fold. First, individuals who are arrested and declared mentally incompetent to stand trial should be deemed not responsible for the charge(s) of which they are accused and remanded to a mental health facility for treatment. Second, for mentally ill individuals who are convicted and sentenced to incarceration, robust mental health services should be made available to them while incarcerated. Third, upon release, mentally ill individuals should be provided with comprehensive and competent mental health services to maximize their likelihood of successfully reintegrating into society, thereby acknowledging that mental health treatment in the United States is woefully inadequate – and a moral failing.

Chapter Highlights

- Society provides insufficient resources for individuals, particularly those in poor communities, to access and receive effective mental health treatment, and prohibits early intervention and commitment by state officials.
- Once arrested, mentally ill defendants often languish for months, if not years, awaiting trial without proper mental health treatment.
- The insanity defense makes it nearly impossible to obtain a verdict of not guilty by reason of insanity, thus subjecting many severely mentally ill defendants to lengthy prison terms where they receive inadequate care, virtually ensuring their psychological and emotional disintegration.
- Even if a defendant is found not guilty by reason of insanity, the resulting period of institutionalization, often at state-run hospitals with inadequately trained personnel, lasts a lifetime and is punitive in nature.
- Upon release, mentally ill offenders receive woefully inadequate support to facilitate their re-entry into society, increasing the likelihood of recidivism and suicide.
- To address these problems, legislators should advocate for laws providing more effective mental health and intervention services at the community level, revising the legal standard for insanity, offering more comprehensive mental health services for mentally ill inmates, and providing follow up and support to ensure successful reintegration into their communities.

Introduction

Marc Lamparello was born on January 28, 1982. He died on April 20, 2020.

His death was preventable. As an article in the *New York Times* describes, the circumstances of his death indict the criminal justice system for its often-deplorable treatment of mentally ill individuals (Ransom, 2020).

In 2012, as a young adult, Marc was diagnosed with schizophrenia and, with the support of his family, sought psychiatric help. He was prescribed anti-psychotic and other medications to control his symptoms and enable him to lead a functional life. And he certainly did, graduating Phi Beta Kappa from Boston College, receiving a master's degree from the University of Pennsylvania, teaching philosophy at Seton Hall University and Brooklyn College, and pursuing a Ph.D. in philosophy from the City University of New York. Unfortunately, he would never graduate and achieve his goal of being a professor of philosophy. Indeed, the journey culminating in his death revealed the shortcomings in how we treat, support, and understand mentally ill persons.

In or around December 2018, Marc, like many who suffer from schizophrenia, stopped taking his medication. In a matter of weeks, Marc began to suffer from hallucinations that interfered with his ability to function and perform satisfactorily in his coursework. These hallucinations increased in frequency and intensity, and in February 2019, Marc drove to the White House and demanded that security officials allow him to speak with then President Donald J. Trump. Obviously sensing that Marc was mentally ill, the security guards detained Marc and returned him to his parents' home the next day.

No further action was taken.

A couple of months later, Marc went to a cathedral in Newark, New Jersey and kneeled in one of the pews for hours. Despite church officials' repeated requests, Marc refused to leave the church, claiming that "God wants me to be here." Marc was arrested. He received a citation and was released into his parents' custody.

No further action was taken.

Approximately two weeks later, in April 2019, Marc drove to St. Patrick's Cathedral in New York City with four gallons of gasoline and two lighters. As he entered the church carrying the gasoline and lighters, church officials stopped him and immediately contacted law enforcement officers, who arrived shortly thereafter. Marc was arrested, jailed, and charged with attempted arson. He faced three to fifteen years imprisonment. He was fired from his job and suspended from his graduate program. In short, he lost everything. In the next year, he would lose his life.

A few weeks after his arrest, Marc was sent to Rikers Island, a notorious prison that is known for its deplorable conditions, insufficient staff, and violence (Kaldheim, 2019). Shortly after his arrival, Marc was assaulted. He received no psychological counseling or other support services and was placed in a room filled with other prisoners awaiting trial, where he languished for weeks.

Eventually, a court ordered a comprehensive psychiatric evaluation of Marc's mental health to determine if he was competent to stand trial. A competency exam determines whether a defendant understands the charges again him or her, and is able to meaningfully assist counsel in defending against these charges. After two psychiatric evaluations, the psychiatrists unanimously agreed that Marc suffered from schizophrenia and was therefore not competent to stand trial.

This determination did not mean that the charges against Marc would be dropped, or that he would be deemed less or even not culpable for his alleged criminal conduct. It only meant that the state had to restore Marc to a minimum level of competency so the trial could proceed before a jury, with the threat of a substantial term of imprisonment likely if the jury returned a guilty verdict.

Over the next few months, Marc was remanded to a state-run mental health facility that provided him with medication to treat schizophrenia and over the next few months his condition improved. However, instead of receiving psychological counseling and other support services, the staff focused almost exclusively on training him to pass the competency examination so that he could be declared competent to stand trial and returned to Rikers Island.

The staff was successful. Marc passed the competency examination and was returned to Rikers Island, where for approximately six months he lived in conditions that bordered on inhumane, awaiting trial. During this time, Marc received his medication, but no further treatment or counseling. Further subjected to minimal recreation time, unhealthy food, indifferent staff, and interminable delays due to a slow-moving and overburdened criminal court system, not surprisingly, Marc decompensated. His symptoms returned. And he understandably lost hope.

Finally, after six months, Marc's attorney agreed to a plea bargain: Marc would be transferred to the jurisdiction of the mental health court system and provided with the intensive mental health treatment that he desperately needed, but had been denied for too long. Under the terms of the plea agreement, Marc would be released, and as a condition of his release, required to undergo outpatient treatment at a mental health facility. If Marc successfully completed treatment, the agreement ensured charges would be dropped and he would have a chance at a normal life again.

However, when Marc was released, nothing happened. The mental health facility entrusted to manage Marc's care required him to quarantine at home – without any treatment for two weeks — to ensure that he was not infected with the coronavirus. The hospital could have scheduled Zoom meetings; they did not. They could have scheduled counseling sessions via telephone; they did not. Thus, Marc languished at home and spent most of his time online, where he discovered dozens of articles that ridiculed and demeaned him in ways that no person with his condition should be forced to endure. As a result, his condition further deteriorated, greatly worrying his family.

After two weeks, the mental health facility still refused to treat him. The facility claimed that Marc had not attended any of his scheduled outpatient sessions during the first two weeks after his release from prison, even though he was required by that very hospital to quarantine at home for those two weeks.

Shortly thereafter, Marc drove to the George Washington Bridge in New York, stopped his car, and tried to jump off the bridge and to his death in the Hudson River. To jump off the bridge, Marc had to climb over a safety net attached to the bridge that had been designed to prevent people from committing suicide. Luckily, law enforcement officers arrived in time to apprehend Marc from the top of the safety net, where he was only seconds away from jumping.

Marc was immediately placed in the same mental health facility that had denied him treatment pursuant to his plea agreement. When he arrived, the doctors conducted no investigation into his medical and mental health background. Instead, they changed his medication, knowing it could take several weeks for the medication to take effect. Then, after only four days, the hospital released Marc. They did no follow-up inquiries.

Two days later, and exactly one year after he was arrested, Marc drove to the Verrazano-Narrows Bridge in New York. This time, law enforcement officers did not arrive in time. He jumped from a height of approximately 240 feet. It took four seconds of free-falling before he hit the water at approximately seventy-five miles per hour. He died of blunt force trauma and drowning.

Alone.
Mentally ill.
Ostracized.
Ridiculed.
Only thirty-eight.
Untreated.

Marc's story is not uncommon, and it highlights the pervasive and woefully inadequate mental health services that ordinary citizens receive in the United States.

The time to solve this problem is now.

***

What reforms should be adopted to increase the effectiveness of mental health services in the United States?

Discussion

At the outset, it is important to recognize that the vast majority of mentally ill individuals do not commit crimes (American Psychological Association, 2014). Rather, they function in and are productive members of society. For this and other reasons, those suffering from mental health illnesses should be neither stigmatized nor ostracized. They should receive the help that Marc was denied. Sadly, in many instances, particularly for low-income citizens, the United States fails to provide affordable, competent, and comprehensive mental health care.

Insufficient Resources Are Dedicated to Mental Health Services in the United States

In the United States, it is nearly impossible for low and modest-income people to access effective mental health treatment because the cost of obtaining private mental health care is staggering.

For example, the cost of a psychiatrist is often between $100 and $300 per session, and the cost of medication, if a person has no insurance, is not just prohibitive (Mukhergee, 2013) but in many cases, impossible to meet. Moreover, the cost of in-patient treatment for individuals who are severely mentally ill is so high that low and moderate-income people have no hope of accessing these services. For example, the cost of in-patient treatment for an eating disorder can be as high as $20,000 per month (MarketWatch, 2018) and worse, many insurance companies refuse to pay for in-patient treatment for eating disorders, or will only pay for a temporary period that is far short of what is necessary to treat the patient effectively (Gordon, 2021).

Furthermore, although government-sponsored programs offer mental health treatment for low-income people, those programs are often ineffective because they are alarmingly underfunded. Table 10.1 illustrates how many states woefully underfund mental health care to an extent that compromises treatment efficacy and availability:

TABLE 10.1 Mental Health Spending Per Capita

State	*Amount*
Florida	$75 or less
Georgia	$75 or less
South Carolina	$75 or less
Kentucky	$75 or less
Ohio	$75 or less
Texas	$75 or less
Oklahoma	$75 or less
Arkansas	$75 or less
Louisiana	$75 or less
Nevada	$75 or less
Idaho	$75 or less
Utah	$75 or less
Indiana	$76 – S105
Illinois	$76 – S105
Alabama	$76 – S105
Missouri	$76 – S105
Tennessee	$76 – S105
West Virginia	$76 – S105

Pan, 2013

These meager funding efforts are woefully inadequate. Mental health treatment does not consist simply of a once-a-month psychiatric visit and adherence to a medication regimen. Rather, a holistic paradigm that involves a combination of psychiatric care and psychological counseling is ideal for maximizing patient outcomes (Lake & Turner, 2017). Low-income individuals, who depend on government assistance to access medical care will receive only the bare minimum: a monthly appointment with a doctor, and medication if necessary. Not surprisingly, this compromises patient care and, ultimately, reduces the likelihood of successful outcomes.

Laws Governing Involuntary Commitment Are Entirely Inadequate

In the United States, the standards governing involuntary confinement fail to provide states with the legal authority to intervene in a timely manner *or* provide comprehensive and sustained mental health services to individuals once confined. Part of the problem results from the United States Supreme Court's decision in *O'Connor v. Donaldson* (1975), where the Court held that individuals cannot be confined involuntarily simply for having a mental illness. Rather, a court must also determine that an individual is a danger to himself or the public. The rationale, of course, is that the government cannot deprive citizens of liberty without a compelling justification, such as the protection of public safety.

Let's examine this a little closer. Marc Lamparello suffered from schizophrenia and traveled to the White House demanding to meet with then President Trump. Additionally, Marc traveled to a church in Newark, New Jersey and refused to leave, claiming that "God wants me to be here." Even at this point, *after* he had stopped taking his medication and manifested symptoms of schizophrenia, *after* he had traveled to the White House, and *after* he had been arrested at the church, he was still ineligible for involuntary confinement because, technically, he had done nothing to suggest that he would harm himself or anyone else.

Does that make sense? No.

When an individual demonstrates through their actions that they are neither rational nor functional, they should be confined because we shouldn't have to wait until a person tries to *kill* himself – or commits a deadly crime – to intervene and provide comprehensive and restorative mental health services. After all, most people do not announce publicly that they intend to commit a crime or kill themselves. Instead, they tend to suffer in silence. They conceal their motives. Essentially, the rule governing involuntary commitment generally requires that we wait for the crime to happen, or the suicide to occur, by which time it is too late. Now, this doesn't mean that the government should be permitted to involuntarily confine any individual who struggles with a severe mental illness, but requiring proof of a danger to self or others ignores that the danger is often hidden while the individual suffers in silence, with no hope for recovery.

Put simply, we should not have to wait until the crime – or suicide – happens (Lamparello, A., 2011).

To make matters worse, mentally ill individuals who are considered a danger to themselves or others often spend mere days in a mental hospital and never receive the comprehensive treatment they require. Consider, again, Marc Lamparello. Think about what happened to Marc: even *after* attempting to jump from the George Washington Bridge to his death, he was only held in a psychiatric hospital for *four days* and then released. Two days later, he jumped again and this time, he succeeded. The hospital that treated Marc stated that they followed *all* of the necessary protocols in providing his treatment.

Think about that for a second – and how ridiculous it sounds. Consider the words of one commentator:

> In Lamparello's case, he was a mentally ill man who needed a lot of extra help that he was not getting. Even after court-mandated psychiatric help, he found countless issues and roadblocks that interrupted his access to care … part of the terms of his release was to get psychiatric care, but when he tried, it was not available. It seems as though the justice system did want him to get the help he needed, however there were so many bumps along the way that ended up being extremely detrimental. This is only one example of someone who could not get the care they needed, and he ended up dead. I am sure there are so many more stories similar to Lamparello's which is devastating to me.
>
> *(Lamparello, M., 2020)*

And to his family.

Upon Arrest, Many Mentally Ill Defendants Languish and Decompensate in Prison While Waiting Months, If Not Years, for Trial

All individuals, regardless of the crime(s) with which they are charged, are presumed innocent until proven guilty, despite the realities of a criminal justice system that demonstrates the polar opposite.

Indeed, the average inmate at Rikers Island Correctional Facility spends *593 days* imprisoned while awaiting trial, often because the inmate cannot afford bail (King, 2015). In fact, as Table10.3 shows, a substantial percentage of the prison population in the United States is comprised of individuals who are presumed innocent, but awaiting trial. The result, sadly, is that many mentally ill prisoners like Marc – who have not been convicted of any crime – deteriorate substantially and sometimes irreparably while awaiting trial. Table10.4 reveals that incarceration is far more harmful to mentally ill individuals than to those who do not suffer from mental illnesses.

Admittedly, inmates receive properly prescribed psychiatric medication, but do they receive psychological counseling? No. Do they receive instruction on coping skills or other topics relating to physical and mental well-being? No. Are they given a substantial amount of time to engage in recreational activities? No. Are they offered reasonably healthy and balanced meals? No. Do inmates spend most of their time in isolation? Yes.

TABLE 10.2 Effects of Incarceration on Mentally Ill Individuals

Incident	*Persons with Mental Illnesses (approximate percentage)*	*Persons Without Mental Illnesses (approximate percentage)*
Injured in a fight while incarcerated	9%	2.5%
Physical assault while incarcerated (perpetrator)	5%	2%
Verbal assault while incarcerated (perpetrator)	5%	1%
Violation of jail rules	19%	9%

And the tragic case of Marc Lamparello shows us exactly what this means for those suffering from a pre-existing mental illness.

To make matters worse, prison is the worst possible environment for individuals with mental health issues, as inadequate mental health services and sustained isolation combine to worsen the conditions from which mentally ill inmates already suffer. Compared to the general population, incarceration has debilitating and often devastating effects even in individuals who do *not* have a mental illness.

Given the effects of prison on the general population, imagine the effects on a mentally ill person confined at Rikers Island for 593 days.

Defendants Found Not Competent to Stand Trial May Still Be Convicted of a Charged Offense

When mentally ill individuals, such as Marc Lamparello, are arrested, they undergo a competency examination shortly thereafter to determine if they are competent to stand trial. Competency to stand trial requires a finding that the defendant has a "sufficient present ability to consult with his lawyer with a reasonable degree of certainty," and a "rational as well as factual understanding of the proceedings against him" (*Dusky v. United States*, 1960). This is a very easy standard to satisfy, as the overwhelming majority of defendants would almost certainly be capable, for example, of telling their attorney about the events resulting in the charge, their personal background, such as a prior criminal record and mental health issues, and other factors that might mitigate the defendant's culpability. Likewise, most, if not nearly all, defendants should be able to understand that they are being charged

TABLE 10.3 Percentage of Inmates with a Mental Illness

Prison	*Percentage of Inmates Who Have a Mental Illness Mentally Ill (approximately)*
Federal Prison	45%
State Prison	56%
Local Jail	64%

Khazan, 2015

TABLE 10.4 The Effects of Incarceration

Condition	*Individuals Incarcerated between ages 14–32 (approximately)*	*Individuals never Incarcerated (approximately)*
Suicidal Tendencies	9%	6%
Depressive Symptoms	24%	15%
Functional Limitations	8%	6%
General Decline in Health	14%	8%

Gago, 2018

with a crime and that there will be a trial to determine whether the defendant is innocent or guilty of that crime.

But Marc was so severely ill that he was found incompetent to stand trial, could not understand that he was being charged with attempted arson, and was not able to communicate with any clarity the circumstances that culminated in his conduct. That meant one thing: he was in a devastating condition when he entered St. Patrick's Cathedral.

The state's response was not to drop the criminal charges, or divert Marc to a mental health court that could design a purposeful plan to provide him with competent and comprehensive mental health treatment. Instead, the goal was to place Marc in a mental health facility and restore him to a minimal level of functionality in order to re-instate the charges and re-initiate the criminal proceeding, which upon conviction would have resulted in a prison term of three to fifteen years. Put simply, even though Marc was so legally incompetent at the time of his crime and arrest, his minimal competence *now* meant that he could face imprisonment even though he was not remotely rational *then*.

That makes no sense.

The Insanity Defense Makes it Nearly Impossible for Mentally Ill Defendants to Obtain a Not Guilty by Reason of Insanity Verdict

The insanity defense serves one primary purpose: to ensure that severely mentally ill individuals have little, if any chance, of obtaining a verdict of not guilty by reason of insanity. It all but guarantees that many mentally ill defendants will spend years in prison rather than receive appropriate treatment at a mental health facility.

Why? Because the insanity defense is nearly impossible to satisfy. Most jurisdictions follow the M'Naghten Rule, which requires mentally ill defendants to demonstrate that: (1) they suffered from a mental illness or defect; and (2) that the mental illness or defect rendered them incapable of conforming their conduct to the law, which means that they could not distinguish right from wrong (*Legal Dictionary*). A minority of jurisdictions use different tests that are broader than the M'Naghten Rule, but the M'Naghten Rule remains the prevalent standard in most jurisdictions.

The problem with this rule is that the vast majority of individuals, including those with severe mental illnesses, know at some level that their conduct is wrong, but that doesn't mean that mentally ill individuals are capable of acting rationally, or understanding the nature of the consequences of their actions.

Consider Marc Lamparello. When asked if he knew that it was wrong to enter St. Patrick's Cathedral with four gallons of gasoline, he responded: "Wrong was completely irrelevant. It was like I was in a fog here; it didn't matter if my actions were wrong." In other words, Marc, who was schizophrenic, technically knew right from wrong, but was not capable of acting rationally and weighing the consequences of those actions. However, under the insanity defense, that wouldn't matter.

Indeed, because it is so difficult to satisfy the M'Naghten Rule, defendants plead insanity in only *1%* of cases and in these cases, juries have found defendants not guilty by reason of insanity only *25%* of the time (Schouten, 2012). Put simply, the insanity defense is not designed to identify defendants whose mental illnesses reduced, if not eliminated, their culpability for a particular crime. It is designed to put the mentally ill in prison.

To be clear, however, many, if not most, mentally ill criminal defendants should not escape culpability – and a guilty verdict – merely because they are mentally ill. To be sure, the overwhelming majority of mentally ill citizens, such as those suffering from depression, anxiety, or bi-polar disorder, never commit crimes. Furthermore, in many cases, the existence of a mental illness does not – and should not – absolve a defendant of blame worthiness for a particular crime because there is no nexus between the illness and the crime. Indeed, to hold that mental illness is *ipso facto* indicative of an inability to conform one's conduct to law unfairly stereotypes and stigmatizes mentally ill individuals. As such, it does make sense to adopt a test for insanity that precludes mentally ill defendants from too readily availing themselves of its protections.

But the M'Naghten Rule goes too far. The requirement that defendants demonstrate that they could not distinguish between right and wrong – and thus conform their conduct to the law – is so difficult to meet that some severely mentally ill defendants who should be found not guilty by reason of insanity are convicted and sentenced to lengthy prison terms. And during this time, they often decompensate to such a degree that successful reintegration into society upon release is nearly impossible.

The difficult but necessary task, therefore, is for legislators and courts to *quantify* the impact that severe mental health issues have on individuals' cognitive and rational decision-making capabilities. Doing so will enable legislators to develop a sensible and fair insanity defense.

How would you distinguish between mental illnesses that may absolve a defendant of responsibility for a crime and those that may not? How would you quantify the influence of the same mental illness in several defendants to determine who should be absolved of culpability and who should not? What standards would use you to make this determination?

Defendants Found Not Guilty by Reason of Insanity Often Spend Decades in a Psychiatric Institution

In the rare instances where a defendant is found not guilty by reason of insanity, the law in most jurisdictions provides that the defendant will be remanded to a mental health facility and released when a court deems the defendant sufficiently stable to rejoin society. Unfortunately, the reality of what occurs after a "not guilty by reason of insanity" verdict often differs from what the law prescribes. In short, it can be the equivalent of a life sentence in which the defendant dies while still institutionalized. Indeed, many defendants found not guilty by reason of insanity spend decades, if not their entire lives, institutionalized, *even though*, if they were found guilty of the charged crime, they would have spent far less time in prison and been released years earlier (McClelland, 2017).For example, John Hinckley, who attempted to assassinate former President Ronald Reagan., was found not guilty by reason of insanity. Hinkley was subsequently committed to a mental health facility, and he spent *thirty-five years* in that facility before being released. Think about that: *thirty-five years.* Either Hinckley had the worst mental illness in the history of the universe, or the doctors treating him were so incompetent that they needed three-and-a-half-decades to help him return to functionality.

Neither explanation makes sense. Hinkley's thirty-five-year stint in a mental health facility was punitive and political. Those overseeing his commitment and potential release knew that, if Hinkley was released too soon, public outrage would be substantial. Undoubtedly, this perception was influenced by the fact that, after the verdict, several states reformed their laws to limit the circumstances in which the insanity defense could be sued (Collins, Hinkebein, & Schorgl, n.d.). Three states abolished the defense. So, they transformed a mental health facility, which is designed to be non-punitive and restorative, into a quasi-prison based on considerations that had nothing to do with Hinckley's mental health or treatment.

So, what's really going on here?

A scam.

A fraud.

One that treats human beings with no dignity or decency.

One that shows infirmities in our mental health system and that requires corrective legislation – immediately.

State-run Mental Health Institutions Are Often Given Immunity from Suit Under State Statutes, thus Precluding Lawsuits for Negligent Conduct

Among the most glaring injustices in the criminal justice system is the near-impossibility of holding hospitals liable for the negligent treatment of patients – like Marc – who desperately need comprehensive and consistent mental health care, often in an inpatient setting. For example, the State of New Jersey, where Marc resided, provides immunity to all state-run psychiatric hospitals absent a finding that a hospital was *grossly negligent* in treating a patient. The result is that many families, who are devastated by the loss of a loved one to suicide, or by their loved one's incarceration, have no legal remedy against these hospitals. Moreover, immunity laws provide no incentive for mental health facilities to improve their treatment protocols, which perpetuates a system in which low and moderate-income people receive, at best, substandard mental health treatment. Marc Lamparello is a perfect example of the inadequacies of New Jersey's mental health services, and its immunities laws only ensure that the quality of such services is not likely to change.

Exercises

Exercise One

David Myers is twenty-one years old and since childhood has suffered from schizophrenia and severe anxiety. David has been on anti-psychotic medications to control the symptoms of schizophrenia, which have included delusional thoughts and hallucinations. Unfortunately, David recently decided to stop taking his medication because he could no longer tolerate the side effects, one of which was tardive dyskinesia, a condition that causes involuntary movements.

Approximately one month after stopping his medication, David began to suffer hallucinations that led him to believe that his best friend John, who had recently confronted David expressing concern about his well-being, was trying to kill him and would do so the next time that he saw David. As a result, David, who believed that John was stalking him, purchased a gun and remained in his home, fearing that if he went outside, John would kill him.

A couple of days later, David noticed John park in the front of his home, exit his car, and walk towards the front door. John did so because he wanted to reconcile with David and offer any help that David might need. When John rang the doorbell, David ran downstairs, opened the door, and fired several shots at John. One of the shots struck David in the head, killing him instantly. Another shot missed David and struck an elderly woman, who was walking her dog, in the head. She died two days later at a local hospital.

***

Should John be prosecuted for two counts of first-degree murder? If so, and if John is convicted, what sentence should he receive? How, and in what manner, should mental health treatment be incorporated into John's sentence?

Exercise Two

Emily Jordan is twenty years old and a junior at Warrior College, where she has achieved a nearly perfect grade point average. She is a member of the school's cheerleading team, and a valued member of the school's debate team. Emily is hoping to gain acceptance to a top-ranked law school upon graduation.

For years, however, Emily has struggled with severe and often debilitating anxiety, and bi-polar disorder. Indeed, Emily's anxiety has, at times, been so severe that, last year at Warrior College's game against rival Wildcat College, she suffered a panic attack during the cheerleading team's halftime show and ran off the field in tears.

In an attempt to overcome her anxiety, Emily joined the debate team at Warrior College in her senior year and despite being extremely nervous, she was determined to conquer her fears and emerge with confidence. Sadly, during several debates with colleges from across the country, Emily suffered panic attacks that substantially affected her and the team's performance. Emily was humiliated and traumatized, but determined to push forward and overcome this debilitating condition.

At the final debate against Wildcat College, which occurred before a crowd of nearly 1,000 spectators, Emily had one of the worst panic attacks of her life during the middle of her debate with Wildcat College's star debater, Jennifer Collins. Emily began sweating and struggled to speak as the crowd grew increasingly concerned. Seconds later, Emily ran off the stage as the crowds laughed and mocked Emily.

After the debate, Emily's teammates approached her, screaming that Emily had been solely responsible for the loss to Wildcat College and was a burden to them and the team. Emily began crying and begged her teammates to stop, but they didn't. In fact, one of her team members, Valerie Griffin, shouted, "I wish you never existed."

Emily snapped. She ran up to Valerie and punched her in the face. Valerie fell backwards and struck her head on the concrete floor, which caused her to suffer a subdural hematoma, which occurs when bleeding occurs inside the skull but outside of the brain. Despite the best efforts of paramedics and physicians, Valerie died three days later. Valerie's family, along with the Warrior College community are devastated.

***

Should Emily be prosecuted for murder or for a lesser crime, such as battery? Depending on your choice, what sentence should Emily receive? Should mental health treatment be incorporated into Emily's sentence? If so, how?

Exercise Three

Recently, the parents of Christopher Mullen, a third-year student at Bearcat High School, contacted law enforcement officers in a state of desperation. Christopher's parents discovered a journal in Christopher's bedroom that contained an entry stating that, "Soon, everyone will know me. I will be famous. The bullies at Bearcat High School are going to die very soon." Law enforcement officers detained Christopher for questioning. During questioning, Christopher stated, "You can't do anything to me. I haven't done anything – *yet*." Based on this statement, Christopher was involuntarily committed at Recovery Hospital and received a comprehensive mental health evaluation. Recovery Hospital is a state-run institution that offers psychiatric and psychological services to teenagers who are struggling with mental illnesses.

The evaluation, which was conducted by the chief of psychiatric services at Recovery Hospital, Charles Meeks, revealed that Christopher suffered from minor depression and narcissistic personality disorder. As a result, Dr. Meeks prescribed Christopher an anti-depressant and suggested that, upon release, Christopher seek counseling from a psychologist that specializes in treating personality disorders.

Additionally, Dr. Meeks was convinced that Christopher's threat was a "transient act of immaturity" and the result of an untreated mental illness. Thus, after three days, Christopher was released to his parents.

Two days later, Christopher walked into Bearcat High School with an AR-15 and killed nineteen students and two teachers.

***

Should Recovery Hospital be held responsible in civil court for the deaths of the students and teachers? Provide the reasoning underlying your decision and address all relevant counterarguments.

Exercise Four

Jason Waterman and Michelle Kelly are high school sweethearts and recently got married at a beautiful ceremony before their friends and family. Over the next year, Jason and Michelle enjoyed a wonderful marriage and recently announced that they were expecting their first child.

A few months later, Michelle stopped at a local supermarket to purchase groceries. After Michelle left and was walking to her car, she was attacked by two men. The men struck Michelle with a baseball bat several times and stole her engagement ring. Sadly, Michelle died one week later at a local hospital. Jason was devastated and became extremely depressed. At the urging of his parents and friends, Jason scheduled an appointment with a psychiatrist, who diagnosed Jason with major depression and post-traumatic stress disorder. The psychiatrist prescribed Jason anti-depressant and anti-anxiety medication, and advised him to seek help from a grief counselor.

Based on eyewitness accounts, the suspects were identified and arrested two months after the murder, and held in the local jail pending a bail hearing. The next day, at the bail hearing, the judge denied bail and ordered the suspects to be held pending trial. However, as the suspects were leaving the courthouse, Jason, who was still suffering from depression and had isolated himself from friends and family, burst through the front door to the courthouse with a rifle and shot the suspects. They died at the scene.

***

Should Jason be prosecuted for murder? If so, what sentence should Jason receive? How, and in what manner, should mental health treatment be incorporated into Jason's sentence?

Exercise Five

Michael and Ricky Morrison are sixteen and seventeen years old, respectively, and live in an affluent suburb of Atlanta, Georgia. Their father, Robert, is a world-renowned heart surgeon and their mother, Diane, is an actress who has appeared in several highly acclaimed movies, including *Terms of the Heart*, which was regarded as one of the best films in years. By all accounts, Michael and Ricky live in the perfect family.

However, Michael and Ricky have been hiding a secret for many years. Throughout their childhoods and continuing into their teenage years, Robert has sexually abused them hundreds of times. In addition, Robert threatened to kill Michael and Ricky if they ever told anyone about the abuse. As such, and because Michael and Ricky suspected that no one would believe them if they accused their father of sexual abuse, they continued for years to endure the abuse. In so doing, they became extremely depressed, as they were unable to cope with or find support for the abuse they endured. To make matters worse, in the last year the instances of abuse have become more frequent – and more violent. After the last incident, Michael and Ricky decided that they had had enough. They would no longer tolerate this horrific abuse and would finally seek justice for the trauma they had been forced to endure throughout their childhood.

A couple of days later, Robert and Diane celebrated their thirtieth wedding anniversary and returned home after dining at the famous restaurant *Love at First Sight*. When they entered their home, Michael and Ricky were waiting, each armed with a rifle. Michael fired first, killing Robert instantly. A few seconds later, Ricky shot Diane, who also died instantly. The neighbors, alarmed at the sounds of gunshots, immediately contacted law enforcement officials, who arrived at the scene within minutes and arrested Michael and Ricky.

Should Michael and Ricky be prosecuted for murder? Is so, what sentence should they receive? How, and in what manner, should mental health treatment be incorporated into Jason's sentence?

Solutions

The above discussion illustrates the significant flaws in how the criminal justice system treats mentally ill individuals. It also helps to identify workable solutions to address the inequities and injustices that currently exist regarding the treatment of mentally ill individuals and offenders.

Building Relationships with Mentally Ill Individuals in the Community and in Mental Health Facilities Is Critical

The famous football coach Woody Hayes once said, "You win with people." He was right.

The best treatment for mentally ill individuals – indeed all individuals – is to provide them with inspirational and dedicated doctors, parents, teachers, and community leaders. The goal is not only to prevent individuals from engaging in criminal conduct, but to help them live happy and productive lives. The best way to do so is by instilling in children at an early age the values that will maximize their likelihood of success, and by providing children, such as those who are mentally ill, with optimal medical and social support.

Legislators should remember that you truly do win with people when they address this and other problems in the criminal justice system. Think about it. Some people have innate talents and qualities that render them ideal for positions that involve treating and supporting mentally ill individuals. Put simply, some things cannot be taught.

Thus, government officials should strive to hire the best and brightest psychiatrists, psychologists, social workers, and teachers, who are those who possess the tangible *and* intangible qualities, such as empathy, to build positive and powerful relationships with those under their care. At the end of the day, the quality of the relationships you build with others influences the quality of recovery – and life – they experience. Thus, reject mediocre people. Find quality people. Build relationships. And remember that you win with people. You can't teach people to be great from a textbook or by giving them multiple degrees. You either have it or you don't.

Cognitive Behavioral Therapy Is Critical

Medication is not the only possible solution to ameliorate the deleterious effects of mental illness. In fact, sometimes, medication does not work at all. The efficacy of medication and the quality of patient outcomes is often enhanced when combined with cognitive behavioral therapy, which helps patients, among other things, to change their thought processes and develop coping skills to overcome adversity (Kingdon, 2009). Put simply, you don't help those with mental illnesses lead functional lives simply by giving them a pill. You help them by equipping them with the cognitive and behavioral tools to cope with life's challenges and lead independent and self-sustaining lives.

Law Enforcement Should Be Permitted to Intervene and Provide In-Patient Treatment to Mentally Ill Individuals Before a Crime Is Committed

Although controversial, this question must be posed: *Why should we wait until the crime happens?* (Lamparello, A., 2011).

We shouldn't.

In some instances, law enforcement officers should have the authority to detain and involuntarily commit severely mentally ill individuals even if there is no evidence that they are a danger to themselves or others. That may sound untenable, but think about Marc Lamparello. He got in his car, drove three hours to Washington, DC, and demanded to see then-President Trump before he was arrested. Shortly thereafter, he refused to leave a church in Newark, New Jersey, claiming that "God wanted him to be there."

Was he a danger to himself or others? *Who cares? It shouldn't matter.*

He was suffering.

He was crying out for help.

He was unable to function.

How could anyone, whether a court or mental health professional, know with precision whether he was likely to harm himself or others *when he had no history of doing so?* The point is that, in circumstances such as these, the government far too often waits until the crime happens – and the harm is done – before intervening. By then, as in Marc's case, it is too late.

Put simply, the government's commitment to providing high-quality treatment to mentally ill individuals – and its decision to involuntarily commit an individual – should not depend on a determination concerning the likelihood of future harm because it is extremely difficult to make this assessment with any degree of accuracy. It should depend on the severity of the illness and the extent to which it is compromising the individual's ability to function and make rational life choices. In Marc Lamparello's case, the answer was clear: he should have been committed involuntarily for a sustained amount of time.

This is not to say, of course, that in these and other cases individuals *do not* pose a harm to themselves or others. It is to say, however, the government should not be required to prove this threat before intervening and involuntarily detaining an individual *if* the evidence demonstrates that the individual lacks the ability to function and act rationally. Also, it most certainly does not mean that anyone with a severe mental illness such as schizophrenia should not be involuntarily committed. But when severely mentally persons do something such as drive to the White House and demand to see the President of the United States, it should not matter whether they are a harm to themselves or others. They are extremely sick. They need help. And they should be involuntarily committed because, in most cases, there is no other way to give them the help they so desperately need.

Marc Lamparello is the perfect example of what can and often does happen when the law prevents the government from involuntarily committing severely mentally ill individuals absent a showing of harm to themselves or others. The argument that individual liberty should be the primary, if not sole, consideration in cases such as Marc's misses the point and misperceives the problem. Mentally ill individuals, such as Marc who suffered from schizophrenia, are not free. Their mind is a prison. Involuntary commitment – for a limited period and with consistent judicial oversight – *is* their path to freedom and liberty.

Mental Health Courts and Treatment Should Be Available to a Wider Array of Criminal Offenders

Many states have created mental health courts that provide certain criminal offenders with comprehensive mental health treatment in lieu of prison. The decision to divert an offender to a mental health court is typically made by a prosecutor based on factors including, but not limited to, the presence of a diagnosed mental illness and the severity of the charged offense. But this approach leads to a profoundly serious problem.

Consider the following hypothetical example: Henry is twenty-five years old and for years has suffered from schizophrenia. One day, Henry hears voices telling him to purchase and experiment with cocaine. Unfortunately, when attempting to purchase cocaine from a well-known drug dealer, Henry is arrested by law enforcement officers who were conducting a sting operation in the area. Because of Harry's mental illness, and because the crime of attempting to purchase cocaine is a misdemeanor under state law, the prosecution agrees to divert Henry to the state's mental health courts, where he receives comprehensive mental health treatment and is released approximately six months later.

Assume the same facts, except that, instead of attempting to purchase cocaine, Henry commits arson by setting fire to a local police station, believing in a delusional state that the police had been following Henry and intended to kill his family. In this instance, Henry is charged with arson and sentenced to ten years' imprisonment, where he receives minimal mental health treatment and decompensates substantially.

How can this be justified? In both examples, Henry had schizophrenia and the delusional thoughts that often accompany this illness caused him to engage in criminal behavior. Thus, the only factor that influenced the prosecutor's decision in each example was the severity of the crime. Is this just? Why should the severity of a crime be a deciding factor in whether a defendant receives treatment through mental health courts?

It makes no sense, but many states restrict eligibility for mental health courts to individuals who commit low-level or misdemeanor offenses (Martinson, 2021). That impermissibly and unjustifiably prohibits individuals, such as those with schizophrenia, from receiving treatment, and subjects them to a prison environment that almost certainly causes them to decompensate and have little chance for successful reintegration into society upon release.

This is not to say, of course, that all or most individuals with mental illnesses should be able to access mental health courts. It does mean, however, that where an individual, such as Henry, is suffering from schizophrenia *and* that condition causes that individual to commit a particular crime, they should be remanded to mental health courts regardless of the severity of the offense. The real challenge is to ensure that the mental health services offered are sufficiently comprehensive and appropriately holistic to maximize the likelihood of positive patient outcomes.

The Competency Determination Should Be Dispositive of the Defendant's Culpability for the Charged Crime

When individuals are arrested and their behavior suggests the presence of a mental illness, the courts order those defendants to undergo a competency examination. The purpose of this examination is to determine whether defendants understand the nature of the charges against them and are able to meaningfully assist their defense counsel, such as by providing relevant facts about the incident that gave rise to the charges. If a defendant is found incompetent to stand trial, the proceedings against the defendant are suspended and the defendant is placed in a mental health facility. Once the defendant is restored to competency, the criminal proceedings resume and, in cases involving serious crimes, the defendant, if convicted, can be subject to a lengthy term of imprisonment.

Thus, a finding of incompetency to stand trial does *not* preclude a defendant from being charged and convicted of a crime. Rather, competency determinations only reflect a decision about the defendant's state of mind at that moment in the criminal proceeding, *not at the time of the crime.*

Does this sound ridiculous? Yes. And it should.

Think about it. Marc Lamparello was suffering from schizophrenia and experiencing delusional thoughts when he walked into St. Patrick's Cathedral with four gallons of gasoline. Thankfully, security officials stopped Marc and he was promptly arrested. A few weeks later, after a comprehensive medical evaluation, Marc was declared incompetent to stand trial due to the hallucinations and delusions he was experiencing at the time. Thereafter, Marc was placed in a mental health facility where the counseling offered was solely on how to pass the state test for competency and thus be declared competent and transferred back to prison while awaiting trial.

So, ask yourself this question: What changed from the moment Marc was arrested and the moment he was declared incompetent to stand trial? Absolutely nothing. Yet, the law states that a determination of incompetency has no relevance to the defendant's mental state at the time of the crime. In other words, the law makes no sense.

A finding of incompetency should, in most cases, end the criminal proceeding. The defendant should not be charged with a crime and should be involuntarily committed to a mental health facility for a period necessary to restore the defendant to a reasonably functional state.

Of course, when such individuals commit serious crimes, the desire for retribution is understandable. But the mob mentality should not trump the fact that some individuals, due to their mental illness, are not culpable for the crime that they are charged with committing.

The Insanity Defense Must Be Changed Because it Makes it Nearly Impossible for Mentally Ill Inmates to Avoid Incarceration

The insanity defense is no defense whatsoever. It is a smokescreen that gives defendants an apparent opportunity to claim that their mental illness rendered them incapable of conforming their conduct to law, namely, understanding the difference between right and wrong.

But it is really no opportunity whatsoever. Even the most mentally ill individuals know, at least on a theoretical level, that a certain action is wrong, but as Marc Lamparello accurately stated, for severely mentally ill individuals the legality of an action is *irrelevant.* It is irrelevant because these individuals are irrational and incapable of conforming their conduct to law – regardless of their knowledge of whether an action is technically right or wrong.

The time has come to expose this charade. The solution is not to create a new test. It is to eliminate the test entirely. After all, in the vast majority of cases mentally ill defendants are technically guilty of the crime with which they are charged *if* the evidence supports the conclusion that their conduct satisfied the elements of that offense. Thus, instead of focusing on guilt or innocence, the law should focus on the mentally ill defendant's *culpability* at the *sentencing phase* and impose a sentence that is commensurate with the defendant's culpability. For mentally ill individuals, this may advise against any term of incarceration and support a period of confinement in a mental institution. And for good reason. It is one thing to be technically guilty of the elements of an offense, but it is an entirely different matter whether those defendants are truly *culpable* and thus deserving of punishment. The criminal justice system should focus on imposing sentences, whether retributive or rehabilitative, that reflect culpability, which is often mitigated, if not eliminated, by the presence of a severe mental illness.

Comprehensive Mental Health Services Must Be More Readily Available to Inmates Suffering from Diagnosed Mental Illnesses

Prisons are perhaps the most destructive environments for mental illnesses. Indeed, inmates with mental illnesses often decompensate rather than rehabilitate, when incarcerated, because the social conditions of incarceration, which include long periods of isolation and minimal social interaction, create an environment that is damaging to recovery and conducive to exacerbating the mental health problems of prisoners.

This must stop. Confining someone who is schizophrenic, for example, and providing that person with no counseling services, no meaningful social interaction, nor consistent periods of recreation, is inhumane and reflects alarming ignorance of the harm that this causes to mentally ill individuals.

Prisoners are people. They still have rights and deserve to be treated with dignity. As such, prisons should design and implement comprehensive treatment protocols that effectively treat inmates' mental health issues *and* provide the support necessary to enhance their stability and functionality while incarcerated. The short and long term benefits would help both inmates and society by increasing the likelihood that mentally inmates, upon release, would be in a better position to successfully reintegrate into society, thus reducing recidivism.

Upon Release, State-Sponsored Re-Entry Programs Should Provide Mentally Ill Individuals with the Medical, Psychiatric, and Social Support to Successfully Reintegrate into Society

When inmates are released from prison, regardless of whether they are struggling with mental illness, they face an uphill battle to successfully reintegrate into society. Many inmates lack family or social support when they are released. Many have little or no money, and when former inmates seek employment or strive to further their education, they are turned away because of their prior conviction. Put simply, upon release, the deck is stacked against former inmates. It should come as no surprise, therefore, that many former inmates commit additional crimes and return to prison; the result is a high recidivism rate.

For mentally ill individuals, reentry into society is even more difficult. In addition to the challenges facing all former inmates, mentally ill individuals require psychiatric care so that they can continue a specific medication regimen. They often require counsel or other support services. If they fail to receive this treatment or these services, they are often left to fend alone in a world that rarely gives people second chances and that turns a blind eye to the struggles of those who were once incarcerated.

The point is as simple as it is obvious: state officials must develop comprehensive and effective reentry programs to assist inmates who, upon release, are striving to find financial, emotional, and social stability.

Remember Marc Lamparello. For one month following his release, Marc received no treatment whatsoever, despite a court order mandating that he receive outpatient treatment upon release. Of course, like most institutions, the personnel at the hospital conveniently used "Covid-19" for apparently rendering them incapable of providing even basic services – even via Zoom or Skype.

On April 20, 2020, Marc committed suicide by jumping off the Verrazano-Narrows Bridge.

The result was tragic, and it was preventable.

Stop Stigmatizing Mental Illness

There is a reason why people with mental illnesses suffer in silence. They know of the societal stigma that mentally ill people wrongfully face. This stigma is the result of ignorance and stupidity, and it is both alarming and appalling. For that reason, many people do not seek mental health treatment because they fear being ostracized and marginalized. That must stop – now. It demonstrates profound ignorance. It causes significant harm. And it causes people to die.

Do you agree with these proposals? Explain your reasoning and address all relevant counterarguments.

***

You are a legislator and have recently been appointed to the United States Mental Health Task Force, which is charged with offering proposals to improve the manner and method by which mentally ill offenders are treated during the trial, correctional, and reentry phases of the criminal justice process, and in the community. You are asked to:

- Create "standard of care" guidelines that specify in detail the procedures that mental health institutions must follow when treating patients who present a risk to themselves or others.
- Design a program that provides comprehensive and effective mental health treatment for incarcerated persons.
- Develop a specific, workable, and detailed re-entry plan that will, among other things, provide effective mental health services to inmates upon release and offer other services to maximize an offender's likelihood of successfully re-integrating into society and leading a productive life.

Write the Proposal.

Note

1 Adam Lamparello was the principal author of this chapter.

References

American Psychological Association (2014, April 15). Mental illness not usually linked to crime, research finds. Available at https://www.apa.org/news/press/releases/2014/04/mental-illness-crime.

Collins, K., Hinkebein, G., & Schorgl, S. (n.d.). The John Hinckley trial and its impact on the insanity defense. University of Missouri-Kansas City Law School. Available at http://law2.umkc.edu/faculty/projects/ftrials/hinckley/hinckleyinsanity.htm.

Dusky v. United States, 362 U.S. 402 (1960).

Gago, I. (2018, April 10). UCLA study links early incarceration with mental, physical health issues. *Daily Bruin*. Available at https://dailybruin.com/2018/04/10/ucla-study-links-early-incarceration-with-mental-physical-health-issues.

Gordon, D. (2021, February 26). Despite progress, patients still struggle with insurance coverage for eating disorder treatment. *Forbes.com*. Available at https://www.forbes.com/sites/debgordon/2021/02/26/despite-progress-patients-still-struggle-with-insurance-coverage-for-eating-disorder-treatment/?sh=6e465a1e22b8.

Kaldheim, P. (2019, August 3). The end of Riker's Island, a stain on New York, can't come soon enough. *Salon.com*. Available at https://www.salon.com/2019/08/03/the-end-of-rikers-island-a-stain-on-new-york-cant-come-soon-enough/.

Khazan, O. (2015, April 7). Most prisoners are mentally ill. *The Atlantic*. Available at https://www.theatlantic.com/health/archive/2015/04/more-than-half-of-prisoners-are-mentally-ill/389682/.

King, S. (2015, June 17). The average inmate at Riker's Island now waiting a ridiculous 593 days for their trial to begin. *Dailykos.com*. Available at https://www.dailykos.com/stories/2015/6/17/1394091/-The-average-inmate-at-Riker-s-Island-is-now-waiting-a-ridiculous-593-days-for-their-trial-to-begin.

Kingdon, D. (2009, April 17). Cognitive behavioral therapy in severe mental illness. *Psychiatric Times*. Available at https://www.psychiatrictimes.com/view/cognitive-behavioral-therapy-severe-mental-illness.

Lake, J. & Turner, M. S. (2017). Urgent need for improved mental health care and a more collaborative model of care. *The Permanante Journal*, 21, 17–24. Available at https://www.ncbi.nlm.nih.gov/pmc/articles/PMC5593510/.

Lamparello, A. (2011). Why wait until the crime happens? Providing for the involuntary commitment of dangerous individuals without requiring a showing of mental illness. *Seton Hall Law Review*, 41, 875–908. Available at https://scholarship.shu.edu/cgi/viewcontent.cgi?article=1390&context=shlr.

Lamparello, M. (2020, June 24). *A Reaction – The prison system: Psyched out!* Available at https://mentalhealthcrime.wordpress.com/2020/06/24/marc-lamparello-a-reaction/.

Legal Dictionary. M'Naghten Rule. Available at https://legal-dictionary.thefreedictionary.com/M%27Naghten+Rule.

MarketWatch (2018, March 3). The unexpected costs of eating disorders. Available at https://www.marketwatch.com/story/the-unexpected-costs-of-eating-disorders-2018-03-01.

Martinson, S. (2021, March 7). Alternative courts not a catch-all fix for mental illness crisis. *Law360*. Available at https://www.law360.com/articles/1356267/alternative-courts-not-a-catch-all-fix-for-mental-illness-crisis.

McClelland, M. (2017, September 27). When "not guilty" is a life sentence. *New York Times Magazine*. Available at https://www.nytimes.com/2017/09/27/magazine/when-not-guilty-is-a-life-sentence.html.

Mukhergee, S. (2013, January). Study: Americans just can't afford mental health treatment. *ThinkProgress*. Available at https://archive.thinkprogress.org/study-americans-just-cant-afford-mental-health-treatment-bf0a3c3d5b2d/.

O'Connor v. Donaldson, 422 U.S. 563 (1975).

Pan, D. (2013, April 9). Map: Which states have cut treatment for the mentally ill the most? *Mother Jones*. Available at https://www.motherjones.com/politics/2013/04/map-states-cut-treatment-for-mentally-ill/.

Ransom, J. (2020, April 30). An arrest at St. Patrick's, a struggle for help, then a suicide. *New York Times*. Available at https://www.nytimes.com/2020/04/30/nyregion/marc-lamparello-suicide-st-patricks-arson.html.

Schouten, R. (2012, August 16). The insanity defense: An intersection of morality, public policy, and science. *Psychology Today*. Available at https://www.psychologytoday.com/us/blog/almost-psychopath/201208/the-insanity-defense.

INDEX

Note: Illustrations and tables are indicated by page numbers in *italics* and **bold,** respectively.